RELIGION, SPIRITUALITY AND SECULARITY AMONG MILLENNIALS

This book explores the world of religion, spirituality and secularity among the Millennial generation in the United States and Canada, with a focus on the ways Millennials are doing (non)religion differently in their social lives compared with their parents and grandparents. It considers the influences exercised on the (non) religious and spiritual landscapes of young adults in North America by the digital age, precarious work, growing pluralism, extreme individualism, environmental crisis, advanced urbanism, expanded higher education, emerging adulthood and a secular age. Based on extensive primary and secondary quantitative data, complemented with high-quality qualitative research, including interviews and focus groups, this book offers cross-national comparisons between the United States and Canada to highlight the impact of different social environments on the experience of religion, spirituality and secularity among the continent's most numerous generation. As such, it will appeal to scholars of religion and sociology, with interests in religious and societal change as well as in religious practice among young adults.

Sarah Wilkins-Laflamme is an associate professor in the Department of Sociology and Legal Studies at the University of Waterloo, Canada. She completed her DPhil (PhD equivalent) in sociology at the University of Oxford in 2015. Her research interests include quantitative methods, sociology of religion, immigration and ethnicity as well as political sociology. Dr. Wilkins-Laflamme is co-author of *None of the Above: Nonreligious Identity in the US and Canada* with New York University Press, and has also published 24 peer-reviewed journal articles and book chapters to date.

Routledge Studies in the Sociology of Religion

A platform for the latest scholarly research in the sociology of religion, this series welcomes both theoretical and empirical studies that pay close attention to religion in social context. It publishes work that explores the ways in which religions adapt or react to social change and how spirituality lends meaning to people's lives and shapes individual, collective and national identities.

A Visual Approach to the Study of Religious Orders
Zooming in on Monasteries
Edited by Marcin Jewdokimow and Thomas Quartier

Bisexuality, Religion and Spirituality
Critical Perspectives
Edited by Andrew Kam-Tuck Yip and Alex Toft

The Transformation of Religious Orders in Central and Eastern Europe
Sociological Insights
Edited by Stefania Palmisano, Isabelle Jonveaux and Marcin Jewdokimow

Society and the Death of God
Sal Restivo

Polish Catholicism between Tradition and Migration
Agency, Reflexivity and Transendence
Wojciech Sadlon

Religion, Spirituality and Secularity among Millennials
The Generation Shaping American and Canadian Trends
Sarah Wilkins-Laflamme

For more information about this series, please visit: https://www.routledge.com/Routledge-Studies-in-the-Sociology-of-Religion/book-series/RRSR

RELIGION, SPIRITUALITY AND SECULARITY AMONG MILLENNIALS

The Generation Shaping American and Canadian Trends

Sarah Wilkins-Laflamme

LONDON AND NEW YORK

Cover image: stock_colors

First published August 2023
by Routledge
4 Park Square, Milton Park, Abingdon, Oxon OX14 4RN

and by Routledge
605 Third Avenue, New York, NY 10158

Routledge is an imprint of the Taylor & Francis Group, an informa business

British Library Cataloguing-in-Publication Data
A catalogue record for this book is available from the British Library

Library of Congress Cataloguing-in-Publication Data
A catalog record has been requested for this book

ISBN: 978-1-032-10602-1 (hbk)
ISBN: 978-1-032-10921-3 (pbk)
ISBN: 978-1-003-21769-5 (ebk)

DOI: 10.4324/9781003217695

Typeset in Bembo
by MPS Limited, Dehradun

CONTENTS

FIGURES

ACKNOWLEDGMENTS

I like to refer to this book as my pandemic baby. When the first COVID-19 lockdown was implemented in Ontario, Canada in March 2020, like many others I suddenly found myself at home, teaching and working remotely, without much capacity or will to go out. I was very fortunate, in that I had a stable job and income, was in a profession easily adapted to remote work, and my extended family and friends stayed healthy and safe in those early days of the pandemic. Nevertheless, I found myself with a lot of time on my hands, and had a hard think about how I would like to fill it. Cooking? Netflix? Working out? Cleaning? Crafting? All these activities played a role in my life during lockdown, but I also decided to finally throw myself into this book project on Millennials and religion I had been contemplating for some time before the pandemic hit. There are always so many things we as academics and researchers would like to do and to write, but finding the time and energy is not always possible. The relative quiet boredom and underlying anxiety of that first phase of the pandemic was the time for me to finally start writing this book. As I now finalize this manuscript at the end of 2021, I am so glad I chose to write this book as my largest pandemic project. Writing this book was a great joy in a difficult time, and provided much comfort and consistency in a period of upheaval. Yet, it also meant I did not get the usual chances to share much of these chapters in progress with my colleagues at conferences and talks. For other writing projects, I would usually thank all those who provided important feedback at such events as the work progressed. For this book though, most will see its contents for the first time upon their reading. I hope you enjoy my research findings and discussion here, and I look forward to when I can chat about them with many of you again in person in the months and years to come.

This said, there are many who made this book possible by their various contributions, despite the abnormal (new normal?) circumstances. A special thank you first of all to the Survey Research Centre at the University of Waterloo (https://uwaterloo.ca/survey-research-centre/) for their key role in the Millennial Trends Survey (MTS) data collection and cleaning in 2019. Also a big thank you to the *Cascadia* research team out West, led by Paul Bramadat from the University of Victoria, and the *Towards the Exit of Cultural Catholicism in Québec* research team led by E.-Martin Meunier from the University of Ottawa. I had the honor and privilege to be a co-investigator on these two SSHRC-funded research projects, and both teams were kind enough to allow me to use some of the focus group and interview data they collected from Millennials to complement and deepen my quantitative data in this book. Thank you to all those on these two research teams who collected and transcribed these high-quality qualitative data.

More broadly, my thanks to all the research teams who have made their survey data available and open access over the years, some survey data which I use in this book to complement my own MTS. These include notably the teams at the American National Election Studies, the Canadian Election Studies, the Pew Religious Landscape Survey, the International Social Survey Programme as well as the American and Canadian General Social Surveys and Census. Many of the quantitative analyses and results found in this book would not have been possible without many organizations making these survey data files freely available to researchers for download. I would sincerely like to thank Statistics Canada, the Pew Research Center, the research teams producing the American National Election Study, the Canadian Election Study, the International Social Survey Programme and the American General Social Survey for their open-access policies and willingness to share when it comes to their data. This open access to good-quality quantitative data has allowed us to strengthen our collective understanding of religion, spirituality and secularity among Millennials in the United States and Canada. In keeping with this open-access principle, I have also shared my 2019 Millennial Trends Survey data file, technical documentation and codebook with the Association for Religion Data Archives (ARDA: https://www.thearda.com/Archive/browse.asp) for all interested researchers to freely access. A big thank you to ARDA for hosting these data files.

Much of my discussion and arguments in this book build on the previous works from many esteemed colleagues (cited throughout this book) and chats I have had with them over the years. These colleagues include, but are not limited to, Joel Thiessen from Ambrose University; E.-Martin Meunier, Lori Beaman and Peter Beyer from the University of Ottawa; Paul Bramadat and Lynne Marks from the University of Victoria; Tina Block from Thompson Rivers University; Jean-Philippe Perreault from Université Laval; Géraldine Mossière from Université de Montréal; Micheline Milot from Université du Québec à Montréal; Sam Reimer from Crandall University; Ryan Cragun from the University of Tampa; Christian Smith from Notre-Dame University; Dick Houtman from the University of Leuven; Jörg Stolz from the University of Lausanne; Nan Dirk de Graaf from the University of Oxford; and David Voas from University College London. Thank you for all of your great work, support and brainstorming over the years. I really do feel this book builds on the shoulders of these and many other giants. I would also like to thank my two PhD students, Jacob Legault-Leclair and Zachary Munro from the University of Waterloo, with whom our discussions have also helped push my thinking forward on many of the topics covered in this book.

I was fortunate to receive a grant from the Social Sciences and Humanities Research Council's (SSHRC) Insight Development Grant program. Without the support SSHRC provides to researchers throughout Canada, I would not have been able to fund and run the 2019 MTS nor write this book.

I want to thank the great editorial team at Taylor and Francis/Routledge, who has been wonderful to work with. Namely, Neil Jordan (Commissioning Editor) and Alice Salt (Editorial Assistant). I also want to thank the external readers who reviewed this manuscript at its various stages for the peer-review process: your thoughtful and thorough feedback helped improved the contents of this book.

Last but certainly not least, a big thank you to all the Millennial research participants—from the surveys, interviews and focus groups—who find snippets of themselves in this book and who were extremely generous with their time and insights into their lives.

DATA AVAILABILITY STATEMENT

The 2019 Millennial Trends Survey (MTS), the main survey dataset used in this book, can be accessed free of charge in Stata format along with the MTS technical documentation and codebook at the Association for Religion Data Archives (ARDA): https://www.thearda.com/Archive/browse.asp

1

MILLENNIAL RELIGION, SOCIALLY LOCATED

"I'm Jeremy. I'm 30. I have a little business here. I do, like web development and stuff, and lots of different work. And I'd also be under the kind of irreligious banner." Jeremy, born in 1988,[1] took part in a focus group conducted by the Cascadia research team in 2018 in the Canadian West Coast metropolitan city of Vancouver,[2] a research team of which I was a member. Jeremy does not typically mention his irreligious identity when introducing himself and interacting with others in everyday life. Yet, he does so when probed with survey, in-depth interview or focus group questions on the topic. Although for the most part an unseen phenomenon in day-to-day life, when we as researchers start asking, we quickly realize that Jeremy is not alone in his irreligion among his generation.

When Statistics Canada asked "What, if any, is your religion?" in its 2018 General Social Survey (GSS; Cycle 33), 43% of teenagers and young adults aged 15–35 years old responded they have no religion. In the United States, the GSS figure for no religion in 2018 stood at 34% among 18–35 year olds. I gave my respondents a multitude of "no religion" options to choose from for such a question in the Millennial Trends Survey (MTS) I ran in 2019 among just over 2,500 18–35 year olds in the United States and Canada. Since I also asked about specific Christian traditions, denominations and groups to discourage nominal affiliation to Christianity as a whole, I found slightly higher rates of nonaffiliation: 44% of Canadian Millennials and 39% of American Millennials said they had no religion.

Nevertheless, putting oneself under the irreligious banner does not mean a life devoid of spirituality for some. Later in the focus group, Jeremy goes on to say:

> And yeah so I mean I'd say I'm also, the spiritual thing, … I like finding meaning in things. I like discussing topics about what life is, purpose and what is this all about. It doesn't matter if the person is religious or not, I'm really interested in that stuff. So, it matters a lot to me anyway.

DOI: 10.4324/9781003217695-1

Of those young adults who said they had no religion in my MTS, 18% of them in turn selected the "spiritual with no religion" answer option: 17% in the United States and 19% in Canada.

Then there are those at the other end of the continuum, like Andrea who was born in 1983, who our Cascadia research team first encountered in Portland, Oregon in June 2018, and who is very devout in her Jewish faith:

> I've been really observing and officially in the Jewish community for 4 or 5 years now. I did convert eventually. I was like, "It's time to take the plunge. It's time to do it." … I feel very, very good about my choice. Now that I do practice a religion, that's made me more curious. I feel like a greater responsibility to know more about other people and other perspectives.

Individuals who are actively involved in a religious group as Andrea is represent a smaller proportion of Millennials than among any older living generation: only 34% of American respondents aged 18–35 said they attend religious services (of any tradition) at least once a month in the 2018 GSS. In Canada, the rate stands even lower at 15%. Still, although they are now a minority among Millennials, those who are actively involved with a religious group are a substantial minority. Additionally, this subpopulation is more diverse than it has ever been, both racially and ethnically along with the wide variety of religious traditions represented. Many nonreligious Millennials like Jeremy, as well as more religious Millennials like Andrea, are also very open toward and willing to engage with views and perspectives different from their own on these matters.

The main objective of this book is to take a deep dive into the fascinating and ever-relevant world of religion, spirituality and secularity among the now most numerous generation in the United States (and fast becoming the most numerous in Canada): Millennials. The focus of the book is on the ways Millennials are doing religion, spirituality and secularity differently in their social lives compared with their parents and grandparents. I will take you on an empirical research journey exploring how the socio-cultural realities of a digital age, precarious work, growing pluralism, extreme individualism, environmental crisis, advanced urbanism, expanded higher education, emerging adulthood and a secular age are reshaping the (non)religious and spiritual landscapes for young adults in North America. We will uncover together what is new among this younger generation that we have never seen before, in terms of broader trends as well as in the more intimate ways Millennials describe their own experiences, hopes and realities.

Outsider Representations

No one really agrees on exactly which year it was in hindsight that newborns switched from being Gen X to Millennials. Some will use Howe's and Strauss' seminal cut-off dates of those born between 1982 and 2004 to group together Millennials (Howe and Strauss 2000; Strauss and Howe 1991). Pew Research

Center (2019) and Twenge (2017) use instead slightly earlier birth periods of 1981–1996 and 1980–1994, respectively. Others still prefer a more even distribution of generations across 20-year periods (Bibby, Thiessen, and Bailey 2019), and so will break down the current living generations in the following manner:

Born between 1906 and 1925 = Greatest Generation

Born between 1926 and 1945 = Silent Generation

Born between 1946 and 1965 = Boomer Generation

Born between 1966 and 1985 = Generation X

Born between 1986 and 2005 = Millennial Generation

Born between 2006 and 2025 = Generation Z

In my view, the exact dates are not all that important to the larger discussion. Any cut-off year is arbitrary in some sense. For practical reasons with the statistics, you will find me using the 1986–2005 birth year range in some cases throughout this book to refer to Millennials. In other instances, I will go with the 18–35 age range for recent survey and interview data which captures most adult Millennials. What is important is to generally encapsulate those individuals who were born and raised in the late 1980s, 1990s and early 2000s. This period marked the beginning of the late capitalist/neoliberal period (Jameson 1991; Scott 2018), the digital age (Prensky 2001) and a period of renewed focus on childhood protection (think of the appearance of Baby on Board car stickers, as well as protective play equipment such as bike helmets; Howe and Strauss 2000) as well as childhood commercialization. These birth cohorts then began to move into young adulthood in the 2000s, 2010s and early 2020s (at the turn of the Millennium, hence the generation's name).

This makes me, born in 1987, an old Millennial. I remember watching *Sesame Street* everyday after school when I was younger in our rural home north of Gatineau, Québec. Then, watching *The Simpsons* everyday after school when my parents decided I was old enough. I remember my grandmother taking my brother and I to church for midnight mass on Christmas Eve while my parents stayed home, and thinking what a weird place a church was (while also dreaming of the presents I was going to get the next day of course). I remember passing *Oui* signs on the way to primary school in 1995, encouraging Québec residents to vote yes for independence from Canada. I remember my family's first Windows 1995 PC arriving at home when I was young, and my older brother and I fighting over who could use the 30 hours of dial-up Internet my parents paid for each month in order to play Blizzard Entertainment's *Diablo* and *Starcraft* online (and our mother yelling at us to get off the Internet so she could use the landline phone). I remember one of the first CDs I got for my birthday: the Spice Girls' debut 1996 album *Spice* (and did I ever drive my dad nuts by listening to it all the time at full volume on my boombox). I remember sitting in math class in high school on the morning of September 11, 2001, and our teacher stopping class to tell us that a pair of passenger planes had struck the Twin Towers in New York City.

These formative childhood experiences of mine were in many ways different from those of younger Millennials born in the late 1990s and early 2000s, and who grew up with such key icons and events as Britney Spears, Jennifer Lopez and Blink 182, iPods, the War on Terror, Hurricane Katrina and the Great Recession. For the longest time, I did not think of myself as a Millennial. We had been called Generation Y while I was growing up, following Generation X. Ironically, it was only when mainstream Millennial anxiety struck older adults in the late 2000s and early 2010s that I, by then in graduate school at university, realized I fell into the first wave of this new Millennial generation others were so worried about. Although in 1990s pop culture Millennials were portrayed as the highly capable child saviors of society's ills (think Lisa Simpson in *The Simpsons*; or Devon Butler in *Cop and a Half*; or Jesse in *Free Willy*; or Roger Bomman in *Angels in the Outfield*; or Hallie Parker and Annie James in *The Parent Trap*; see Scott 2018, 87–94), by the late 2000s the shine had worn off. Suddenly, we were Generation Me (Twenge 2006): selfish, coddled, entitled, over-confident, morally uncertain, miserable and far removed from the practical realities of the world according to members of older generations (Alsop 2008; Eyre and Eyre 2011; Manne 2014; Tulgan 2009). We were labeled snowflakes: told too often by our parents that we were each unique and special, and thus supposedly growing up too fragile for the real world. Jeremy's irreligion became one of a number of highly worrisome Millennial trends. We were different from older generations in all the wrong ways. Marketers sold us stuff with this in mind. Members of the business community lamented our many faults as emerging workers in their eyes. Books and articles proposed solutions where the onus was on young individuals to lower their expectations and change their approach to better fit the current market economy.

OK Boomer. As can be the case, antagonism and targeting from outside groups (in this case, older adults in mainstream culture) reinforced for many the sense of community within our own generation, shoring up in-group and out-group identity boundaries. Offended by these negative stereotypes, I took on the Millennial identity in university and have owned it since. For some at least, this became a moment "… when individual members of a generation become conscious of their common situation and make this consciousness the basis of their group solidarity" (Mannheim 1952, 290); when, to continue in Mannheim's (1952) words, generation location was transformed into membership of a generation as an actuality. Because whether you like it or not, we Millennials are now the most numerous adult generation in the United States, and fast becoming so in Canada with ongoing immigration trends. When we decide to show up and vote (and voting is accessible to us and our votes are counted), we change the outcome of elections. When we take out our (e)wallets and flex our consumer muscle, companies and capitalism pay attention. And, as discussed in the later chapters of this book, when we choose to stay away from churches, many of these churches consequently have to close their doors permanently.

This Millennial awakening also began to show up in a variety of more academic works in the 2010s. Works such as those of Bibby, Thiessen, and Bailey (2019), Cairns (2017), Giroux (2013), Hancock (2011) and Scott (2018) pushed back against the prevailing myth of Millennial entitlement. Some did so by arguing that Millennials are not that different from previous generations in terms of their values and behavior, so older adults need not worry (Bibby, Thiessen, and Bailey 2019; Environics 2017). Many others though argued instead that Millennials are different because they are in fact facing never-before-seen challenges tied to the excesses of neoliberalism, economic austerity, work precarity and the decline of the welfare state across Western nations (Barr and Malik 2016; Cairns 2017; Giroux 2013; Hancock 2011; Raynor 2016; Scott 2018; Silva 2013). Rather than proposing young individuals simply lower their standards to worsening economic, social and environmental conditions, these scholars (many of them Bernie Sanders supporters in the United States) are now calling for political action from Millennials to help solve these issues or at least help improve these conditions.[3]

Although I am sympathetic to many of these calls for political action, and find much of this work very relevant for my own study in this book, part of me (the somewhat cynical part if I'm honest) still hears a bunch of older adults squabbling about how Millennials should be defined and what their political and social priorities should be. It is only very recently that we have started hearing from Millennial researchers themselves: the contemporary historical and cultural analysis by Scott (2018) being an important example here. The goal of my book is to do away with this baggage of both an extreme anxiety of stereotypes and a utopian hope for a perfect future found among older generations dreaming (or nightmaring) about the young, and instead examine how things really are regarding religion, spirituality and secularity for members of my own Millennial generation.

The Millennial Social Location

There currently exists a number of important social divides in the United States and Canada along which strong differences in values and behavior appear between individuals, and according to which social experiences and opportunities vary greatly. These include notably race, gender and socio-economic status. Although these key socio-demographic determinants and their intersections will come into play throughout this book, the main focus here is nevertheless on another important fracture line: that of generation. As we will see in the chapters to come, generational effects are especially crucial for understanding differences in (non) religious and spiritual identity, beliefs and practices in today's North American societies. It is with a new generation raised in "… a common location in the historical dimension of the social process …" (Mannheim 1952, 290), and "… differentiated by the changing content of formal education, by peer-group socialization, and by idiosyncratic historical experience …" (Ryder 1965, 843), that changes in (non)religiosity and spirituality become especially apparent.

According to the classic German sociologist of generations and social change Karl Mannheim, members of a same generation share in common a similar social location:

> The fact that people are born at the same time, or that their youth, adulthood, and old age coincide, does not in itself involve similarity of location; what does create a similar location is that they are in a position to experience the same events and data …. (Mannheim 1952, 297)

Especially crucial for Mannheim are those experiences which happen during childhood: first impressions which are key in the formation of consciousness during primary socialization, which Mannheim refers to as part of the "primary stratum":

> Early impressions tend to coalesce into a *natural view* of the world. All later experiences then tend to receive their meaning from this original set, whether they appear as that set's verification and fulfilment or as its negation and antithesis. Experiences are not accumulated in the course of a lifetime through a process of summation or agglomeration, but are 'dialectically' articulated in the way described. (Mannheim 1952, 298, italic emphasis by original author)

Consequently, individuals who are born and raised during the same period of time in a shared social environment are likely to experience aspects and events of this social environment as formative, and thus may go on to resemble each other in their attitudes and behaviors in key ways distinct from other older and younger generations not sharing this same social location. Strauss and Howe (1991, 32) put it this way:

> We explain how a generation is shaped by its 'age location' – that is, by its age-determined participation in epochal events that occur during its lifecycle. During childhood and, especially, during the coming-of-age experiences separating youth from adulthood, this age location produces what we call a 'peer personality' – a set of collective behavioral traits and attitudes that later expresses itself throughout a generation's lifecycle trajectory.

This book focuses on one generation specifically, which Strauss and Howe (1991) originally coined as the Millennial generation. Yet, unlike Strauss and Howe, my goal is not to find some repeat pattern between constellations of four generations throughout history to order the past and to make predictions about what Millennials will end up being in the future: accurate predictions which Strauss and

Howe, and most scholars for that matter, were not all that successful in making about Millennials back in the 1990s and early 2000s. My objective is rather to explore with recent empirical data how Millennials are different from the generations who have come before, since these differences are currently and will continue to have a significant impact on shifting American and Canadian religious and spiritual landscapes.

What is new and distinct about the Millennial social location, coming back to Mannheim's terminology, making their lives different from those of their parents and grandparents? I examine eight interconnected societal trends here that are especially being felt by Millennials. This is by no means an exhaustive list of all things new. Indeed, Wuthnow (2007), for example, identifies many of these same trends as influential for the lifeworlds of young adult members of Generation X. This said, the following eight interconnected trends are key elements of our current social world that have had an especially profound impact on Millennials. It is members of this younger generation who have been socialized within this new social environment during their childhood, teenage and young adult years, and who are being shaped in all aspects of their lives by these trends, including in their (non)religion and spirituality. I introduce these eight trends here in this chapter, as illustrated in Figure 1.1, and return to each throughout the book as we examine different aspects of the lives of religious, spiritual and secular Millennials.

A Digital Age

A Millennial colleague of mine in the neighboring history department at the University of Waterloo, Ian Milligan, likes to say that no one can do adequate contemporary history from the 1990s onward without studying and taking into account the Internet. He believes so strongly in this that he has dedicated a large part of his career to finding ways to record, archive and preserve it (yes, the whole Internet; Milligan 2019). Millennials are the first generation to grow up with computers, the Internet, cellphones and social media in their homes, to the point that these technologies are as prevalent and crucial to their everyday lives as key technologies from prior childhoods, such as paper, landlines, bicycles, cars, radios, TVs and home appliances.

The online world is now firmly weaved into the real worlds of work, food, family, friends, our bodies, leisure, pets, sports, music, religion, education, politics, health, market consumerism, transportation and even our experiences of nature. Finding and booking a campsite or a day hike often happens now online. As an avid outdoors person myself, I do not even notice anymore when people whip out their smartphones for a selfie with their favorite view, tree, flowers or wildlife to post on social media. It happens so often (and yes, I am also guilty of it at times). To go out on a day trip or extended expedition without a cellphone, GPS or some other communication or tracking tech on one's person is virtually unheard of now, or at the very least strongly discouraged by park officials.

FIGURE 1.1 Eight key trends of the Millennial social location

In many instances, the bricks and mortar of stores, restaurants, schools, community centers, health clinics, churches, offices and more continue to give way to digital spaces. One can focus on and lament the decline of older institutions and ways of doing, which many members of older generations do, and there is no doubt loss that accompanies this decline. Still, one can also look at it from the opposite direction: think instead about the rise of online shopping, food delivery apps, online courses, fitness and health wearables, gaming, music and video streaming, social media and virtual social gatherings, virtual doctor appointments and health advice, virtual faith services and materials, and remote online work from home. All these digital realities are molded by and are in turn shaping almost everyone, but especially today's emerging adults.

Religion and spirituality are most definitely not immune to this digital age. Like many (if not all) other forms of community now, religious groups are weaving online resources and content into their in-person activities to reach and connect their members. Yet, the impact of the digital age also goes far beyond this.

For Millennials, digital communities, including those which revolve around (non)religion and spiritualities, have in many instances replaced in-person gatherings. If someone now has an interest in faith matters, the first port of call for information gathering and understanding is often the Internet, rather than in-person consultation with faith leaders and community members. If someone wants to discuss and share their experiences of faith, they may very well turn to a Reddit forum. If someone wants to take part in a group prayer or meditation session, they may do so virtually, or in a pop-up in-person session organized on social media. Many holy sites may also be visited virtually, if the physical trek cannot be made.

In an ever-more individualized choice-based and consumer-based society, the Internet and social media provide resources (of varying quality) for teenagers and emerging adults who choose to go the involved seeker route. Digital faith communities and networks are not bound by the limits of physical location, and so can often reach a larger number of people further afield and around the world. But Cimino and Smith (2014) and Environics (2017, 45–46) also argue these are more precarious forms of community involvement than in-person religious groups, and Millennials tend to drop in and out of these digital spaces as they please without developing strong communal ties that lead to more engaged forms of faith and local community activity. In addition, faith networks are just one type of a whole variety of digital communities available to individuals now, competing in a sense for an individual's time and attention with others such as fandom groups; gaming networks, atheist, secularist and humanist organizations; cooking and foodie channels; outdoor enthusiasts; fashionistas; real-estate and home improvement buffs; kitten and puppy lovers; so much more; and my personal favorite these past few weeks, filmed, edited and commentated sand rallies of racing marbles (yes, it is a thing ... with dedicated fans).

Neoliberalism and Economic Precarity

Cairns (2017), Giroux (2013) and Scott (2018) are a few key works which map out the shifting market economy and role of the State that have paralleled the rise of the digital age so far since the 1980s, and the impact of this change on Millennials: a shift from the New-Deal inspired, achievable middle-class, single-bread winner, manufacturing-focused economic system of the late 1940s to 1970s United States to the deregulation and austerity-driven neoliberalism of the 1980s to today. The most pronounced example of this turn is the new gig economy, which has encompassed over a third of the American workforce in recent years (Forbes 2018). A gig economy based on the ideals of freedom, freelance passion-driven work, flexibility and creativity, but often put into practice as a mostly unregulated model of precarious work characterized by the prevalence of temporary contract positions, unpaid internships, part-time work and low pay paired with poor or non-existent benefits for most not lucky and skilled enough to access the high-paying Silicon Valley style information and technology jobs.

Overall, earnings are lower among American Millennials compared with when their older counterparts were their age, and debt load is higher (Kurz, Li, and Vine 2018). In Canada, median income in general is not necessarily lower among Millennials, but the gap between low- and high-income households is growing (Heisz and Richards 2019). The Great Recession of 2007–2009 was a key moment which accelerated this shift, and had a large impact on the first wave of Millennial adults just arriving on the job market at the time. The COVID-19 pandemic, its lockdowns and she-cessions are shaping up to be another key moment in accelerating this market shift further: destabilizing once again the job market for the younger wave of Millennials just reaching adulthood now, disproportionately favoring the home delivery and online shopping sectors of the gig economy as everyone goes even more digital and virtual due to restrictions on in-person activities, and this time disproportionately affecting female workers with children at home as well as in the service industry.

This shift to more precarious work and less State public support has been experienced to a greater extent in the United States than in Canada, where the Canadian federal and provincial welfare state has remained more pronounced with public healthcare and subsidized higher education (and is looking to actually grow with hundreds of billions of dollars of pandemic public spending). Nevertheless, Canada has not been immune to these changes either over the last few decades. I see it among my many friends and peers who are still struggling to find stable work in their thirties and forties. I see it in universities and colleges around me which are hiring more contract sessionals to teach their courses rather than creating permanent, better-paid, tenure-track professor positions with benefits. We also all saw it in the thousands of dead from COVID-19 in public and private long-term care homes in Ontario and Québec in 2020–2021, care homes which have been chronically underfunded over the past several decades. These are but a few examples among many.

There are different schools of thought on the impact this growing economic precarity is having on individual religiosity. Some will argue growing material insecurity will play to religion's advantage: that, faced with more difficult economic times and a weakened welfare state, more people will seek out comfort, support and social capital among faith groups. This is the other side of the coin to the argument that growing material security and a growing welfare state over the last couple of centuries have been key factors in the secularization of many Western societies; that people's need for religion as a coping mechanism and as an afterlife safety net is reduced as their economic conditions improve (Hirschle 2013; Höllinger and Muckenhuber 2019; Immerzeel and Tubergen 2013; Norris and Inglehart 2011; Ruiter and Tubergen 2009; Storm 2017).

Yet, there is little empirical evidence in developed nations of a resurgence of religion in economically difficult times. Frequent religious service attendance has only continued to decline among younger generations despite their economic precarity and during periods of economic downturn such as the Great Recession in both Canada and the United States. It is also not the poorest individuals in these two countries who are the most religious. For example, only 19% of Canadian respondents with family incomes of less than $25,000 in the 2018 GSS attended religious services at least once a month, compared with 23% among the $25,000–$49,999 income bracket and 22% among the $50,000–$74,999 income bracket. In the 2018 U.S. GSS, 38% of respondents with family incomes lower than $25,000 attended religious services at least monthly, which is the same proportion as among those in the $25,000–$49,999 income bracket and lower than the 44% who attend monthly or more frequently among the $50,000–$89,000 income bracket.

Growing material security may only have a negative impact on individual religiosity when transitioning out of a base threshold of abject poverty, individuals no longer having to face starvation, widespread disease and low life expectancy. Additionally, this may also be a case of asymmetrical causality (Lieberson 1987). An increase in material security in societies may lead to decline in individual religiosity for some, but a subsequent decrease in material security may not necessarily lead to a return to religion. Those Millennials socialized in more secular social environments without religion may very well turn to other sources of comfort and opportunity in times of hardship; and/or religion may be blamed by many for the decline in material security (the discourse that political leaders are relying on blind faith rather than on science and social policy for example).

Some religious traditions have positioned themselves as a source of resistance to neoliberalism, such as Pope Francis strongly and regularly criticizing the excesses of the current market economy. Yet others, including many White evangelical groups in the United States, have instead strongly aligned themselves with the Republican Party, accepted uncritically most of its policy positions, and so either consciously or unconsciously end up being mouth pieces for many of the party's neoliberal economic values as well; neoliberal economic values that a majority of Millennials do not seem to share in both the United States and Canada (Bibby, Thiessen, and Bailey 2019; Frey 2018; Pew Research Center 2010). Nicholas, born in 1990 and one of the research participants of a Millennial focus group conducted in Vancouver, British Columbia in April 2018, highlights this:

> … our age group as far as I am aware, is the most anti-capitalistic, maybe, I don't know. … we grew up in 2008, that happened just as I was getting an awareness of what the world is, so fundamentally grew up with a realization that this system is bullshit.

Growing Pluralism Paired with Ongoing Systemic Racism and Inequalities

William Frey (2018) coined the concept "cultural generation gap" to refer to the divide between the racially diverse youth population and the older, still predominantly white population in America. Millennials are the most racially and ethnically diverse adult generation the United States (and Canada) have ever seen, and this trend is set to continue among post-Millennial generations as well. Among 15–34 year olds in the 2016 Canadian Census, 26% are visible minorities, and another 6% are Indigenous (First Nations, Métis or Inuit). In the largest metropolitan area, the Greater Toronto Area, these percentages stand at 56% and 1%, respectively. According to 2015 U.S. Census Bureau population estimates, 14% of 18–34 year olds are Black, another 21% are Hispanic, 6% are Asian, and 3% are of another non-White ethno-racial background (Frey 2018, 256). Frey sees Millennials as a bridge generation, acting as a social, economic and political link between older, whiter populations and the next, even more racially diverse, post-Millennial younger generation.

This growing pluralism extends to religion as well. Non-Judaeo-Christian religions represent an estimated 6% of those born between 1986 and 2005 and residing in the United States in 2018, compared with 3% among Gen Xers and 2% among Boomers. In Canada, affiliation to non-Judaeo-Christian religions encompasses an estimated 14% of Millennials in the 2018 GSS. The largest religious tradition among these, Islam, is held in turn by 1% of American and 4% of Canadian Millennials. We explore these trends of growing religious diversity in more detail in the next chapter.

This factual pluralism is also complemented by the positive attitudes most Millennials in both the United States and Canada have toward minority groups, immigration and issues of equality. Jeremy's and Andrea's openness to perspectives different from their own, discussed at the start of this chapter, are examples of this. In Canada, Bibby, Thiessen and Bailey (2019, 84) find for example that 83% of Millennials indicate racial and cultural diversity as good for the country, compared with 78% of Gen Xers and 73% of Boomers. Seventy-four percent of Millennials say in turn that, on the whole, immigration is a good thing for Canada, compared with 66% among Gen Xers and 67% among Boomers. In the 2018 U.S. GSS, 81% of Millennials agree or strongly agree that homosexuals should have the right to marry, compared with 69% of Gen Xers and 60% of Boomers.

In many instances, the higher levels of pluralism among Millennials have also highlighted ongoing systemic racism in both the United States and Canada. Although Millennials overall have the most positive attitudes toward immigration, multiculturalism and equality among adults, this in itself does not solve important inequalities in society. Black Lives Matter and other anti-black racism protests that saw a resurgence in the summer of 2020, driven in large part by Millennial activists of color, highlighted once again how the color of someone's skin (along with their gender, religion, ethno-racial background and sexual orientation) still severely affects their treatment by police and the justice system, their educational and job opportunities, their access to high-quality healthcare and more.

For some, religion has been a source of empowerment in the face of these inequalities. Reverend Al Sharpton, a key figurehead and voice of the Black Lives Matter movement in the aftermath of the police shooting of George Floyd in Minneapolis, personifies this. Yet for others, religion is just another cog in the problematic system. President Trump (for whom only 37% of the American Millennial electorate voted in 2016; Galston and Hendrickson 2016) disrupting peaceful anti-black racism protests in Washington, D.C. with security forces and police to get a photoshoot holding a Bible outside St John's Church in June 2020 became a key moment to this effect.

Religious pluralism is also having another major impact on the (non)religious and spiritual landscape, in addition to diversifying it. In his classic 1967 work *The Sacred Canopy*, Peter Berger argued that pluralism would lead to a "crisis of credibility" and be a key factor in subjective secularization:

> Religion no longer legitimates 'the world.' Rather, different religious groups seek, by different means, to maintain their particular subworlds in the face of a plurality of competing subworlds. Concomitantly, this plurality of religious legitimations is internalized in consciousness as a plurality of possibilities between which one may choose. *Ipso facto*, any particular choice is relativized and less than certain. (Berger 1967, 152)

This theory was heavily criticized by supply-side religious market scholars in the 1980s, 1990s and 2000s (Bibby 2004; Iannaccone 1994; Stark and Finke 2000), to the point that Berger recanted his initial argument in his 1999 paper *The Desecularization of the World*. The supply-side religious market theorists' counter-argument is that pluralism, framed as a more open religious marketplace, in fact leads to greater religious vitality since a larger array of religious "products" were now available to "consumers" to better fit their spiritual wants and needs. With this better-quality selection available, a majority of individuals were thus expected to find a religious group that they perceived as worth the associated time and resource costs in order to reap the related spiritual and social benefits.

This said, in the 2010s, the pendulum swung again. After having disqualified most of the supply-side market theorists' empirical evidence for their pluralism = religious vitality argument, which was shown to be based on faulty measures (Voas, Olson, and Crockett 2002), better-quality qualitative and quantitative evidence began to appear supporting the original 1967 Berger idea. Few individuals were switching religions to find better-suited options, and many more were instead disaffiliating altogether. Many nonreligious interviewees speak of how they became aware of perspectives different from their own during their childhood, teenage and early adult years, and how this weakened the legitimacy of their own religious beliefs and led them to doubt their prior religious worldview (Baggett 2019, 64; Thiessen and Wilkins-Laflamme 2017, 2020). Olson et al. (2020) show with nation-wide quantitative longitudinal Religious Congregations and Membership Studies data from the United States that "… greater county-level religious diversity is followed by later declines in county-level religious participation rates." Lim and de Graaf (2021) also find that greater out-group presence and diversity in U.S. counties negatively impact religiosity indicators among Protestants and Catholics.

Kamal, a practicing Muslim born in 1989 and who took part in a focus group of Millennials in April 2018 in Vancouver, British Columbia, touches on this mechanism of pluralism driving a decline in religion. Kamal discusses the cognitive work and effort that goes into understanding and coexisting peacefully with those who have different religious worldviews and beliefs from your own, and how this might turn off many individuals: "It's much easier to be like, 'I don't believe, I'm out of here. My spirituality is individual,' because the hard work is dealing with other people, who have different ideas, so it's much easier to peace out from that … ." On the other side of Canada, Jason, born in 1994, describing himself as an atheist and living in Montréal, Québec took part in a series of life history interviews conducted among Millennials and Gen Xers in the province by another research team I was involved with in 2018–2020 and led by E.-Martin Meunier at the University of Ottawa as well as by Jean-Philippe Perreault at the Université Laval. Jason describes how growing religious pluralism in his extended family, notably the arrival of in-laws from religions outside of Catholicism and Christianity, led the family to stop attending mass at Easter and Christmas later in Jason's childhood so the non-Christian in-laws would feel included in their family celebrations of the holidays. Even though religion had not played a large role for Jason's family in his earlier childhood years, growing religious pluralism within the family was a factor in the dispearance of the last remnants of religious service attendance during special holidays. Jason describes this as happening relatively quietly and mostly indifferently within the family, without any real discussion of the issue having taken place.

Individual Choice and Consumerism

This fourth shift has been happening for many generations now, but is at its most advanced among Millennials. This generation often scores higher on values of individualism such as independence and self-achievement (Arnett 2015; Bibby, Thiessen, and Bailey 2019; Pew Research Center 2010). Identity self-construction, autonomy and personal choice as highly prized values in our societies, with the ultimate goals of personal happiness and "authentic" experiences, and authority ultimately lying with the individual rather than with an external source such as a parent, a religious leader, a political leader or even God, are themes that permeate the very fabric of our current-day Western societies since the 1960s, and are paired with our consumer market economy (Berger 1979; Heelas and Woodhead 2005; Taylor 1991).

As mentioned previously, supply-side religious market theorists thought that this availability of choice when it came to religious and spiritual traditions, or "products," would lead to a revival of faith among most individuals, or "consumers," in society. However, they neglected to include in their equations the fact that a variety of nonreligious choices are now also available and socially acceptable in our societies, especially among the Millennial generation. Individuals may shop around and pick and choose *à la carte* different religious and spiritual elements to build their own personal faith systems, what Wuthnow (2007) calls *tinkering*. Yet, individuals may also choose to stay away from religion and spirituality altogether, in many cases with little or tolerable social penalty, and instead find meaning in other areas of life such as with friends, family, food and fido (pets) to use Drescher's (2016) terminology.

Many examples of this came through during the Cascadia research project's focus groups and life history interviews with Millennials. Rachel, born in 1992 and who took part in a focus group in Portland, Oregon, in June 2018, states:

> We put out a study recently looking at the Jewish population here in Portland, and a lot of Jews are unaffiliated with a synagogue or an organization and one of their theses is that maybe those Jews just find a service that was previously provided by a Jewish place, but now it's, you could find it easily elsewhere. If it's closer to you, or if it's cheaper, then you should go.

Kayla, born in 1995 and who took part in a focus group in Victoria, British Columbia in April 2018, says:

> I also find in my circles that a lot of my friends' parents are still going to church, but with, like, maybe dubious commitment to the theology, but are still in it for the community? And a lot of people my age kind of say, well, like, "Well, that's fine. Like, I go to knitting group. I'm taken care of." At least, in university, like, I do not feel as though I have any of the arguments that my mother has for going to church every Sunday, because I feel as though I have people that see me all the time when I'm in school, that are looking out for me. And that serves a lot of the similar purposes that churches used to serve.

Kelly, born in 1992 and who sat down with historian Lynne Marks for a life history interview in Seattle, Washington in May 2018, says:

> However, I think living here and with the culture of what you do on Sunday, you go to brunch, you don't go to church, you know? Or you go hiking, or you go, if it's a nice day you go to the beach and you dink around at the beach.

My co-author Joel Thiessen and I in our previous book *None of the Above: Nonreligious Identity in the US and Canada* explored how parents giving choice to their children in matters of religion was a key factor for some in their religious disaffiliation (Thiessen and Wilkins-Laflamme 2020, 31–32). Parents would initially religiously socialize their children by taking them along to religious services and involving them in other religious activities within and outside the home. Then, in their children's pre-teen or teen years, many parents would give them the choice of continued religious involvement or not, unlike in previous generations for which it continued to be a family and social obligation. Some of these children took this opportunity to step away from their religious group.

For others though, heightened individualism and choice have led to a more engaged relationship with their faith. Andrea was able to explore different faiths during her teenage and young adult years, and ended up converting to Judaism in her early thirties. She appreciated the more open intellectual and social space she was given to explore:

> … I think sometimes you do need that time to figure out where that community has meaning for you and why you find it meaningful to be part of your community. … you're able to be untethered and you're able to find that solitary space, you're allowed that intellectual space to come back to [religious community], like, "Oh yeah. I would really like it if I could back into that." … because you have to continue to negotiate it, but it can also be really good for one to have that clear space, that clear moment where nothing's around you so you can find that again and come back to where you're supposed to be.

Victoria, born in 1992 and a self-identifying Protestant who took part in another focus group conducted by the Cascadia research team in Portland, Oregon in June 2018, describes her church life and that of her fellow Millennials as follows: "I think now it's more about you individually seeking something, rather than your community experience of being born into something, having these traditions." These more religious seeking individuals, like Andrea and Victoria, represent a much smaller portion of the young adult population than was anticipated by supply-side religious market theorists, but are nevertheless a substantial and important minority to consider.

For others still, expressive individualism and valued choice have led to an exploration of more personalized forms of spirituality. For example, this can include belief in a personal god, supernatural being or higher power, belief in an interconnected natural world and universe, belief in some form of afterlife, prayer, meditation, mindfulness activities or other spiritual identities and self-help materials and behaviors. Stephanie, a self-identified spiritual but not religious individual who was born in 1986 and who took part in a focus group led by the Cascadia research team in Seattle, Washington in May 2018, says:

> I tend to get a 'hippie' label in my group of friends, you know, so if I start spouting off something about, you know, Mother Universe and us all going back to the same dust that we came from and being part of one big energy that we can't really explain, … I've considered Buddhism, I guess, especially, or just meditation practice … I guess things like convening with nature and being in nature and playing music to me are my everyday spiritual practices. And I find meditation and activity and being with other people in my own

> way – I haven't felt compelled to seek some other kind of structured community that's specific to a religious creed. … it's like I was raised by two people from very different cultures from this region, and I've never really felt like I had a culture that I inherited. For me, it was very much that I built my own culture, beliefs, philosophy, from the ground up. That like, obviously all of our parents influenced us, but I feel like my culture comes very much from myself. And there's definitely a strong vein … of getting back to authentic culture that stems from people's actual needs, and feelings, and behaviours, …

Luckmann (1967) famously refers to this phenomenon as "invisible religion," Heelas and Woodhead (2005) as the "spiritual revolution" and Watts (2022) as the "religion of the heart." Houtman and Aupers (2007, 305) argue that their cross-national findings from Europe provide evidence for a surge in post-Christian types of spirituality, and "… confirm the theory of detraditionalization, according to which a weakening of the grip of tradition on individual selves stimulates a spiritual turn to the deeper layers of the self." More on this is given in Chapter 4.

Other populations still, notably Indigenous peoples, have begun to revisit and reinfuse their nations' traditional spiritualities and ways of life that were overtly suppressed and decimated for so long by colonial powers. Many First Nations, Métis and Inuit, 30% of whom were between the ages of 12 and 29 in Canada in 2016, find in these spiritualities a source of resistance to the excesses of individualism and the White Man's consumer market economy, as well as a source of empowerment to combat ongoing cultural genocide and systemic racism. These spiritualities, defined at their core by the virtues of humility, honesty, bravery, respect, generosity, love and wisdom (Stonechild 2016), are also proving to be a key resource in the fight against another and connected current-day existential crisis: that of environmental destruction.

Environmental Degradation and Climate Change

Air, water and land pollution, the extinction of species, the destruction of wild habitat, the depletion of natural resources and of course climate change are considered by many in society, especially among Millennials, to be the crisis of our age. Raised to care about the environment by the Boomer green movement that began in the 1960s and 1970s, and facing severely worsening environmental conditions as they age throughout the 21st century, 59% of 18–35 year olds in the 2016 American National Election Study think the federal government should increase spending to protect the environment, a proportion that reached 78% among the same age group in the 2019 Canadian Election Study.

Greta Thunberg, a late Millennial born in 2003, is a voice heard and valued especially by members of her generation and who personifies the environmental crisis and the need for wide-scale action. Salient imagery of the crisis that Millennials have been regularly exposed to for most of their childhood, teenage and emerging adult years includes the clear-cut forest, the starving polar bear, the quickly disappearing wild tiger and the melting glacier.

A number of religious and spiritual traditions and leaders have played key roles in the environmental movement and its message. One example among many includes the Tsleil-Waututh Nation elders and the *Kwekwecnewtxw*, a traditional cedar watch house, they constructed to protest the Kinder Morgan Trans Mountain pipeline expansion in spring 2018 in Burnaby, British Columbia.[4] Another example is the large number of American faith leaders from mainline Protestant, Catholic, Jewish, Muslim and Hindu organizations who denounced President Trump's withdrawal from the Paris climate agreement in 2017. Victoria, introduced earlier from the Portland, Oregon focus group, is very environmentally minded and engaged, and works "... for an earth keeping organization that's a Christian organization that does environmental work."

Yet, in other instances, because of the environmental movement's alignment with the scientific community, notably, for example, the widespread scientific evidence supporting the existence of human-driven climate change, some religious groups and leaders who tend to present their faith in opposition to science will equally deny or downplay the existence of climate change and the need to urgently address this and other environmental crises. It is not all Evangelicals who think this in the United States, but many do and it often accompanies their more conservative value orientation in general (Pew Research Center 2015). This Christian-Right-inspired opposition to climate change action also seems to get more attention in mainstream and social media, and thus has a disproportionate impact on many Millennials' overall perception of religion and what it stands for.

Further Urbanism and Cosmopolitanism

At the same time as the environment has become a key socio-political issue, more and more individuals, especially Millennials, are living further away from wild, natural and rural spaces. Just over 80% of American and Canadian populations now live in urban areas (Plecher 2020; U.S. Census Bureau 2012). This proportion is even higher, closer to 90%, among 18–35 year olds in both countries in recent years. Some Millennials have moved back to more rural areas with the possibilities offered by online remote work, as well as the draw of a back-to-the-land and back-to-nature lifestyle (paired with affordable housing). But more have chosen to remain in or move to big cities and their burbs, driving a continued urbanization trend into the 21st century.

The cities are where most of the jobs are, where the diverse peoples, food, shopping and entertainment are, where many of the social services are (good-quality schools, universities and healthcare, for example), where the airports for world travel are, where the high-speed good-quality Internet is, where the various modes of public transit are and more. Most Millennials are not willing to leave this behind to chance it in the distant countryside, especially when the city is all they have known since childhood.

This continued trend of urbanization, dating back to the late nineteenth and early twentieth centuries in the United States and Canada, has completely changed the name of the game for religious groups. European settler Christianity arrived in North America and became entrenched as the center of socio-political life in the form of the village church(es). Often the only institution offering social services and community space, many of the big mainline Christian traditions in America and Canada developed and thrived in this rural, agricultural lifeworld of the 19th century.

We just do not live in that kind of society anymore. Many of the old liberal Protestant and Catholic churches surrounding my childhood area in the rural Gatineau Hills are left abandoned and crumbling, along with many of the old wooden barns and cabins from over a century ago. A few are bought up by those with wealth from nearby cities to convert into ultra-modern farmhouse-styled weekend and vacation homes. And in population centers, religious groups are now competing with a wide variety of more secular social institutions, spaces and activities that can entirely frame individuals' wants and needs.

Religious groups, including from Christianity and many other traditions, are gaining though in metropolitan centers from an influx of actively religious immigrants from Central and South America, Africa, the Middle East, Eastern Europe, as well as South and South-East Asia. Forty-seven percent of those who attend religious services at least once a month and who live in Canadian cities are born outside the country. In the United States, this rate stands at 18%. In Canada and the United States, 27% and 23%, respectively, of these foreign-born actively religious urban adults are under the age of 36 years. Racial and ethnic pluralism are becoming key realities for religion in general in the two countries, with millions of Hindus, Buddhists, Sikhs and especially Muslims arriving and becoming established over the last few decades. Immigration is also bringing new vitality and ways of practicing to Christian traditions struggling to reach many of their traditional base of European-origin populations. Many churches are either going mega in a sense, or are going broke and being converted into condos and high-end hipster restaurants in these urban areas.[5]

Expanded Higher Education

One of the many draws of urban centers for emerging adults is the colleges and universities more often found within city limits. Thirty percent of 18–35 year olds had a post-secondary degree in the 2018 U.S. GSS, and 47% of the same age group had one in the 2016 Canadian Census. Further, 15% and 24%, respectively, were in the process of getting one at the time of these data collections. Millennials are the most educated living adult generation on average in American and Canadian history. College and university years have become important life transitions for a large portion of this generation, and graduation from higher education a key rite of passage along with the formation of long-term romantic relationships (often at college or university) and the birth of one's child. Higher education is giving access to a whole world of knowledge and skills to more people of this generation than ever before.

But not all Millennials have the financial means or life opportunities for higher education, and are often severely penalized for it in terms of their later job prospects, more so than any other generation before. Greater access to higher education has meant an inflation of degrees, where many post-secondary diplomas do not give a young person access to as many jobs as they once did. It has also meant that those without a university degree have access to even less, especially with the job market shift from manufacturing to service, information and technology work over the last half-century (Côté and Allahar 1994).

There is ongoing debate about the effects of higher education on individual religiosity. On one side of the debate, Smith and Snell (2009, 250) for example argue that "While the transition from the teenage to the emerging adult years does entail an overall decline in religious involvement, …, attending college per se is not an experience that particularly contributes to that decline." On the other side of the debate though, the years spent at college and university, especially nondenominational (non-Christian) institutions of higher education, are considered a time in an emerging adult's life when religious ties may weaken (Glanzer, Hill, and Ream 2014; Hill 2011; Mayrl and Oeur 2009). Many college and university students are no longer living with their parents near their original religious group or congregation; they have other social and educational demands on their time; and they are regularly exposed to new, notably critical and scientific, worldviews in classes and among their peers.

More widespread and longer higher education, along with the trend toward precarious work explored earlier in this chapter, are additionally delaying Millennials' transition from their teenage years to full adulthood, an extended life phase during their late teens, twenties and early thirties that Jeremy Arnett (2015) has coined as "emerging adulthood."

Emerging Adulthood as an Extended Life Stage

Emerging adulthood is defined by Arnett (2015) as the post-teenage stage of life now extending from the age of 18 years old to the mid- or late twenties (or even early thirties for some) during which marriage and parenthood are postponed, post-secondary education and training are often acquired, and during which there is usually prolonged job instability for the individual. William, born in 1984 and interviewed about his life history in June 2018 in Laval, Québec, talks about this period of his life:

> … I think my adult life started pretty late because of my full-time studies up until I was 26 years old. I then started looking for a [teaching] job and I had to take substitute positions left, right and center. It's only in the last 4 or 5 years [since William was 30 years old or so] that things are a bit more stable.… in my head it was very clear [during his early 20s] that I didn't know where I was going to live, that I was probably going to live in another country, alone I don't know where so all the family aspect, the romantic

> aspect, I put it aside in that sense because I told myself "I don't know what's going to happen, I don't know where I'll end up, maybe I will leave and I don't want to be stuck here" … (translated from French).

This extended emerging adulthood life phase is a relatively new social phenomenon, distinct to many Gen Xers and Millennials especially. For most members of the Silent and Boomer generations, it was typical to be married (or almost married), to have a child (or to be expecting a child), to own their home and to have a stable role in the labor force or as a homemaker by their early twenties. Now, emerging adults are likely to live with their parents well into their twenties, and may sometimes even boomerang back to their parental household after their higher education, during an unemployment phase, facing unaffordable housing and/or with COVID-19 pandemic lockdowns. Many first-wave Millennials born in the late 1980s are now transitioning out of this emerging adulthood and starting families of their own, becoming homeowners and achieving more stable work in their thirties. But most members of the Millennial generation still remain in this emerging adulthood stage of life in the early 2020s.

Arnett identifies four key changes in the 1960s and 1970s in the United States and other Western nations that laid the groundwork for this extended emerging adulthood life phase for later generations: (1) the Technology Revolution, referring to the automation of manufacturing and the subsequent shift from a manufacturing-based labor force to a service economy which requires more individuals now to gain post-secondary education and higher-level information and technology skills training before career employment; (2) the Sexual Revolution and the widespread availability of birth control, which allows individuals (and women especially) to be sexually active while delaying child-rearing; (3) the Women's Movement and the subsequent expansion of young women's educational and job opportunities beyond homemaking; and (4) the Youth Movement which exalted being, feeling and acting young, and represented full adulthood as an end to independence, to spontaneity and to wide-open possibility.

In addition to pushing back the age of marriage and parenthood, this extended emerging adulthood life stage will have many lasting effects for Millennials. One series of lasting effects, not discussed by Arnett, may be on the religious and spiritual lives of this generation. Extending the life period of job and financial uncertainty for emerging adults means that many are unable to "settle down," own their own home and feel economically secure enough to start a family of their own in their twenties and thirties. This in turn could have a negative impact on individual religiosity, with religious service attendance usually going hand in hand with weekly family life and a stable home location near one's local religious group. Hiemstra, Dueck, and Blackaby (2018), Smith and Snell (2009, 75), Smith et al. (2011) as well as Wuthnow (2007) argue that the social, institutional and geographical disruptions and transitions experienced in this now extended life phase of emerging adulthood can correlate negatively with religious practices.

BOX 1.1 THE IMPACT OF COVID-19.

The COVID-19 pandemic, which I lived through as I wrote this book, does not seem to have brought about fundamental change to any of the eight societal trends that I list as key to the Millennial social location. Indeed, so far it seems to have exasperated many of them instead. We will have to wait and see if the travel and immigration restrictions as well as greater national protectionism tied to the pandemic will have a lasting effect on migration, cosmopolitanism and pluralism in North America. We will also have to wait and see if office buildings staying shut in downtown cores during the pandemic will impact urban populations in the long run. However, what we do know at the moment is that younger Millennials were arriving on the job market in one of the worst economic recessions in living memory. Much of the (precarious) work in the service, hospitality and tourism sectors all but dried up for many months, and does not look like it will return to pre-COVID levels anytime soon. The lack of benefits, notably paid sick leave and other healthcare benefits, as well as chronic low pay were especially felt by front line workers in grocery stores, in Amazon and other online shopping warehouses, in long-term care homes, and in many other essential industries as workers were exposed to and fell ill with the virus. The digital age has become even more salient for our lives, notably with vastly expanded online shopping, remote online work, and virtual social, religious, artistic and cultural activities now being the norm. Many forms of environmental action and funding have been sidelined by authorities and politicians in favor of dealing with the immediate urgency of the pandemic and recovering economically from its effects, at the same time as we experienced one of the worst Atlantic hurricane seasons on record in 2020 along with one of the worst wildfire season on the West Coast of the United States in the summer and fall of 2020, due at least in part, as most scientific experts agree, to human-driven climate change. Also, with lockdowns and strict limits on in-person gatherings that lasted the better part of two years, social isolation and the extremes of individualism were felt by many like never before.

These and other COVID-19 pandemic experiences impacted everyone, including Millennials, but the largest formative influence may be on the next generation, Generation Z born roughly between 2006 and 2025. Many among this youngest living generation are currently in their prime childhood socialization years when their experiences will have a lasting influential impact on the rest of their lives. The COVID-19 pandemic will affect some of how Millennials see and live in the world for years to come, but probably not as much as it will affect the formative social location of the next generation.

Religion among Millennials

So far in this introductory chapter, my aim has been to demonstrate that religion, spirituality and secularity are not separate isolated phenomena only marching to their own beat among Millennials. Instead, they are interconnected with key societal transformations over the past few decades which characterize my generation's social location. Consequently, when I explore distinct aspects of the Millennial (non)religious and spiritual experience from now on, it is with the understanding that these aspects are tied to other socio-political upheavals.

What has been the main focus to date among prior research on Millennials and religion? The most common story so far has been one of religious decline (Jones, Cox, and Banchoff 2012; Pew Research Center 2010, 85–109; Sherkat 2014; Smith and Snell 2009; Twenge 2017; Voas and Chaves 2016; Wittberg 2021). Millennials score lower on a whole range of religiosity indicators compared with members of older generations, including religious affiliation, frequent religious service attendance, belief in God or a higher power, salience of religion in their lives and personal prayer. We will explore these empirical trends in more detail in the next chapter.

Religious decline among Millennials in the United States and Canada fits into and is explained by the broader secular transition framework. Like with the more classic secularization theories of Weber's (1993) disenchantment and Berger's (1967) collapse of the sacred canopy, modernization is understood in secular transition theory as the root cause of religious decline, including its "… mix of industrialization, democratization, urbanization, rationalization, cultural diversity, expanded education, and increased prosperity …" (Voas and Chaves 2016, 1522). These modern processes, pushed to their limits and even taking on new forms in the Millennial social location, are argued to undermine identities, beliefs and behavior related to the superempirical and transcendent. Debate rages on in a number of more recent quantitative cross-national and longitudinal studies as to which of these processes is most influential in driving the decline of religiosity indicators among (mostly Western) populations (see notably Stolz (2020) for a summary of this debate). Nevertheless, there are three main arguments put forward by the secular transition framework on how religious decline unfolds that form more of a consensus among those currently within the secularization paradigm. Taking inspiration from Martin's (1978) seminal work, secular transition theory first argues that religious decline can be triggered at different moments in different regions, and proceed at different speeds depending on the specific socio-historical context (Brauer 2018; Stolz, Pollack, and de Graaf 2020; Voas 2008):

> Every country's experience of secularization is unique when it comes to specifics like the onset of decline, the rate of decline, and contingencies that may accelerate or offset cohort-driven decline in a particular time and place.… although historical, political, cultural, social, and economic differences among the dozens of European countries produced substantial

> variation in the onset of secularization across the continent, once it begins the pattern of change looks very similar in all of them. The differences are a matter of history and culture, and explaining them always requires a combination of the general and the particular. But these differences should not obscure the reality that there is a general pattern of religious decline that characterizes the West, including the United States. (Voas and Chaves 2016, 1549)

The second main argument put forward by this secular transition framework, also mentioned in the previous quote, is one of generational religious decline. Although the timing may vary between regions and countries, once underway a process begins where "... each successive cohort is less religious than the preceding one. America is not an exception. ... The common story is decline driven by cohort replacement ..." (Voas and Chaves 2016, 1517, 1520). This process achieves fruition when many parents with weakened religiosity from their now more secular social environment have (Millennial) children of their own and raise their children without explicit religious socialization in markedly more secular surroundings. Declining levels of religious socialization during childhood are considered a key factor in understanding these inter-generational decreases in religion. Within the secular transition framework, religious and spiritual needs among individuals are understood as socially constructed; usually only present among adults who learnt them during childhood. Individuals born and raised in more religious social environments and families tend to be those who go on to be more religious and spiritual as adults. Secular transition argues that this is less and less the case for larger and larger portions of younger generations who do not receive such a socialization.

The third main argument is that the secular transition would affect all forms of religion and spirituality in society. The popularity of more fuzzy forms of fidelity, as Voas (2009) names them, would only be a transitional phase in the process of decline: populations having been religiously socialized as children but no longer religiously active in the conventional sense as adults would be those especially likely to practice more individualized forms of personal spirituality (Bruce 2017). As younger birth cohorts receiving less or no religious socialization as children begin to replace these older cohorts though, secular transition theory expects in-person and digital forms of less conventional religion and spirituality to also begin declining cross-generationally. Voas and Crockett (2005) for example argue that religious and spiritual beliefs are also on the decline across birth cohorts, along with religious identity and behavior. More on this secular transition framework is given in Chapter 5.

Seen instead in a more substantive or positive light focused not on decline but on what has been gained among members of this generation, Millennials can be understood as the inheritors of their Boomer parents' (and grandparents' in some instances) counter-cultural revolution that de-emphasized traditional social institutions, including more traditional forms of Judaeo-Christianity, in the 1960s, and brought about a society more characterized by progressive sexual and family morals, individual choice and authenticity with the ultimate goal of personal happiness, and a consumer market economy on steroids. Gauthier and Perreault (2013) for example argue that the socio-cultural differences between Millennials, Gen Xers and Boomers are not that large, rather that the key generational split was between Boomers and older adults in the 1960s.

Liberal Protestantism has been the main loser in some sense from the 1960s cultural shift: it is this Christian tradition in both the United States and Canada that has seen the most declines over the last half-century or so. The number of mainline Protestant affiliates in Canada for the United, Anglican, Presbyterian, Lutheran and Baptist Churches combined declined by 39% between 1971 and 2011 (Clarke and Macdonald 2017), while the general population in the country grew by 56% over the same period. In the United States, liberal and moderate Protestants, Episcopalians as well as Lutherans combined went from representing 31% of the general population in the 1970s to only 20% in the 2000s (Sherkat 2014, 37).

Yet, in another sense, liberal Protestantism is a big winner. As Demerath (1995) and Smith and Snell (2009, 287–289) argue, liberal Protestantism has declined as a series of religious organizations, but its ideas and values of individualism, pluralism, emancipation from authorities, tolerance, more progressive social values, free critical inquiry, and the importance of human experience now permeate mainstream culture, and are especially prevalent among Millennials.

Additionally, just because there is some religious decline across generations, this does not mean that religion and spirituality have disappeared entirely among today's emerging adults. Smith and Snell (2009, 154–155) show with their 2007–2008 National Study of Youth and Religion (NSYR) data that many first-wave American Millennials (born 1984–1990) are followers of what the authors call Moralistic Therapeutic Deism (MTD). This MTD is characterized by five key beliefs: (1) a God exists who created and orders the world and watches over human life on earth; (2) God wants people to be good, nice and fair to each other, as taught by most world religions; (3) the central goal of life is to be happy and to feel good about oneself; (4) God does not need to be particularly involved in one's life except when God is needed to resolve a problem; and (5) good people go to heaven (or another similar good place) when they die.

> Most emerging adults are okay with talking about religion as a topic, although they are largely indifferent to it—religion is just not that important to most of them. So for the most part, they do not end up talking much about religion in their lives. To whatever extent they do talk about it, most of them think that most religions share the same core principles, which they generally believe are good. But the particularities of any given religion are peripheral trappings that can be more or less ignored. The best thing about religion is that it helps people to be good, to make good choices, to behave well. (Smith and Snell 2009, 286)

Based on the in-depth semi-structured interviews that were also conducted as part of the 2007–2008 NSYR, Smith and Snell (2009, 166–179) classify 18–23 year olds into six major religious types: *committed traditionalists* who have strong religious beliefs and actively practice their faith;[6] *selective adherents* who pick and choose only certain elements of their faith to believe and practice; the *spiritually open* who are not that committed to a religion, but are receptive and somewhat interested in spiritual and religious matters; the *religiously indifferent* who do not care about practicing a religion nor opposing religion; the *religiously disconnected* who have virtually no connection to any aspect of religion; and the *irreligious* who are openly skeptical toward religion.

For those among the Millennial generation who are more religious and/or spiritual, Gauthier and Perreault (2008, 2013) add that young adult religiosity today is for the most part de-institutionalized (takes place more and more away from organized religion); is much more transnational and global in focus (rather than centered on ethno-national religions of the past); is heavily entwined with mass media (the Internet, social media and the digital age), the market economy and consumerism; is a source of distinct and niche identities for individuals; and emphasizes above all else personal experiences (of revelation), emotion and experimentation. Wuthnow (2007) refers to young adults today as predominantly *tinkerers*, who pick and choose their spiritual identities, beliefs and rituals from what is on offer in order to create a specific construct that addresses their own needs.

Another common thread for religious and spiritual Millennials is that they are regularly grappling with wider secular culture among their generation, in order to justify why they are religious and/or spiritual and to build and maintain their own distinct identities as individuals. Many Christian Millennials see themselves as going back to the core teachings and origins of the religious tradition, similar to when Jesus walked the Earth in Roman times with only a small dedicated and holy following in a larger world of heathens and pagans. They see this as a much more engaged and authentic form of their faith, compared with the masses in prior generations nominally carrying out church teachings and the will of religious leaders. Smith (1998) in turn uses subcultural identity theory to explain how Evangelicals leverage an embattled narrative with the rest of secular society in their own identity formation and differentiation. This may be especially the case for Evangelical Millennials who form a smaller proportion of their generation (Putnam and Campbell 2010; Sherkat 2014; Smith and Snell 2009). More broadly, Smith and Snell (2009, 239) describe a cognitive resistance to modern secular culture among religious emerging adults characterized by "… strong resistance to the authority claims of the modern secular, religiously liberal, or even indecisively religious outlook." This is a mostly newer phenomenon, or at least is more pronounced now compared with religious members of the Silent and Boomer generations who were (or at least felt like and were told they were) the majority, not a minority.

The Impact of a Secular Age

Taylor (2007) raises this point in his examination of the current "secular age." Taylor argues that, rather than there being a default one way or another toward belief or nonbelief, toward what he refers to as open (belief) or closed (non-belief) world structures, our current societies are instead characterized first and foremost by their coexistence. Over the last few centuries, there has been a transition in the West from "... a society in which it was virtually impossible not to believe in God, to one in which faith, even for the staunchest believer, is one human possibility among others ..." (Taylor 2007, 3). No matter if someone is a believer or a nonbeliever in the transcendent, everyone experiences the "cross pressures" from the other side: believers are aware of nonbelieving worldviews, and vice versa. These cross-pressures in turn create a context of uncertainty for many: no worldview is free from the cross-pressures that can throw someone's (non)beliefs into doubt (Taylor 2007, 539–593).

Yet, I argue in this book that this uncertainty has a greater impact on belief than on nonbelief. Faith requires a level of certainty in the existence of the transcendent, of a higher power, of the supernatural, without the support of empirical evidence: that is the very nature of what faith is. Although not impossible to achieve in our current Western societies, as many hundreds of millions of ardent believers who are certain in their faith in North America prove, it is nevertheless more difficult to maintain in a context where uncertainty reigns with the coexistence of other (nonreligious) worldviews. As this uncertainty begins to permeate belief, one of the outcomes seems to be that many younger individuals are more inclined to leave aspects of religious practice and identity to the wayside. With less or no normative pressure toward practicing a religion over any other, or at all, a larger segment of the population moves away from other dimensions of religiosity and spirituality while still maintaining their belief. But, as seen with secular transition theory earlier in this chapter, this belief may be more difficult to pass on to the next generation with less of an institutional or communal framework to support this transmission, and without practice and identity to reinforce it. More members of younger generations are thus inclined toward nonbelief and a nonreligious, nonspiritual worldview (think YOLO, You Only Live Once, among others). Consequently, over the last few generations at least, this context of cross-pressures and uncertainty seems to be favoring nonbelief.

The main argument here then is that the shift toward nonreligion that has been happening over a number of generations is now tipping the scales and becoming the new default option among Millennials. This is a generation characterized by high retention rates of nonreligion among those raised without religion, and high disaffiliation rates among those socialized with religion (as we will explore in detail in Chapter 6). As discussed earlier, this default has not come out of nowhere, but is instead tied at least in part to Millennials' social location in the United States and Canada. I will unpack, explore in-depth and provide systematic empirical evidence for this argument throughout this book, so stay tuned and read on.

Once again, I repeat my earlier statement for emphasis: this does not mean that religion and spirituality have or will disappear altogether among Millennials. Instead, these phenomena are shaped by the new secular default as much as by growing pluralism, which in turn gives religion and spirituality a new flavor among today's emerging adults. This book brings important updated data to the works of Gauthier and Perreault (2008), Smith and Snell (2009) and Wuthnow (2007) 10–15 years on. This said, I also deviate from these researchers' approaches by focusing on what is new and distinct about the religious and spiritual flavor that will most likely last a Millennial's lifetime, now that many Millennials are at the cusp of middle age, rather than on seeing these differences only as emerging adult life cycle effects that may disappear as individuals grow older. I also bring in cross-national comparisons between the United States and Canada to highlight the impact of different social environments on these generational effects. My goal is not to argue if generational differences regarding religion, spirituality and secularity among Millennials are a good or a bad thing, but rather to pinpoint and better understand them along with their socio-political context and impact.

Heading Down the Yellow #Lit Road ...

In order to achieve this research goal, I draw on a series of primary and secondary sources of high-quality and complementary quantitative and qualitative empirical data from both the United States and Canada. My main data source is the earlier mentioned MTS. I administered the MTS online between 4 and 27 March 2019 in both English and French. The survey questionnaire contained a total of 69 questions on the respondent's sociodemographic characteristics, (non)religious and (non)spiritual affiliations, beliefs and practices, friendship networks as well as inclusivity attitudes. The complete MTS questionnaire, technical documentation and initial results can be found in an open-access online research report (Wilkins-Laflamme 2019).

A total of 2,514 respondents (1,508 from Canada and 1,006 from the United States) aged 18–35 years old completed the 15-minute web survey. Respondents were recruited through Léger's panel of members (leger360.com) to complete the survey hosted by the University of Waterloo's Survey Research Centre (uwaterloo.ca/survey-research-centre/). Potential respondents were sent an e-mail invitation to complete the web survey, and then were sent reminders up to two times, if necessary. Age, gender, regional and education level strata were applied during the initial random selection of respondents, and later monitored as responses came in to adjust further recruitment efforts and complete.[7] Post-stratification weights were then created and applied to the statistical analyses in this book in order to achieve greater young adult population representativeness on the variables of country of birth, household income and race/ethnicity.[8] The final response rate for the MTS was 6.5%: lower than the 10–15% response rates common for online surveys, mainly because of the additional recruitment efforts to fill some of the harder-to-reach strata (notably young adult males with no university education). This survey was reviewed and received ethics clearance through the University of Waterloo's Research Ethics Committee.

I supplement this MTS data with other quantitative sources to capture trends over time and between generations. These additional open-access quantitative sources include the American and Canadian General Social Surveys (NORC 2020; Statistics Canada 2020), Canadian Census (Statistics Canada 2015a, 2015b), Pew Research Center's Religious Landscape Survey in the United States (Pew Research Center 2014), International Social Survey Programme (2018), American National Election Study (2016) and Canadian Election Study (Stephenson et al. 2020).

I also complement this quantitative data with a series of focus groups and life history interviews conducted among Millennials in two other research projects I have been involved in over the past five years; some research participants who we have already heard from earlier in this chapter, and more who we will hear from throughout this book. First, the *Cascadia* research project, led by Paul Bramadat at the University of Victoria, British Columbia. Between April and June 2018, Paul Bramadat and Chelsea Horton conducted a series of eight focus groups in the Canadian West coast and American Pacific Northwest cities of Victoria, Vancouver, Portland and Seattle among both Millennials and active religious adherents, and on the topics of religion, spirituality, secularity and society in the Pacific Northwest. For the same research project, West coast historian Lynne Marks also conducted 39 life history interviews with non-religious individuals in the region, four of which were with research participants 18–35 years old and whose interviews I use in this book. For more detailed information on this Cascadia research project, see Bramadat, Killen, and Wilkins-Laflamme (2022).

Second, the *Towards the Exit of Cultural Catholicism in Québec* research project led by E.-Martin Meunier at the University of Ottawa, Ontario. Between May 2018 and August 2020, E.-Martin Meunier, Jean-Philippe Perreault and their research team conducted 37 life history interviews with Gen Xers (20) and Millennials (17; nine men and eight women) from the province of Québec on their relationship with religion and spirituality. I refer to the translated interviews of the Millennial research participants, born between 1983 and 1998, at times throughout this book. Sixteen of these 17 Millennial research participants are from Catholic backgrounds, and one experienced a nonreligious upbringing as a child. Eight of the interviewees were still actively involved with a religious group as young adults, whereas nine were not very or not at all involved with a religious group at the time of the interviews. Throughout this book, the names of interviewees and focus group participants are pseudonyms to protect their confidentiality. All of these qualitative data will allow us to hear from Millennial research participants in their own words, will provide real-world examples of the wider statistical trends we are seeing in the survey data, and will offer insight into the decision-making and life processes at play among Millennials.

The rest of the book will unfold as follows. Chapter 2 contains an examination of some of the key trends in religious identities, behaviors, beliefs and attitudes among Millennials, with a special focus on two distinct dynamics among this generation: growing religious pluralism paired with the decline of organized religion. Using quantitative analysis techniques, I group Millennials into a typology of four well-defined categories: religious, spiritual seeker, cultural believer and nonreligious Millennials. The in-depth exploration of these types and each group's key features then structure the following chapters of this book.

Chapter 3 will focus on an important milieu for Millennials who are more actively religious: digital communities. How are religious Millennials using the online world for their faith? To what extent is digital religion the sole domain of Millennials who are also more actively religious in person, or instead extends to other less traditionally religious young adults in the United States and Canada? This chapter also explores the implications of living among an increasingly secular generation and social world for the experiences of religious Millennials, giving religion both a more left-leaning and defensive flavor among this generation. Religious identities become an important, but not exclusive, source of identity differentiation in societies that now highly value and promote perceived individual uniqueness.

Chapter 4 makes a conceptual distinction between organized religion and more individualized, unchurched, spiritualities, even if in practice many Millennials combine the two in their everyday lives. How do many Millennials develop and use their more individualized forms of spirituality? There will be a special focus in this chapter on nature and outdoor spaces as important milieus for spiritual experiences, and how this plays out among the youngest living adult generation.

Chapter 5 examines the significant proportion of young adults who identity with a religion and have some religious beliefs, but pair this with little to no religious or spiritual behavior. This group, known as marginal, nominal, cultural or fuzzy affiliates in the existing literature, is often lumped together with nonreligious individuals. Yet, there are some important distinctions to make between these two types of individuals. Religious identity plays an important cultural and family heritage role for the cultural believer Millennial, giving them a sense of belonging and place in the world. It also in turn tends to affect their attitudes toward others considered as outsiders or members of out groups, such as religious minorities and immigrants. The cultural believer Millennial also acts as a bridge in many ways between more religious and spiritual Millennials on the one hand, and nonreligious Millennials on the other; as a transitional group toward nonreligion.

In Chapter 6, I explore how the nonreligious Millennial is fast becoming the default option in many ways among the youngest living adult generation. I show this notably through (non)religious switching and retention rates among Millennials: that disaffiliation rates from parents' religion are especially high, and that retention rates of parents' nonreligion are also very high … the highest they have ever been among any living generation. I also examine the different forms this nonreligion can take among young adults.

Chapter 7 concludes the book by bringing all these research findings together, and detailing their implications for both the main argument of this book as well as for society more broadly. What does Millennial religion, spirituality and secularity really mean for our socio-political realities in North America? Where are Millennials steering the (non)religious and (non)spiritual landscapes both in the United States and Canada for the years to come? We continue the early stages of this journey now by first getting a better grasp in the next chapter of the key trends and dynamics that define religion, spirituality and secularity for a generation.

Notes

1 I first introduced readers to Jeremy in Wilkins-Laflamme (2022).
2 This Cascadia research project was led by Paul Bramadat from the University of Victoria, and the focus groups conducted between April and June 2018 by Paul Bramadat and Chelsea Horton. For more details on this research project, see Bramadat, Killen, and Wilkins-Laflamme (2022).
3 I am writing this introduction in October 2020, at the beginning of the second wave of COVID-19 cases among young adults here in Ontario, Canada. I still see this tug of war play out in the media and in public health messaging between views of entitled stereotypes on the one hand and sympathy due to never-before-seen challenges on the other hand regarding Millennials. Many in the media, including journalists, politicians and doctors, are chastising Millennials and their supposed laissez-faire party lifestyle as the main cause for a rise in COVID-19 cases. They repeatedly call for young adults to "smarten up" and for tougher enforcement of anti-gathering city bylaws. By contrast, others are pointing out that many young adults are the ones working on the front lines of the pandemic in grocery stores, hospitals, long-term care homes and schools, and do not have the luxury of staying home and isolating like many older adults who have more secure white-collar employment or pensions. The latter commentators want to see policy improvements to help address issues such as precarious work, paid sick leave and overcrowding on public transit.
4 See notably https://www.indianz.com/News/2018/03/14/yes-magazine-elders-and-warriors-keep-cl.asp
5 See, for example, the C3 mega church in Toronto (https://gem.cbc.ca/media/cbc-docs-pov/season-4/episode-2/38e815a-012df4c995a); as well as the conversion of All Saints Anglican Church in Ottawa, Ontario, to a restaurant and event space (https://www.cbc.ca/news/canada/ottawa/recipe-grilled-peach-prosciutto-salad-1.5215327); or the conversion of St. John's Evangelical Lutheran Church in Chicago into high-end condos (https://chicago.curbed.com/2019/8/6/20757368/ukrainian-village-church-condo-conversion-revival).
6 Environics (2017, 9) refers to a similar group of Canadian Millennials, "new traditionalists," who make up an estimated 11% of this generation in the country.
7 Strata sizes were based on Statistics Canada Census and U.S. Census Bureau American Community Survey data with regards to the size of young adult subpopulations, and are available in the MTS's technical documentation: https://uwspace.uwaterloo.ca/handle/10012/15102
8 Post-stratification weights were based on Statistics Canada Census and U.S. Census Bureau American Community Survey data with regards to the size of young adult subpopulations. Two weighting variables were generated based on young adult (18–35) population age, gender, Census region of residence, level of education, country of birth, household income and race/ethnicity parameters: one for the Canadian subsample, and one for the American subsample. These weighting variables were generated using a sequential iterative technique.

References

Alsop, Ron. 2008. *The Trophy Kids Grow Up: How the Millennial Generation Is Shaking Up the Workplace*. San Francisco, CA: Jossey-Bass.

American National Election Study. 2016. University of Michigan, and Stanford University. *ANES 2016 Time Series Study*. Ann Arbor, MI: Inter-university Consortium for Political and Social Research [distributor]. doi:10.3886/ICPSR36824.v2

Arnett, Jeffrey Jensen. 2015. *Emerging Adulthood: The Winding Road from the Late Teens through the Twenties*. New York, NY: Oxford University Press.

Baggett, Jerome P. 2019. *The Varieties of Nonreligious Experience: Atheism in American Culture*. New York, NY: New York University Press.

Barr, Caelainn, and Shiv Malik. 2016. "Revealed: The 30-Year Economic Betrayal Dragging Down Generation Y's Income." *Guardian*, March 7, 2016. https://www.theguardian.com/world/2016/mar/07/revealed-30-year-economic-betrayal-dragging-down-generation-y-income

Berger, Peter. 1967. *The Sacred Canopy: Elements of Sociological Theory of Religion*. Garden City, NY: Doubleday.

Berger, Peter. 1979. *The Heretical Imperative: Contemporary Possibilities of Religious Affirmation*. New York, NY: Doubleday.

Bibby, Reginald W. 2004. *Restless Gods: The Renaissance of Religion in Canada*. Toronto, ON: Novalis.

Bibby, Reginald W., Joel Thiessen, and Monetta Bailey. 2019. *The Millennial Mosaic: How Pluralism and Choice Are Shaping Canadian Youth and the Future of Canada*. Toronto, ON: Dundurn.

Bramadat, Paul, Patricia Killen, and Sarah Wilkins-Laflamme, eds. 2022. *Religion at the Edge: Nature, Spirituality, and Secularity in the Pacific Northwest*. Vancouver, BC: University of British Columbia Press.

Brauer, Simon. 2018. "The Surprising Predictable Decline of Religion in the United States." *Journal for the Scientific Study of Religion* 57 (4): 654–675. doi:10.1111/jssr.12551

Bruce, Steve. 2017. *Secular Beats Spiritual: The Westernization of the Easternization of the West*. New York, NY: Oxford University Press.

Cairns, James Irvine. 2017. *The Myth of the Age of Entitlement: Millennials, Austerity, and Hope*. Toronto, ON: University of Toronto Press.

Cimino, Richard, and Christopher Smith. 2014. *Atheist Awakening: Secular Activism and Community in America*. New York, NY: Oxford University Press.

Clarke, Brian, and Stuart Macdonald. 2017. *Leaving Christianity: Changing Allegiances in Canada since 1945*. Montréal, QC: McGill-Queen's University Press.

Côté, James E., and Anton L. Allahar. 1994. *Generation on Hold: Coming of Age in the Late Twentieth Century*. Toronto, ON: Stoddart.

Demerath, N. Jay. 1995. "Cultural Victory and Organizational Defeat in the Paradoxical Decline of Liberal Protestantism." *Journal for the Scientific Study of Religion* 34 (4): 458–469. doi:10.2307/1387339

Drescher, Elizabeth. 2016. *Choosing Our Religion: The Spiritual Lives of America's Nones*. New York, NY: Oxford University Press.

Environics. 2017. *Canadian Millennials: Social Values Study*. Accessed December 2, 2020. https://www.environicsinstitute.org/docs/default-source/project-documents/canadian-millennial-social-values-study/final-report.pdf?sfvrsn=394cf27a_2

Eyre, Richard, and Linda Eyre. 2011. *The Entitlement Trap: How to Rescue Your Child with a New Family System of Choosing, Earning, and Ownership*. New York, NY: Penguin.

Forbes. 2018. "57 Million U.S. Workers Are Part of the Gig Economy." Article written by TJ McCue. Accessed October 26, 2020. https://www.forbes.com/sites/tjmccue/2018/08/31/57-million-u-s-workers-are-part-of-the-gig-economy/

Frey, William H. 2018. *Diversity Explosion: How New Racial Demographics Are Remaking America*. Washington, DC: Brookings Institution Press.

Galston, William A., and Clara Hendrickson. 2016. *How Millennials Voted This Election*. Brookings Institution. Accessed November 5, 2020. https://www.brookings.edu/blog/fixgov/2016/11/21/how-millennials-voted/

Gauthier, François, and Jean-Philippe Perreault, eds. 2008. *Jeunes et religion au Québec*. Québec, QC: Presses de l'Université Laval.

Gauthier, François, and Jean-Philippe Perreault. 2013. "Les héritiers du *baby-boom*. Jeunes et religion au Québec." *Social Compass* 60 (4): 527–543. doi:10.1177/0037768613504042

Giroux, Henry A. 2013. *Youth in Revolt: Reclaiming a Democratic Future*. Boulder, CO: Paradigm Publishers.

Glanzer, Perry L., Jonathan Hill, and Todd C. Ream. 2014. "Higher Education's Influence Upon the Religious Lives of Emerging Adults." In *Emerging Adults' Religiousness and Spirituality: Meaning-Making in an Age of Transition*, edited by Carolyn McNamara Barry and Mona M. Abo-Zena, 152–167. New York, NY: Oxford University Press.

Hancock, Ange-Marie. 2011. *Solidarity Politics for Millennials: A Guide to Ending the Oppression Olympics*. New York, NY: Palgrave Macmillan.

Heelas, Paul, and Linda Woodhead. 2005. *The Spiritual Revolution: Why Religion Is Giving Way to Spirituality*. Oxford, UK: Blackwell.

Heisz, Andrew, and Elizabeth Richards. 2019. "Economic Well-being Across Generations of Young Canadians: Are Millennials Better or Worse Off?" *Economic Insights*. Statistics Canada, 11–626-X No. 092. Accessed October 26, 2020. https://www150.statcan.gc.ca/n1/pub/11–626-x/11–626-x2019006-eng.htm

Hiemstra, Rick, Lorianne Dueck, and Matthew Blackaby. 2018. *Renegotiating Faith: The Delay in Young Adult Identity Formation and What It Means for the Church in Canada*. Toronto, ON: Faith Today Publications. Accessed December 15, 2021. www.RenegotiatingFaith.ca

Hill, Jonathan P., 2011. "Faith and Understanding: Specifying the Impact of Higher Education on Religious Belief." *Journal for the Scientific Study of Religion* 50 (3): 533–551. doi:10.1111/j.1468-5906.2011.01587.x

Hirschle, Jochen. 2013. "'Secularization of Consciousness' or Alternative Opportunities? The Impact of Economic Growth on Religious Belief and Practice in 13 European Countries." *Journal for the Scientific Study of Religion* 52 (2): 410–424. doi:10.1111/jssr.12030

Höllinger, Franz, and Johanna Muckenhuber. 2019. "Religiousness and Existential Insecurity: A Cross-National Comparative Analysis on the Macro-and Micro-Level." *International Sociology* 34 (1): 19–37. doi:10.1177/0268580918812284

Houtman, Dick, and Stef Aupers. 2007. "The Spiritual Turn and the Decline of Tradition: The Spread of Post-Christian Spirituality in 14 Western Countries, 1981–2000." *Journal for the Scientific Study of Religion* 46 (3): 305–320. doi:10.1111/j.1468-5906.2007.00360.x

Howe, Neil, and William Strauss. 2000. *Millennials Rising: The Next Great Generation*. New York, NY: Vintage Press.

Iannaccone, Laurence R. 1994. "Why Strict Churches Are Strong." *American Journal of Sociology* 99 (5): 1180–1211. doi:10.1086/230409

Immerzeel, Tim, and Frank Van Tubergen. 2013. "Religion as Reassurance? Testing the Insecurity Theory in 26 European Countries." *European Sociological Review* 29 (2): 359–372. doi:10.1093/esr/jcr072

International Social Survey Programme. 2018. *Religion IV* [dataset]. Accessed May 25, 2021. http://w.issp.org/menu-top/home/

Jameson, Fredric. 1991. *Postmodernism, or the Cultural Logic of Late Capitalism*. Durham, NC: Duke University Press.

Jones, Robert P., Daniel Cox, and Thomas Banchoff. 2012. *A Generation in Transition: Religion, Values, and Politics among College-Age Millennials. Findings from the 2012 Millennial Values Survey*. Public Religion Research Institute and Georgetown University's Berkley Center for Religion, Peace, and World Affairs. Accessed December 15, 2021. https://repository.library.georgetown.edu/bitstream/handle/10822/1052347/120419BC-PRRIMillennialValuesSurveyReport[1].pdf?sequence=1

Kurz, Christopher, Geng Li, and Daniel J. Vine. 2018. "Are Millennials Different?" *Finance and Economics Discussion Series 2018-080*. Washington: Board of Governors of the Federal Reserve System. Accessed October 26, 2020. https://www.federalreserve.gov/econres/feds/files/2018080pap.pdf

Lieberson, Stanley. 1987. *Making It Count: The Improvement of Social Research and Theory*. Berkeley, CA: University of California Press.

Lim, Chaeyoon, and Nan Dirk de Graaf. 2021. "Religious Diversity Reconsidered: Local Religious Contexts and Individual Religiosity." *Sociology of Religion* 82 (1): 31–62. doi:10.1093/socrel/sraa027

Luckmann, Thomas. 1967. *The Invisible Religion: The Problem of Religion in Modern Society*. London, UK: MacMillan.

Manne, Anne. 2014. *The Life of I: The New Culture of Narcissism*. Melbourne, Australia: Melbourne University Press.

Mannheim, Karl. 1952. *The Sociology of Knowledge*. London, UK: Routledge & Kegan Paul Ltd.

Martin, David. 1978. *A General Theory of Secularization*. New York, NY: Harper & Row.

Mayrl, Damon, and Freeden Oeur. 2009. "Religion and Higher Education: Current Knowledge and Directions for Future Research." *Journal for the Scientific Study of Religion* 48 (2): 260–275. doi:10.1111/j.1468-5906.2009.01446.x

Milligan, Ian. 2019. *History in the Age of Abundance?: How the Web is Transforming Historical Research*. Kingston, ON: McGill-Queen's University Press.

NORC. 2020. *General Social Survey 1972–2018 Cross-Sectional Cumulative Data* [dataset]. https://gss.norc.org/

Norris, Pippa, and Ronald Inglehart. 2011. *Sacred and Secular: Religion and Politics Worldwide*. 2nd ed. New York, NY: Cambridge University Press.

Olson, Daniel V.A., Joey Marshall, Jong Hyun Jung, and David Voas. 2020. "Sacred Canopies or Religious Markets? The Effect of County-Level Religious Diversity on Later Changes in Religious Involvement." *Journal for the Scientific Study of Religion* 59 (2): 227–246. doi:10.1111/jssr.12651

Pew Research Center. 2010. *Millennials: A Portrait of Generation Next. Confident. Connected. Open to Change*. Accessed December 2, 2020. https://www.pewsocialtrends.org/2010/02/24/millennials-confident-connected-open-to-change/

Pew Research Center. 2014. *Religious Landscape Study* [dataset]. https://www.pewforum.org/about-the-religious-landscape-study/

Pew Research Center. 2015. *Religion and Views on Climate and Energy Issues*. Accessed October 28, 2020. https://www.pewresearch.org/science/2015/10/22/religion-and-views-on-climate-and-energy-issues/

Pew Research Center. 2019. *Defining Generations: Where Millennials End and Generation Z Begins*. Accessed October 26, 2020. https://www.pewresearch.org/fact-tank/2019/01/17/where-millennials-end-and-generation-z-begins/

Plecher, H. 2020. *Urbanization in Canada 2019*. Statista. Accessed November 5, 2020. https://www.statista.com/statistics/271208/urbanization-in-canada/#:~:text=In%202019%2C%2081.48%20percent%20of,in%20Canada%20lived%20in%20cities.&text=Canada%20is%20one%20of%20the,land%20area%2C%20second%20behind%20Russia

Prensky, Marc. 2001. "Digital Natives, Digital Immigrants Part 1." *On the Horizon* 9 (5): 1–6.

Putnam, Robert, and David Campbell. 2010. *American Grace: How Religion Divides and Unites Us*. New York, NY: Simon and Schuster.

Raynor, Jennifer. 2016. *Generation Less: How Australia Is Cheating the Young*. Carlton: Black Inc. Books.

Ruiter, Stijn, and Frank Van Tubergen. 2009. "Religious Attendance in Cross-National Perspective: A Multilevel Analysis of 60 Countries." *American Journal of Sociology* 115 (3): 863–895. doi:10.1086/603536

Ryder, Norman B. 1965. "The Cohort as a Concept in the Study of Social Change." *American Sociological Review* 30 (6): 843–861.

Scott, Shaun. 2018. *Millennials and the Moments that Made Us*. Washington: Zero Books.

Sherkat, Darren E. 2014. *Changing Faith: The Dynamics and Consequences of Americans' Shifting Identities*. New York, NY: New York University Press.

Silva, Jennifer. 2013. *Coming Up Short: Working-Class Adulthood in an Age of Uncertainty*. New York, NY: Oxford University Press.

Smith, Christian. 1998. *American Evangelicalism: Embattled and Thriving*. Chicago, IL: University of Chicago Press.

Smith, Christian, with Karl Christoffersen, Hilary Davidson, and Patricia Snell Herzog. 2011. *Lost in Transition: The Dark Side of Emerging Adulthood*. New York, NY: Oxford University Press.

Smith, Christian, and Patricia Snell. 2009. *Souls in Transition: The Religious and Spiritual Lives of Emerging Adults*. New York, NY: Oxford University Press.

Stark, Rodney, and Roger Finke. 2000. *Acts of Faith: Explaining the Human Side of Religion*. Berkeley, CA: University of California Press.

Statistics Canada. 2015a. *1971, 1981, 1991 and 2001 Census of Population [Canada] Public Use Microdata Files (PUMF): Individual Files (Province Level)* [datasets]. Accessed via Statistics Canada's Research Data Centre.

Statistics Canada. 2015b. *2011 National Household Survey [Canada] Public Use Microdata File (PUMF): Individual File* [dataset].

Statistics Canada. 2020. *General Social Survey, Cycles 1–32 (1985–2018)* [datasets]. Accessed via the South-Western Ontario Research Data Centre at the University of Waterloo, Ontario.

Stephenson, Laura B., Allison Harell, Daniel Rubenson, and Peter John Loewen. 2020. 2019 Canadian Election Study - Phone Survey [dataset]. doi:10.7910/DVN/8RHLG1, Harvard Dataverse, V1.

Stolz, Jörg. 2020. "Secularization Theories in the Twenty-First Century: Ideas, Evidence, and Problems. Presidential Address–Karel Dobbelaere Conference." *Social Compass* 67 (20): 282–308. doi:10.1177/0037768620917320

Stolz, Jörg, Detlef Pollack, and Nan Dirk de Graaf. 2020. "Can the State Accelerate the Secular Transition? Secularization in East and West Germany as a Natural Experiment." *European Sociological Review* 36 (4): 626–642. doi:10.1093/esr/jcaa014

Stonechild, Blair. 2016. *The Knowledge Seeker: Embracing Indigenous Spirituality*. Regina, SA: University of Regina Press.

Storm, Ingrid. 2017. "Does Economic Insecurity Predict Religiosity? Evidence from the European Social Survey 2002–2014." *Sociology of Religion* 78 (2): 146–172. doi:10.1093/socrel/srw055

Strauss, William, and Neil Howe. 1991. *Generations: The History of America's Future, 1584 to 2069*. New York, NY: William Morrow and Company.

Taylor, Charles. 1991. *The Ethics of Authenticity*. Cambridge, MA: Harvard University Press.

Taylor, Charles. 2007. *A Secular Age*. Cambridge, MA: The Belknap Press of Harvard University Press.

Thiessen, Joel, and Sarah Wilkins-Laflamme. 2017. "Becoming a Religious None: Irreligious Socialization and Disaffiliation." *Journal for the Scientific Study of Religion* 56 (1): 64–82. doi:10.1111/jssr.12319

Thiessen, Joel, and Sarah Wilkins-Laflamme. 2020. *None of the Above: Nonreligious Identity in the U.S. and Canada*. New York, NY: New York University Press.

Tulgan, Bruce. 2009. *Not Everyone Gets a Trophy: How to Manage Generation Y*. San Francisco, CA: Jossey-Bass.

Twenge, Jean M. 2006. *Generation Me: Why Today's Young Americans Are More Confident, Assertive, Entitled – and More Miserable Than Ever Before*. New York, NY: Atria.

Twenge, Jean M. 2017. *iGen: Why Today's Super-Connected Kids Are Growing Up Less Rebellious, More Tolerant, Less Happy–and Completely Unprepared for Adulthood–and What That Means for the Rest of Us*. New York, NY: Simon and Schuster.

U.S. Census Bureau. 2012. *United States Summary: 2010*. Washington, DC: U.S. Government Printing Office. Accessed November 5, 2020. https://www.census.gov/prod/cen2010/cph-2-1.pdf

Voas, David. 2008. "The Continuing Secular Transition." In *The Role of Religion in Modern Societies*, edited by Detlef Pollack and Daniel V. A. Olsen, 25–48. New York, NY: Routledge.

Voas, David. 2009. "The Rise and Fall of Fuzzy Fidelity in Europe." *European Sociological Review* 25 (2): 155–168. doi:10.1093/esr/jcn044

Voas, David, and Mark Chaves. 2016. "Is the United States a Counterexample to the Secularization Thesis?" *American Journal of Sociology* 121 (5): 1517–1556. doi:10.1086/684202

Voas, David, and Alasdair Crockett. 2005. "Religion in Britain: Neither Believing nor Belonging." *Sociology* 39 (1): 11–28. doi:10.1177/0038038505048998

Voas, David, Daniel V.A. Olson, and Alasdair Crockett. 2002. "Religious Pluralism and Participation: Why Previous Research is Wrong." *American Sociological Review* 67 (2): 212–230. doi:10.2307/3088893

Watts, Galen. 2022. *The Spiritual Turn: The Religion of the Heart and the Making of Romantic Liberal Modernity*. New York, NY: Oxford University Press.

Weber, Max. 1993. *The Sociology of Religion*. Translated by Ephraim Fischoff. Boston, MA: Beacon Press.

Wilkins-Laflamme, Sarah. 2019. *Religion, Non-Belief, Spirituality and Social Behaviour among North American Millennials*. UW Space. https://uwspace.uwaterloo.ca/handle/10012/15102

Wilkins-Laflamme, Sarah. 2022. "Second to None: Religious Non-Affiliation in the Pacific Northwest." In *Religion at the Edge: Nature, Spirituality, and Secularity in the*

Pacific Northwest, edited by Paul Bramadat, Patricia Killen, and Sarah Wilkins-Laflamme, 101–123. Vancouver, BC: University of British Columbia Press.

Wittberg, Patricia. 2021. "Generational Change in Religion and Religious Practice: A Review Essay." *Review of Religious Research* 63: 461–482. doi:10.1007/s13644-021-00455-0

Wuthnow, Robert. 2007. *After the Baby Boomers: How Twenty- and Thirty-Somethings Are Shaping the Future of American Religion*. Princeton, NJ: Princeton University Press.

2

DIFFERENT APPROACHES TO MILLENNIAL RELIGION, SPIRITUALITY AND SECULARITY

There are two main trends that distinguish Millennials' religion in many ways in both the United States and Canada; two trends which are much more pronounced among this younger adult generation than among older individuals. These include greater religious diversity paired with a decline in many (especially Christian) forms of religious identities, practices and convictions. These key trends are seen in Millennials' own characteristics as well as in their greater public opinion acceptance of pluralism and nonreligion in others around them. This chapter begins with an overview of how these main trends play out more specifically among the three key dimensions of religion—belonging, behavior and belief (the three Bs as they are often referred to in sociology of religion and religious studies)—as well as among Millennial attitudes toward religion, spirituality and secularity in society. Once this overview of religiosity and spirituality indicators among Millennials in the United States and Canada is complete, I will then tie this mass of data together by drawing out some crucial patterns and establishing a typology of ways Millennials approach religion, spirituality and secularity.

Identifying with and Belonging to Religion

The two trends that distinguish Millennials' religion, growing religious diversity and nonreligion, are immediately apparent when examining religious (non)affiliation data from both the United States and Canada. As indicated in Table 2.1 with results from the 2018 American GSS, although a majority of U.S. Millennials are still affiliated with a Christian tradition, this Christian majority is now only a slim one. In Canada (Table 2.2), Millennials are the first generation where Christian affiliation has fallen below 50% of the general population. Fed by immigration notably from Africa, the Middle East, South Asia and South-East Asia as

DOI: 10.4324/9781003217695-2

TABLE 2.1 Religious affiliation by generation, U.S. GSS 2018

	Millennials (born 1986–2000)	*Gen Xers (born 1966–1985)*	*Boomers (born 1946–1965)*	*Silent generation and older (born before 1946)*
Protestant	34.8%	45.9%	54.2%	63.7%
Roman Catholic	22.1%	23.4%	24.4%	21.6%
Christian/inter-denominational	1.1%	2.0%	1.0%	0.0%
Jewish	1.9%	0.8%	2.3%	1.4%
Muslim	1.2%	0.8%	0.5%	0.2%
Buddhist	1%	0.6%	0.5%	1.4%
Other religion	3.4%	2.3%	1.2%	0.9%
No religion	34.5%	24.2%	15.9%	10.8%
Total	*100%*	*100%*	*100%*	*100%*

N Millennials = 521; *N* Gen Xers = 789; *N* Boomers = 755; *N* Silent Generation and older = 262. Percentages weighted to be representative of the general population.

TABLE 2.2 Religious affiliation by generation, Canadian GSS 2018

	Millennials (born 1986–2003)	*Gen Xers (born 1966–1985)*	*Boomers (born 1946–1965)*	*Silent generation and older (born before 1946)*
Catholic	19.8%	27.0%	37.5%	37.1%
Anglican	0.9%	2.5%	5.4%	7.3%
United Church	0.8%	1.8%	5.8%	8.7%
Baptist	0.6%	1.1%	1.8%	2.9%
Presbyterian	0.8%	0.8%	1.8%	2.3%
Christian Orthodox	0.7%	1.1%	1.2%	2.5%
Pentecostal	0.3%	0.9%	0.9%	0.9%
Other Christian	18.2%	19.4%	17.0%	17.4%
Jewish	0.6%	0.7%	0.8%	1.7%
Muslim	4.3%	4.3%	1.8%	1.1%
Buddhist	1.8%	1.2%	1.3%	1.5%
Hindu	2.0%	2.2%	1.4%	0.5%
Other religion	6.4%	5.0%	3.0%	1.9%
No religion	42.9%	31.9%	20.1%	14.3%
Total	*100%*	*100%*	*100%*	*100%*

N = 14,387. Percentages weighted to be representative of the general population. Any discrepancies in totals are due to rounding.

well as higher birth rates among these first-generation immigrants once they arrived in North America, non-Judaeo-Christian traditions still represent a minority of Millennials, but a much larger minority than among older generations. Consequently, we can extend Frey's (2018) concept of the cultural generation gap, originally defined by the author to refer to the greater racial and ethnic diversity among younger generations in America, to the domain of religion as well.

Yet, the growth of non-Judaeo-Christian traditions in North America is not the only source of growing diversity among Millennials when it comes to their religious identities. Another important source of this diversity comes, somewhat paradoxically, from their nonbelonging, which brings us to our second trend found especially among Millennials. While the decline of Christianity has opened new spaces for non-Judaeo-Christian religions, it is nevertheless nonreligion that now occupies much of this vacant space within the Millennial generation. Rates of religious nonaffiliation have been climbing rapidly in the United States since the 1990s and in Canada since the 1970s, and have been more pronounced for each successive generation as seen with secular transition theory in the previous chapter and in Tables 2.1 and 2.2 here. These rates of religiously unaffiliated individuals now reach their highest adult levels among Millennials, with just over a third in the United States saying they have no religion in the 2018 GSS, and 43% saying the same in Canada.

It is Protestants, notably liberal Protestants, whose share of the population has been steadily declining since the 1960s and 1970s in both countries (Clarke and Macdonald 2017; Sherkat 2014), and whose decline is feeding this continued trend of growing nonreligion among Millennials. White Catholics and White Evangelicals have also experienced declines among Millennials, but declines within these wider religious traditions have been offset somewhat by higher birth rates and higher levels of young Hispanic Catholics and Black Protestants in the United States (Putnam and Campbell 2010; Sherkat 2014). Religious decline among Millennials, or the growth of nonreligion when seen from the opposite direction, is a theme that will come back in the following sections for the dimensions of religious behavior and believing as well.

Let us now add a few more layers of information about (non)religious identity among Millennials by bringing in data from the Millennial Trends Survey (MTS) I ran back in 2019 (Figures 2.1 and 2.2). When the religious affiliation question and its answer options are formulated a bit differently from those in the GSSs, namely multiple no religion answer options are provided and respondents are asked to specify the Christian tradition they say they belong to (potentially discouraging broad nominal affiliation to Christianity), nearly half (44%) of the Canadian young adults in the MTS selected one of the "no religion" options provided; and well over a third (39%) of the U.S. young adults did the same. We can see from these results that not all respondents who self-select into one of the "no religion" categories are self-identified atheists. In fact, "no particular preference" is the most popular of the no religion options in both countries, followed by atheist/secular humanist, agnostic and then spiritual with no religion.

Levels of non-Judaeo-Christian affiliations are also slightly higher in this MTS sample than in the U.S. GSS, encompassing 9% of U.S. respondents. In turn, a slim majority in the United States identify with Christian denominations and traditions, and this rate of Millennial Christians in Canada slips just below the 50%

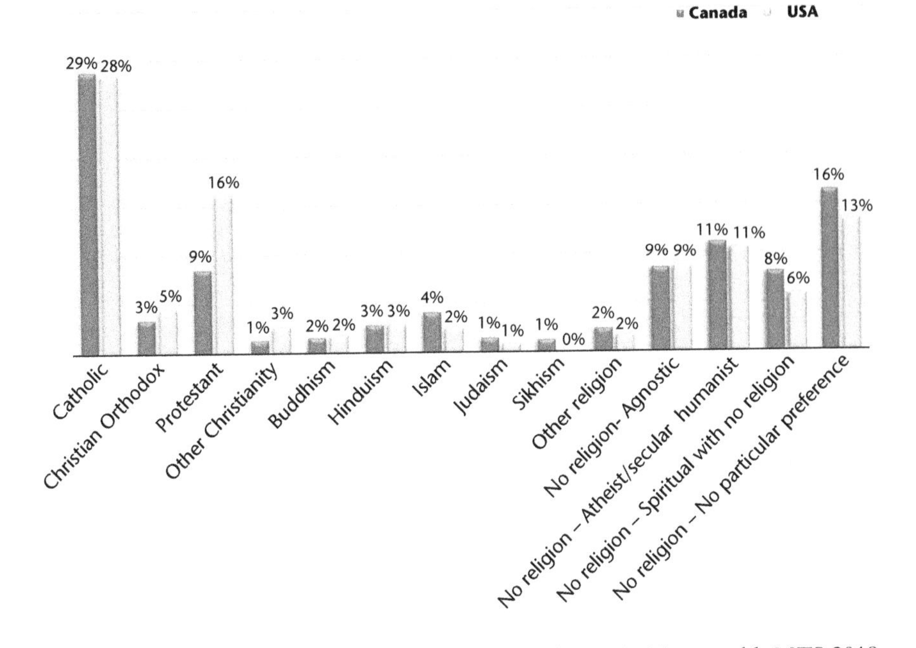

FIGURE 2.1 "What, if any, is your religion?" respondents 18–35 years old, MTS 2019

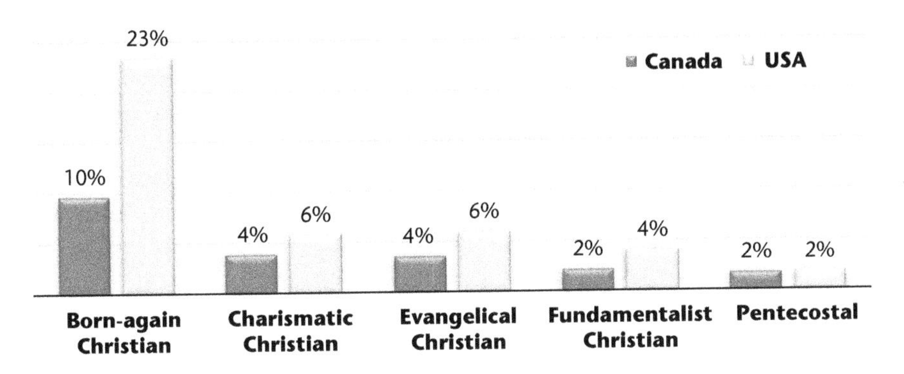

FIGURE 2.2 "Do you identify as (select all that apply)," respondents 18–35 years old, MTS 2019

mark in the MTS. Just under 30% in both countries identify as Catholic; 16% in the United States and 9% in Canada identify with a Protestant tradition; and 8% in the United States and 4% in Canada belong to another Christian tradition. Specifically, 36% of the American and 18% of the Canadian young adult respondents in the survey identify as either a born-again Christian, charismatic Christian, evangelical Christian and/or fundamentalist Christian. Born-again Christians are the most common among these categories in both countries, with 23% of U.S. and 10% of Canadian respondents identifying with this group, which includes some Catholics.

Lori Beaman refers to the increasing size of (non-Christian) minorities, mainly fed by first- and second-generation immigration, the growth of nonreligion as well as the growing public presence and recognition of Indigenous spiritualities especially in countries such as Canada and Australia as a new form of more complex diversity: "new diversity" (Beaman 2017). The coexistence of these key demographic and socio-political trends is having widespread effects notably on education, health, politics and the law. It is driving a redefinition of what is considered religion, its role in the public sphere, as well as how (non)religious minorities are accommodated in social institutions. This new diversity seems to be especially pronounced (and often publicly celebrated) in Canada, with its even higher levels of religious diversity and nonreligion. Nevertheless, it is also beginning to permeate U.S. society. And it is most present among the Millennial generation. Although it would be a mistake to assume that tensions are nonexistent among Millennials, there does appear to be what religious studies researcher Géraldine Mossière calls a live-and-let-live cosmopolitan universalism and sociability that is a prevalent mindset among many of these young adults who coexist in, encounter daily and for the most part value this new diversity (Meintel and Mossière 2013; Mossière 2021).

Doing Religion

Nonetheless, this valuing of diversity and cosmopolitan sociability is accompanied for the most part by relatively low levels of religious behavior among Millennials. Traditional indicators of religious practice, like service attendance and prayer, reach their lowest levels for the most part among this younger adult generation as illustrated in Tables 2.3 and 2.4 with 2018 GSS data.

In the United States, weekly religious service attendance is down among Millennials; never attending levels are up; and infrequent attendance levels are similar (even a bit higher in some instances) to those of older generations. In Canada in 2018, the break seems to be especially between members of the Silent

TABLE 2.3 Frequency of religious service attendance by generation, U.S. GSS 2018

	Millennials (born 1986–2000)	*Gen Xers (born 1966–1985)*	*Boomers (born 1946–1965)*	*Silent generation and older (born before 1946)*
At least once a week	14%	21%	28%	41%
At least once a month	20%	20%	19%	14%
At least once a year	25%	22%	25%	16%
Less than once a year or never	42%	37%	29%	30%
Total	*100%*	*100%*	*100%*	*100%*

N Millennials = 525; *N* Gen Xers = 788; *N* Boomers = 758; *N* Silent Generation and older = 261. Percentages weighted to be representative of the general population. Any discrepancies in totals are due to rounding.

TABLE 2.4 Frequency of religious service attendance by generation, Canadian GSS 2018

	Millennials (born 1986–2003)	*Gen Xers (born 1966–1985)*	*Boomers (born 1946–1965)*	*Silent generation and older (born before 1946)*
At least once a week	11%	14%	14%	25%
At least once a month	6%	8%	8%	9%
At least three times a year	8%	8%	9%	8%
Once or twice a year	16%	16%	15%	12%
Not at all	59%	54%	55%	46%
Total	*100%*	*100%*	*100%*	*100%*

N = 14,872. Percentages weighted to be representative of the general population.

TABLE 2.5 Frequency of prayer by generation, U.S. GSS 2018

	Millennials (born 1986–2000)	*Gen Xers (born 1966–1985)*	*Boomers (born 1946–1965)*	*Silent generation and older (born before 1946)*
At least once a day	37%	59%	68%	73%
At least once a week	23%	15%	13%	14%
Less than once a week	15%	10%	9%	7%
Never	26%	16%	10%	7%
Total	*100%*	*100%*	*100%*	*100%*

N Millennials = 523; *N* Gen Xers = 791; *N* Boomers = 758; *N* Silent Generation and older = 261. Percentages weighted to be representative of the general population. Any discrepancies in totals are due to rounding.

Generation and younger individuals. Levels of frequent religious service attendance are almost as low among Gen X and Boomers as among Millennials, whereas these levels are higher among those born prior to 1946, an indication of the earlier generational beginnings of this decline in Canada than in the United States.

In turn, levels of frequent prayer and other personal religious practices are down among Millennials in both the United States and Canada compared with members of older generations (Tables 2.5 and 2.6). It is important to note here that, although trends of decline are present among Millennials in both countries when it comes to frequent attendance and prayer, levels of these two measures remain higher among U.S. young adults than among Canadians of the same age group.

Smith and Snell (2009, 281) make the claim for the U.S. context that "… today's emerging adults do not appear to be dramatically less religious than former generations of emerging adults have been, at least going back to the early 1970s." The findings here contradict this claim to a certain extent though, as illustrated in Tables 2.7 and 2.8. I find instead that, for the indicators of frequency of religious

TABLE 2.6 Frequency of religious or spiritual practices on one's own (such as prayer, meditation, etc.) by generation, Canadian GSS 2018

	Millennials (born 1986–2003)	*Gen Xers (born 1966–1985)*	*Boomers (born 1946–1965)*	*Silent generation and older (born before 1946)*
At least once a day	11%	17%	20%	30%
At least once a week	10%	11%	11%	12%
Less than once a week	19%	19%	18%	16%
Not at all	60%	53%	51%	42%
Total	*100%*	*100%*	*100%*	*100%*

N = 14,836. Percentages weighted to be representative of the general population. Any discrepancies in totals are due to rounding.

TABLE 2.7 Rates of frequent religious behavior among 20–29 years old respondents across generations, U.S. GSS

	Monthly or more frequent religious service attendance	*Weekly or more frequent prayer*
1988 GSS: Late Boomers and Early Gen X (born 1959–1968)	44%	68%
1998 GSS: Gen X (born 1969–1978)	34%	66%
2008 GSS: Late Gen X and Early Millennials (born 1979–1988)	35%	63%
2018 GSS: Millennials (born 1989–1998)	31%	58%

TABLE 2.8 Rates of religious affiliation and regular religious behavior among 20–29 years old respondents across generations, Canadian GSS

	Religiously affiliated	*Monthly or more frequent religious service attendance*
1986 GSS: Late Boomers (born 1957–1966)	86%	32%
1998 GSS: Gen X (born 1969–1978)	75%	19%
2008 GSS: Late Gen X and Early Millennials (born 1979–1988)	66%	19%
2018 GSS: Millennials (born 1989–1998)	55%	15%

service attendance and prayer in the United States at least, Millennials are less religious than their prior birth cohort counterparts were in the past at the same age. The same goes for Canadian Millenials in their twenties in 2018 for the indicators of religious affiliation and frequency of religious service attendance.

The 2019 MTS asked respondents about a larger number of religious and spiritual practices, the results of which can be found in Figures 2.3, 2.4, 2.5

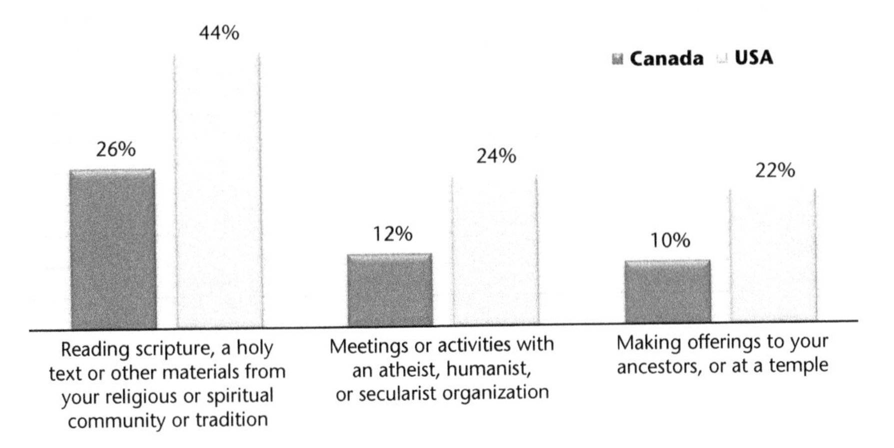

FIGURE 2.3 In the past year, practiced or took part in the following activities at least once a month, respondents 18–35 years old, MTS 2019

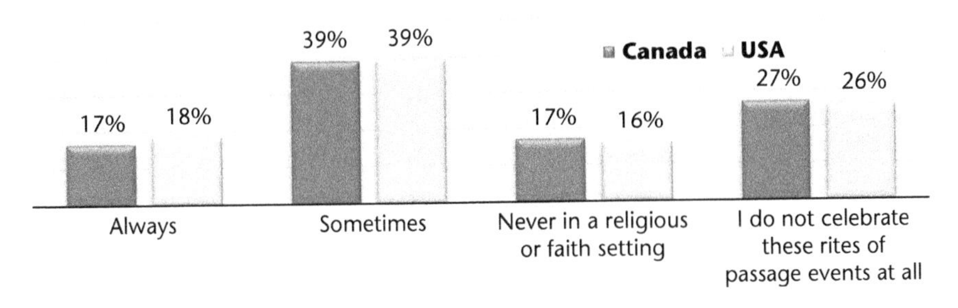

FIGURE 2.4 "How often have you ever celebrated, or plan to celebrate in future, your own rites of passage events with a religious or faith group?" respondents 18–35 years old, MTS 2019

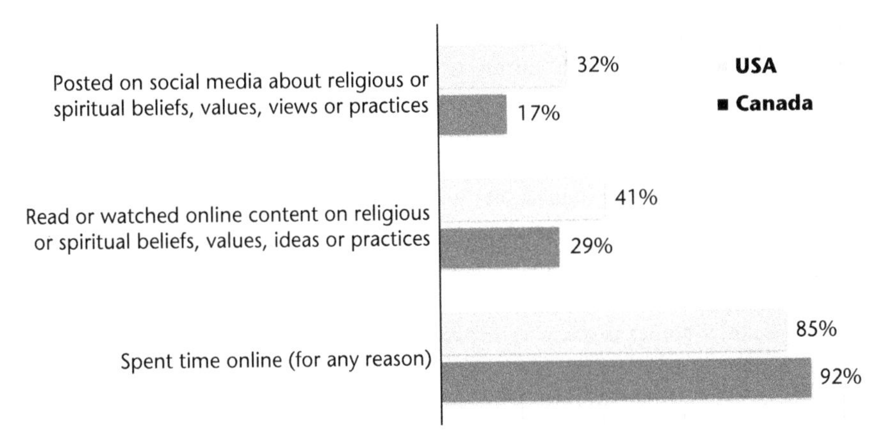

FIGURE 2.5 In the past year, did the following on the Internet at least once a month, respondents 18–35 years old, MTS 2019

TABLE 2.9 Activities identified and defined as practiced spiritual activities in the past 12 months, respondents 18–35 years old, MTS 2019

	Canada	*United States*
Meditation, mindfulness and breathing activities	22%	14%
Yoga	14%	10%
Religious practices (attending church, reading the Bible, Indigenous spiritual practices, etc.)	12%	10%
Outdoor/nature activities	13%	7%
Prayer	8%	12%
Art, writing and dance	6%	4%
Making or listening to music	3%	2%
Rites of passage (baptisms, marriages, funerals)	3%	2%
Friends, family and relationships, including special events/parties	2%	2%
Brainstorming, thinking or reading	2%	2%
Sports/workout	3%	1%
Volunteering, charitable giving, community participation or service	2%	1%
Home/everyday activities (cooking, sharing on social media, organizing, video games, etc.)	1%	1%
Consumption of drugs or other substances	1%	1%
Traveling	1%	0%
Visit sacred sites	0%	0%
I did not take part in any spiritual activities in the past 12 months	52%	55%

and Table 2.9. Like for the indicators of religious service attendance and prayer seen earlier, Canada remains the less religiously active nation for other religiosity measures as well: these include reading religious and spiritual materials as well as making offerings to one's ancestors or at temple monthly or more frequently. Rates for these two indicators in the United States remain higher among young adults than in Canada. These lower levels of regular activity among Canadian Millennials can also be found at the other end of the (non)religious spectrum: monthly or more frequent participation in organized atheist, humanist or secularist meetings and activities is higher in the United States (24%) than in Canada (12%). It would seem then that Canada is generally a country where many citizens, including Millennials, are less involved with organized groups when it comes to their religious or secular belief systems and worldviews.

Yet, when it comes to the past or planned future celebration of rites of passage with religious or faith groups (for example, a wedding, birth/initiation/baptismal rites for a child or funeral), rates are similar among young adults in both countries: just under a fifth say they always celebrate their rites of passage in religious or faith settings; just over a third say sometimes; just under a fifth say never in a religious or faith setting; and just over a quarter say they do not celebrate rites of passage events at all, either in a religious/faith setting or otherwise.

I also aimed to capture less conventional religious and spiritual activities potentially practiced by young adults with the 2019 MTS. In order to do so, respondents were asked in a short-answer open-ended question to list up to three of their group or individual activities, practiced at least once in the past 12 months, that they consider spiritual experiences according to the following definition: "a profound and usually positive experience that helps individuals find their authentic self, as well as connects them to a mysterious, universal, and overarching reality."

The results from this question can be found in Table 2.9. Just over half of young adult respondents in the United States (55%) and Canada (52%) say they did not take part in any spiritual activities so defined in the year prior to the survey. Among the large minority in both countries who did identify at least one spiritual practice in the past year, those activities listed as examples in the survey question were the most commonly identified by respondents in both countries, including meditation, mindfulness and breathing activities, yoga, outdoor nature activities and artistic creation. Prayer and other more conventional religious practices were also among the most commonly identified by respondents. Among those who did identify at least one spiritual activity, the average practice rate of this activity was once a week in both Canada and the United States.

Apart from prayer, which is a more common practice in the United States than in Canada, spiritual activities and experiences seem to be slightly more prevalent among young adult Canadians than their American counterparts. It would seem then that practices tied to more organized forms of religion are more prevalent among U.S. Millennials, and spiritual practices less tied to organized religion are slightly more common among Canadians.

These SBNR (Spiritual But Not Religious) phenomena as they are known in the literature (Ammerman 2014; Drescher 2016; Fuller 2001) definitely appear to be important to many Millennials' lives, but not necessarily to a majority of Millennials though. Although these SBNR phenomena are eclectic and touch many aspects of life for some, as illustrated by the results in Table 2.9, most scholars in the existing literature on the topic agree that there are elements common to these more individualized spiritual endeavors: a search for one's authentic self, valuing personal authenticity above conformity to external religious norms and authorities, and relocating the sacred from the external and transcendent to the internal and immanent (Heelas and Woodhead 2005; Houtman and Aupers 2007; Taylor 2007; Watts 2022). These spiritual activities can be undertaken in a larger search for meaning; they can and often are also undertaken with the goals of self-help (think de-stressing and relaxation, improving physical and mental health, etc.), self-achievement and self-understanding. Stephanie, who we met in the last chapter, speaks about her road biking and being out in nature in many of these ways:

> ... that's definitely like an everyday spiritual experience for me, is just the experience of getting somewhere on my own power, and also seeing this

> nature that I know is connected to me and all of life in mysterious ways that I can't understand. It's like, I mean, to me the great mystery is part of the fun, and maybe part of what draws me to my unidentified spirituality, is that it's almost a relief to me to say, "Yes, there's something out there that's bigger than me, and that I am part of, and I can't understand it and that's okay." And, like, letting that go is almost, like, the comfort that I find in that.

This quote from Stephanie highlights the fact that spiritual activities are not necessarily just private affairs which appear during special and distinct moments in an individual's life. Ammerman (2014) and Drescher (2016) draw attention to the nuanced ways in which individuals, particularly those with weak or no ties to institutional religion, invoke the sacred in the ordinary everyday aspects of life, from life at home to work, relationships, food, art, nature, exercise and health. In these ways, spirituality moves beyond a strictly individualized endeavor and involves others as well. Spiritual practices are "… neither utterly individual or strictly defined by collective tradition … people draw on practices that they learn about from others, both inside and outside traditional religious communities; and occasionally they come up with something genuinely new" (Ammerman 2014, 290).

Another important space for religious and spiritual activity among Millennials is the Internet. Forty-one percent of U.S. MTS respondents say they read or watch online content on religious or spiritual beliefs, values, ideas or practices at least once a month, compared with 29% in Canada; 32% of U.S. young adult respondents post on social media about religious or spiritual beliefs, values, views or practices at least once a month, compared with 17% in Canada. Although it seems that frequent participation in digital religion and spirituality has not become the new normal among a majority of Millennials, it is a substantial phenomenon among an important proportion of them. Additionally, like with the more conventional religious practices seen earlier, this appears to be more so the case among U.S. Millennials than among Canadian ones. Digital is an important way of doing religion and spirituality among Millennials, but is also not for everyone of this generation. We explore this digital religion and spirituality in more detail in the next chapter.

To wrap up this section on religious and spiritual behavior, it is worth mentioning that some other activities not captured by the 2019 MTS did come up during the religious adherents focus groups out West as well as the life history interviews among practicing Catholic Millennials in Québec. Many of these individuals were part of groups or organizations with religious ties and doing various work in their local communities. A couple of the Québec research participants had been on a pilgrimage during their lifetimes, a couple more on trips to the Vatican, and a few more on spiritual retreats; all considered by the research participants as extremely important for the development and nurturing of their faith. Daniel, born in 1993 and living in Montréal, listens to gospel choir music each morning, and Solange, born in 1987 and living in St-Lambert, is a member of her parish choir. Solange has also attended a number of World Youth Day (WYD) gatherings across the globe over the years, took part in a Catholic street procession in downtown Montréal in June 2013, and makes a point of dressing modestly in her everyday life. All the more actively religious Catholics in the Québec study practice lent before Easter in some way, and most also say grace before their evening meal as their parents and grandparents often had during their childhood. Three of the less conventionally religious Québec research participants described having experienced some form of paranormal activity themselves during their lives, or knew of close friends or family members who had.

Believing Religion

Like with many religious behaviors characteristic of Christianity (weekly religious service attendance, daily prayer, etc.), more traditional Christian beliefs are also on the decline among Millennials. Belief in God or a higher power, in Heaven, in Hell, in the Bible as the word of God, and in religious miracles are all still found among a majority of young adults in the United States, but among a smaller majority than for older generations. These results are found in Table 2.10. In fact, for belief in religious miracles Millennials seem to be the first adult generation among whom levels have fallen.

This does not mean though that all religious and spiritual beliefs are on the decline. Levels of belief in life after death in the United States are quite similar among Millennials compared with those among older adults. Rates of belief in the supernatural power of one's deceased ancestors, a belief found in many Asian and Indigenous spiritual traditions as well as in many pop culture references (including ghosts), are substantially higher among the more racially, ethnically and religiously diverse Millennials (reaching 47%) than among older generations. Bibby, Thiessen, and Bailey (2019, 175–179) find similar belief trends among Canadian Millennials, including a decline in rates of belief in God, in the divinity

TABLE 2.10 Beliefs by generation, U.S. GSS 2018

	Millennials (born 1986–2000)	*Gen Xers (born 1966–1985)*	*Boomers (born 1946–1965)*	*Silent generation and older (born before 1946)*
God or a higher power	85%	90%	91%	94%
Heaven	76%	83%	83%	87%
Hell	67%	74%	70%	82%
Bible is the inspired or literal word of God	71%	77%	84%	84%
Religious miracles	68%	80%	80%	80%
Life after death	83%	81%	81%	83%
Supernatural power of deceased ancestors	47%	37%	32%	25%

of Jesus, and in miraculous healing; yet a stability, even a slight increase, in rates of belief in life after death as well as some beliefs in the paranormal (such as communication with the dead and precognition).

In the 2019 MTS, I asked a more general worldview question, providing respondents with answer options ranging from a more religious belief in God, to more spiritual beliefs in mystery and connection, to a material and scientific worldview, to indifference. The results of this question are included in Table 2.11. With the way the worldview question was worded and with the MTS sample, just over two thirds (68%) of U.S. young adult respondents say they first believe in God or a higher power, with belief in God according to the teachings of their religion being the most popular of these belief systems. By contrast, just over half (56%) of Canadian young adult respondents say they first believe in God or a higher power, with belief in God in the respondent's own way being the most popular in Canada.

Among the four nonbelief (do not believe in God or a higher power) categories respondents could choose from, the more material and scientific worldview that life on Earth is purely the result of complex biological, physical and material processes is the most popular category among U.S. respondents. Yet, among Canadian young adults, it is the mystery worldview (we are all part of a mysterious and connected natural world and universe) that is the most popular. Another instance then of less religious Canadian Millennials showing slightly higher levels of preference for unchurched spirituality.

Among those U.S. and Canadian young adult respondents who do have religious or spiritual beliefs, a majority consider these beliefs to be somewhat or very important in the way they lead their lives (Figures 2.6 and 2.7). This salience of beliefs is most pronounced in the United States: overall, 51% of Canadian respondents consider their religious or spiritual beliefs to be somewhat or very

TABLE 2.11 "Which of the following statements would you say best applies to you?" respondents 18–35 years old, MTS 2019

	Canada	*United States*
I believe in God, according to the teachings of my religion	22%	35%
I believe in God, but in my own way	26%	26%
I believe in a higher, transcendent power or being(s), but I would not call this power or being(s) God	8%	7%
I do not necessarily believe in God or a higher power, but I do believe that we are all part of a mysterious and connected natural world and universe	18%	8%
I believe that life on Earth is purely the result of complex biological, physical and material processes	14%	11%
I have not made up my mind about my beliefs	9%	7%
I have never thought about it and it does not make any difference to me	4%	5%
Total	*100%*	*100%*

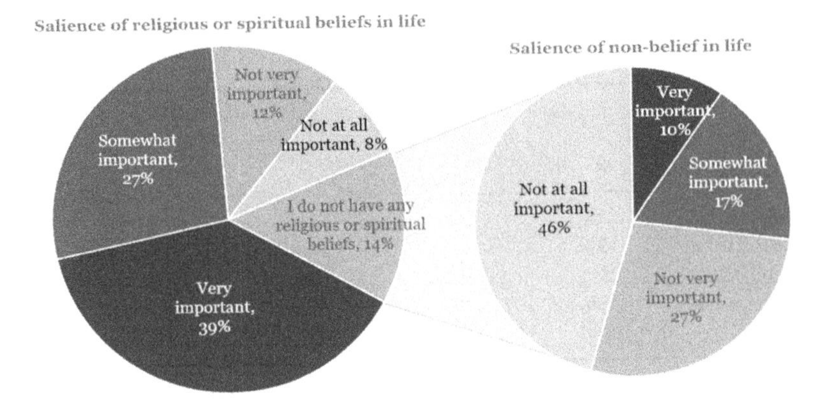

FIGURE 2.6 "How important are your religious or spiritual beliefs (or not having any) to the way you live your life?" respondents 18–35 years old, United States, MTS 2019

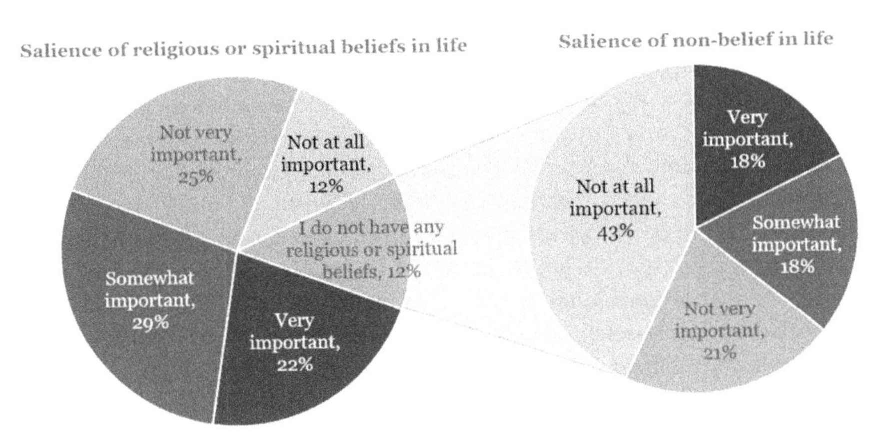

FIGURE 2.7 "How important are your religious or spiritual beliefs (or not having any) to the way you live your life?" respondents 18–35 years old, Canada, MTS 2019

important in the way they lead their lives, compared with 66% of U.S. respondents who say the same. This also means that 37% of Canadian and 20% of U.S. respondents say that their religious or spiritual beliefs are not very or not at all important to the way they live their lives.

Another 12% in Canada and 14% in the United States say they do not have any religious or spiritual beliefs at all. Among these nonbelieving respondents, just over a third (36%) in Canada and just under a third (27%) in the United States consider this nonbelief as something more substantive that they say is somewhat or very important to the way they lead their lives.

The 2018 Canadian GSS (Cycle 32) also contains a question on the salience of religious and spiritual beliefs in life (but without the option of saying one has no religious or spiritual beliefs). These survey data indicate that Millennials have the lowest salience of beliefs levels among all living adults (Table 2.12).

TABLE 2.12 Salience of religious and spiritual beliefs in life, by generation, Canadian GSS 2018

	Millennials (born 1986–2000)	*Gen Xers (born 1966–1985)*	*Boomers (born 1946–1965)*	*Silent generation and older (born before 1946)*
Very important	22%	26%	34%	44%
Somewhat important	22%	26%	29%	28%
Not very important	21%	19%	16%	14%
Not at all important	35%	29%	22%	14%
Total	*100%*	*100%*	*100%*	*100%*

N = 20,116.[1] Percentages weighted to be representative of the general population. Any discrepancies in totals are due to rounding.

Attitudes toward Religion

Growing nonreligion among Millennials in terms of higher rates of religious nonaffiliation as well as lower rates of Judaeo-Christian religious practices and beliefs does not necessarily mean a growing anti-religious sentiment among young adults. Smith and Snell (2009) found that emerging adults generally had a positive outlook toward religion when asked, if mostly indifferent toward it in their everyday lives. As discussed earlier in this chapter, the general Millennial mindset on these issues is much more one of cosmopolitan universalism and sociability than of anti-religion rationalism and secularism, although this later approach is not entirely absent among Millennials either. This said, positive attitudes toward religiosity and spirituality among the Millennial generation do not extend to all dimensions of religion in society, and some less positive attitudes remain toward certain religious groups. The following 2019 MTS results explore this in more detail.

In terms of attitudes toward public dimensions of religion in society, a majority of young adult respondents in both Canada (60%) and the United States (64%) agree or strongly agree that government employees should be allowed to wear religious symbols or clothing, and only 19% in Canada and 13% in the United States disagree or strongly disagree with this statement (Figure 2.8). However, support for religious or faith groups receiving government subsidies for the social services they provide (for example, running immigrant settlement programs, soup kitchens and shelters for the homeless, educational programs, etc.) is not quite as high: just under half of respondents (45%) in both countries either agree or strongly agree with these types of government subsidies for religious groups, and a quarter disagree or strongly disagree with them. The least support is reserved for religious or faith groups receiving tax exemptions full stop. Only 16% of Canadian and 33% of U.S. young adult respondents agree or strongly agree with these tax exemptions for religious or faith groups (Figure 2.9).

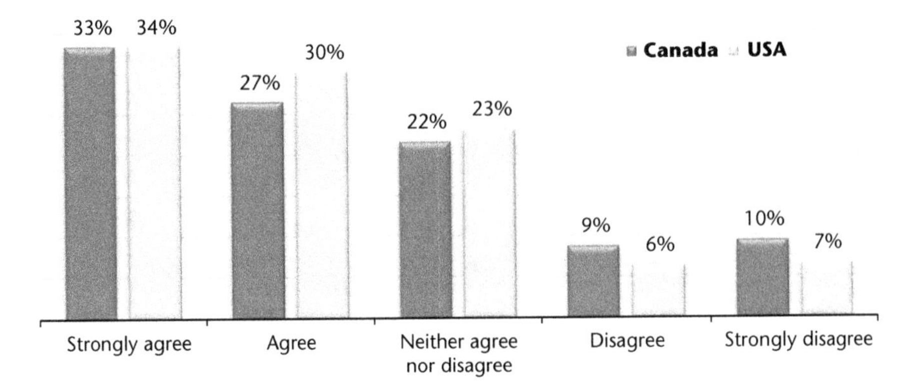

FIGURE 2.8 "Government employees should be allowed to wear religious symbols or clothing while they are working, such as a Christian cross, a turban (Sikh head covering), a kippah (Jewish head cap), or a hijab (Islamic headscarf)," respondents 18–35 years old, MTS 2019

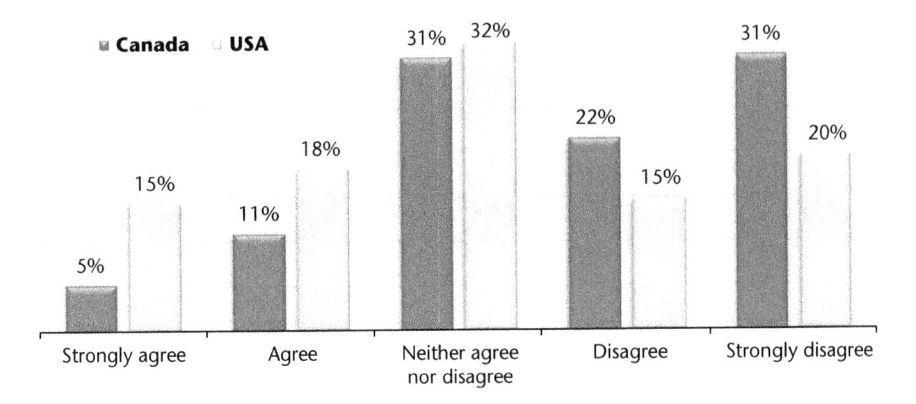

FIGURE 2.9 "Religious or faith groups should receive tax exemptions," respondents 18–35 years old, MTS 2019

Respondents in the 2019 MTS were also presented with a list of 27 words in random order (see horizontal *x* axis in Figure 2.10 for this list) and asked to select which of these words have positive associations or meanings for them, and which have negative associations or meanings. Each word was then assigned a +1 for each 1% of respondents who selected it for positive associations; a −1 for each 1% of respondents who selected it for negative associations; and 0 for each 1% of respondents who did not select it at all. These points were then tallied to create this word's average feeling score in both the United States and Canada. For example, in the United States, 16% of respondents indicated negative associations for "religion" (−16), 56% did not select this word for positive or negative associations (0) and 27% had positive associations with "religion" (+27), which gives a total feeling score of +11 for "religion" in the United States.

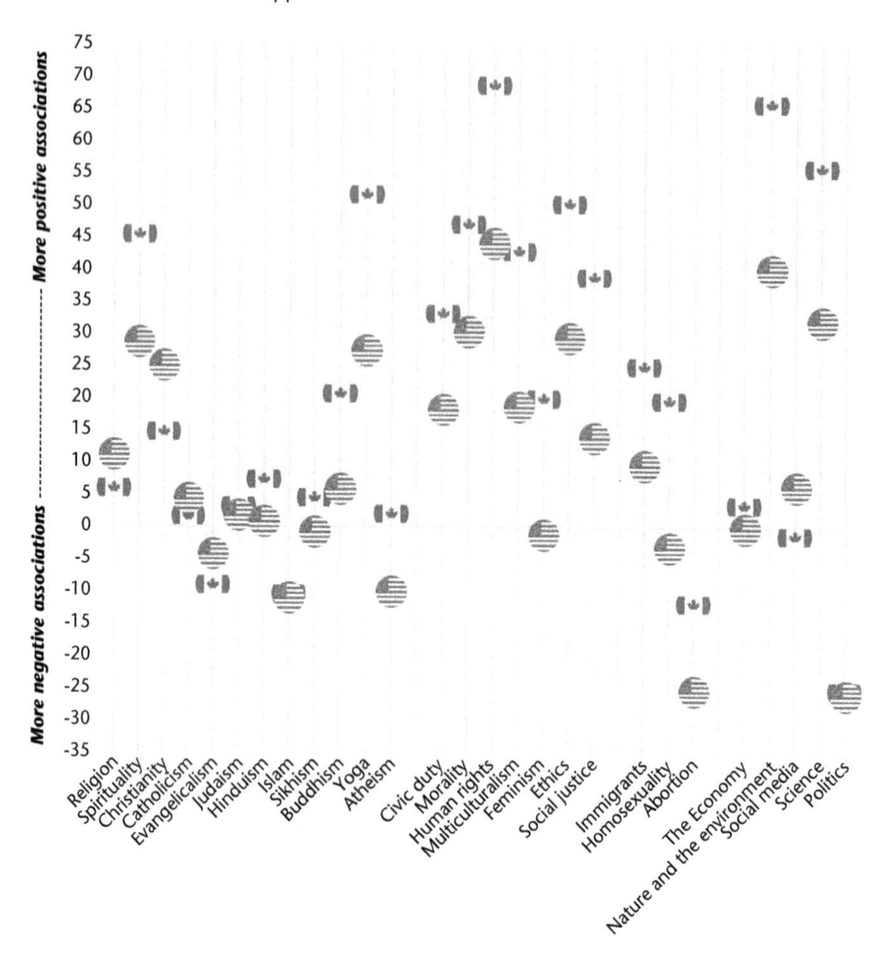

FIGURE 2.10 Average feelings scores, "Select all words that generally have positive or negative associations or meanings for you," respondents 18–35 years old, MTS 2019

In terms of the different (non)religions and spiritual traditions provided, most received feeling scores close to 0 (within the range of −9 to +9) from young adult respondents, indicating overall neutral feelings toward these traditions. Exceptions to this include "spirituality" and "yoga" which for many have positive connotations, especially in Canada (+45 and +52, respectively); along with "religion" receiving a positive score just above +10 in the United States, but only +6 in Canada. Another example then of Canadian Millennials' greater preference for unchurched spirituality. "Islam" received a substantial negative score in both Canada (−10) and the United States (−11), an indication of Islamophobic attitudes even among some of the most tolerant adult living generation today, and even in Canada where multiculturalism is often touted by many as a prized value. Atheism received an overall negative score of −10 in the United States, but +2 in Canada, showing continued greater support (or at

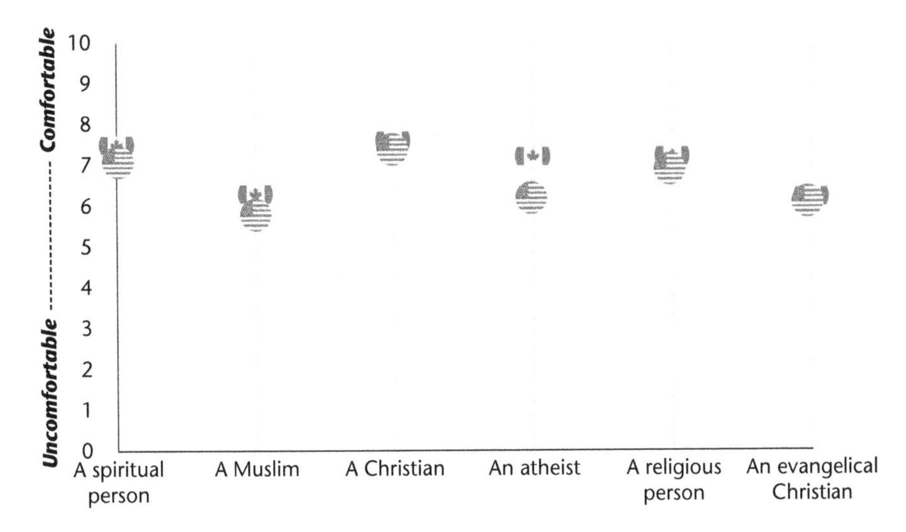

FIGURE 2.11 "On a scale from 0 to 10 (0 indicating very uncomfortable; 10 indicating very comfortable), indicate what level of comfort you would feel if the following type of person became your relative by marriage (in-law)," respondents 18–35 years old, MTS 2019

least greater tolerance) for this nonreligious identity north of the 49th parallel among Millennials, a national trend that is also found among older generations (Thiessen and Wilkins-Laflamme 2020).

It is worth mentioning that some other words score much more positively among Millennials in both countries than the (non)religious and spiritual traditions, including notably human rights, nature and the environment, and science. Still, other words score much more negatively than the (non)religious and spiritual traditions, including notably abortion in the United States and politics in both countries.

MTS respondents were then asked how comfortable they would feel on a scale from 0 to 10 if a member of a specific (non)religion or spiritual tradition were to become their relative by marriage (0 indicating very uncomfortable; 10 indicating very comfortable). The results in Figure 2.11 show that spiritual persons and Christians score the highest on average (most comfort) in both the United States and Canada. Muslims and Evangelicals in both countries, as well as atheists in the United States, score the lowest (least comfort), but it is also important to note that none of the average scores for these groups fall below 5. Once again, Millennials are on average the most tolerant generation to members of many of these (non) religious and spiritual traditions (Young and Shipley 2020), but some differences in attitudes between groups still remain.

Toward a Latent Class Typology

You may at this point feel like you are beginning to buckle under the weight of all these data. Even I, an unabashed data lover, can admit that this is a lot of information to process. To help with this information crunch and to better grasp the different ways Millennials do religion, spirituality and secularity, I now turn to the tried-and-tested way in sociology of making sense of a lot of data coming from individuals: by creating a typology. Now that we have explored some of the trends in religious identity, behavior, believing as well as public opinion, the next important step in the analysis is to combine the data on some of the key presented indicators. This will allow us to build categories of Millennials' approaches to the dimensions of (non)religion and (non)spirituality.

To borrow wise words from Smith and Snell (2009, 166):

> Every typology is of course an oversimplification and needs to be used with caution. Not every last person falls neatly within one category or other. Some people seem to straddle types, and others are simply very unique. Nevertheless, empirically informed categories that represent major differences in groups of people can bring helpful analytical clarity to what would otherwise be a complex mass of data.

As discussed in the previous chapter, Smith and Snell establish a religious typology of six categories among emerging adults based on their qualitative interviews. I instead use latent class analysis for my 2019 MTS quantitative data. A latent class analysis is a type of statistical model that looks at how respondents answered a series of questions on the survey, and from this information extracts a number of underlying groups (or latent classes). In other words, this type of statistical analysis identifies patterns in respondents' answers to survey questions, and groups them accordingly into different underlying categories (or classes) of individuals.

Table 2.13 contains the list of variables included in the latent class analysis. These are variables of (non)religious and (non)spiritual belonging, worldviews and religious and spiritual behaviors. Based on how respondents answered this set of survey questions, underlying latent groups of young adults were identified by the statistical analysis. Four of these latent groups, or classes, emerged from the analysis, which I name as follows: religious Millennials, spiritual seeker Millennials, cultural believer Millennials and nonreligious Millennials.[2] Table 2.13 also contains the predicted probabilities and means of how each latent class scores on each variable included in the analysis. Let us examine each group in a bit more detail here.

The Religious Millennial

Young adult respondents who are more likely to fall into this group than any of the other three show the highest probabilities of being religiously affiliated, and of believing in God according to the teachings of their religion. Without exception, these respondents also score highest on all religious behaviors contained in the analysis, including the more personal, group and digital religious practices. There is also a 25% probability that these respondents will take part in

TABLE 2.13 Predicted probabilities of religious identity, believing and behavioral indicators among the four latent classes of Millennials, MTS 2019

	Religious Millennial	*Spiritual seeker Millennial*	*Cultural believer Millennial*	*Nonreligious Millennial*
Religiously affiliated	93%	70%	82%	2%
Spiritual with no religion	2%	10%	9%	12%
Other no religion identity	5%	20%	9%	86%
Believe in God, according to the teachings of my religion	70%	14%	18%	1%
Believe in God, but in my own way	21%	47%	47%	8%
Believe in a higher, transcendent power or being(s), but I would not call this power or being(s) God	4%	10%	9%	10%
Do not necessarily believe in God or a higher power, but do believe that we are all part of a mysterious and connected natural world and universe	2%	15%	10%	24%
Believe that life on Earth is purely the result of complex biological, physical and material processes	1%	5%	6%	31%
I have not made up my mind about my beliefs	1%	7%	8%	14%
I have never thought about it and it does not make any difference to me	1%	2%	2%	12%
Unchurched spiritual activity in past year	25%	40%	23%	28%

(Continued)

TABLE 2.13 (Continued): Predicted means of religious behavioral indicators among the four latent classes of Millennials, MTS 2019

	Religious Millennial	*Spiritual seeker Millennial*	*Cultural believer Millennial*	*Nonreligious Millennial*
Frequency of prayer	At least once a week	At least once a month	A few times a year	Not at all
Frequency of religious service attendance	At least once a week	A few times a year	Once a year	Not at all
Frequency of reading religious or spiritual materials	At least once a week	At least once a month	Not at all	Not at all
Frequency of making offerings to your ancestors, or at a temple	A few times a year	Once a year	Not at all	Not at all
Frequency of reading or watching online content on religious or spiritual beliefs, values, ideas or practices	At least once a week	A few times a year	Once a year	Once a year
Frequency of posting on social media about religious or spiritual beliefs, values, views or practices	At least once a month	Once a year	Once a year	Not at all
Frequency of celebrating rites of passage with religious group	Sometimes	Sometimes	Never in a religious or faith setting	Never in a religious or faith setting
Frequency of discussing religion or spirituality with friends	At least once a month	A few times a year	Once a year	Once a year

unchurched spiritual activities as well (spiritual activities included in Table 2.9, minus those designated as "religious practices"), on top of more traditionally religious ones. This latent class of religious Millennials is closest to the committed traditionalists identified by Smith and Snell (2009) in their typology of emerging adults.

Andrea, introduced in the previous chapter, is an example of a religious Millennial. Kamal, born in 1989 and who took part in one of the focus groups conducted in Vancouver, British Columbia, by the Cascadia research team in April 2018, is another example of someone who personifies this latent class:

> I think growing up post 9/11 there's a lot of media attention on what it is to be Muslim and I think it became a strong part of my identity because of that. … I go to the mosque on the Friday, pray in congregation … when Ramadan comes around, I don't want to be breaking fast by myself in my apartment, I want to be with people who have also been fasting.

The Spiritual Seeker Millennial

This second latent class is also characterized by higher probabilities of religious affiliation, although not quite as high as among the religious and cultural believer groups. Belief in God in their own way is highest among this spiritual seeker latent class, with probabilities for believing in God according to the teachings of their religion as well as for the mystery worldview also being substantial. This group has mid-level averages for the various religious behaviors, but the highest probabilities of taking part in unchurched spiritual activities of all the four latent classes. This latent class of the spiritual seeker seems to be a combination of the selective adherent and spiritually open types identified by Smith and Snell (2009). It is important to note here that these Millennials' spiritual seeking often appears to be done partly within traditional religious groups, and partly without.

Stephanie, introduced in the last chapter and who we heard from again earlier in this chapter, would fall into this spiritual seeker type. Nicholas, born in 1990 and part of an April 2018 Vancouver focus group, is another example of a spiritual seeker Millennial:

> … some of my most powerful spiritual experiences have been on the moors in Britain, … the Rockies are for me a religious experience, I don't know if I want to say like spiritual, I want to say religious experience, because that's like a church …

The Cultural Believer Millennial

This third latent class is characterized by very high probabilities of religious affiliation, high probabilities of belief in God in their own way (with an additional

18% probability of belief in God according to the teachings of their religion), but relatively low average frequency of religious behaviors. These averages are not as low as among the nonreligious Millennial, but still lower compared with the religious and spiritual seeker Millennials. Such cultural believer individuals are often referred to as marginal, nominal, fuzzy or cultural religious affiliates in the existing literature (Meunier and Wilkins-Laflamme 2011; Smith et al. 2014; Thiessen 2015; Voas 2009). They often link their religious affiliation and some of their beliefs to their family, regional and/or cultural heritage and values, but for the most part do not pair this with frequent religious or spiritual activities. When comparing with the Smith and Snell (2009) typology, they seem to be a combination of the selective adherent and religiously indifferent. Andrew, born in 1988, who identifies as Jewish and who took part in one of the Cascadia focus groups in Seattle, Washington, in May 2018 personifies many of the dimensions of the cultural believer Millennial when he says:

> I used to pray, I don't any more outside rare occasions in community space, then it's communal-driven that's for sure. ... I think I take part in ... rituals spaces but as a shared cultural experience, which I think is often bolstered by a certain nostalgia or continued tradition or whatever the thing is that makes us do things when we wouldn't otherwise because it's what we grew up with because we share that familiarity within a space.

The Nonreligious Millennial

This fourth and final latent class is characterized, in contrast to the other three, by very high probabilities of religious nonaffiliation. Predicted averages of all religious behaviors without exception are at their lowest among nonreligious Millennials, often with these behaviors being completely absent altogether. There is, however, a 28% probability among this group of taking part in unchurched spiritual activities, and a 12% probability of identifying as spiritual with no religion. The most common worldview is the material and scientific one, with a 24% probability also going to the mystery worldview. This latent class is also characterized by the highest probabilities among all four groups of uncertainty surrounding beliefs (14%) and indifference toward beliefs (12%). This latent class appears to make up a combination of the religiously indifferent, religiously disconnected and irreligious types put forward by Smith and Snell (2009).

Jeremy, introduced in the previous chapter, is an example of a nonreligious Millennial. Kelly, born in 1992 and who was interviewed by Lynne Marks about her life history in May 2018, is another example. When asked how she would define herself in relation to religion, Kelly answers:

> I don't, I wouldn't describe myself as anything. I don't, I don't really know. I haven't been exposed to different [religions]. So I don't really know what I, what I define myself as. ... I just really wasn't exposed to it [religion}. I

> don't really, I've never taken the time to learn about it enough for me to create an opinion or educate myself on it. It hasn't been something that I have found to be necessary for me to live comfortably here in the city. Or to even, like, find friends or anything like that.... And we've kind of as a family kind of concluded that if there was some greater power or some God, then things that are so horrible wouldn't be happening to people.

Sarah, born in 1986 and who took part in one of the focus groups conducted in Portland, Oregon, in June 2018, takes a bit more of an irreligious stance when she talks about her dislike of Christianity:

> ... for me religion had always been about the symbolism, and then going to church had been about family. And about community. And so, when I stopped, when I went away and went to college, I lost that connection to that family, so there was no real reason for me to go to a church, because all the—the ritual is fine, and some of the songs are really comforting because they're part of my childhood. But, for me, the whole—in the teaching of Christianity, there's just not much there for me. It doesn't serve my needs, and there's too much I find really repulsive, and really antagonistic towards queer people like me, and towards women, and just unsuitable to living a life in this world, where we need to get along with each other, and where we need to really respect our relationships with other creatures and other beings, whether or not they're sentient. And so I've always erred more towards science and looking for ways to show that empathy is more important than religion. Or empathy is more important than winning. That if we want to survive, we should be looking out for the best for everybody. So even though I'm not religious, I have very strong convictions about morality and justice and the common humanity among people.

For the most part, these four latent classes seem to fit along a spectrum of religiosity, from most to least religious, as illustrated at the bottom of Figure 2.12. Most of the variables included in the latent class analysis show this linear pattern between the four latent groups: for example, most of the religious behaviors are highest in their average frequency among the religious Millennial, and then decline steadily from the spiritual seeker, cultural believer to the nonreligious Millennial. This said, there are some important exceptions to this trend, which is why I chose to analyze the data as four separate latent classes rather than an underlying latent scale (or factor) of religiosity. Religious identity appears to be more common and especially important among the cultural believer, more so than among the spiritual seeker. The spiritual seeker in turn scores highest on unchurched spiritual activities; higher than the religious Millennial. Additionally, worldviews also do not follow a linear progression from religious to spiritual to secular between the spiritual seeker and the cultural believer.

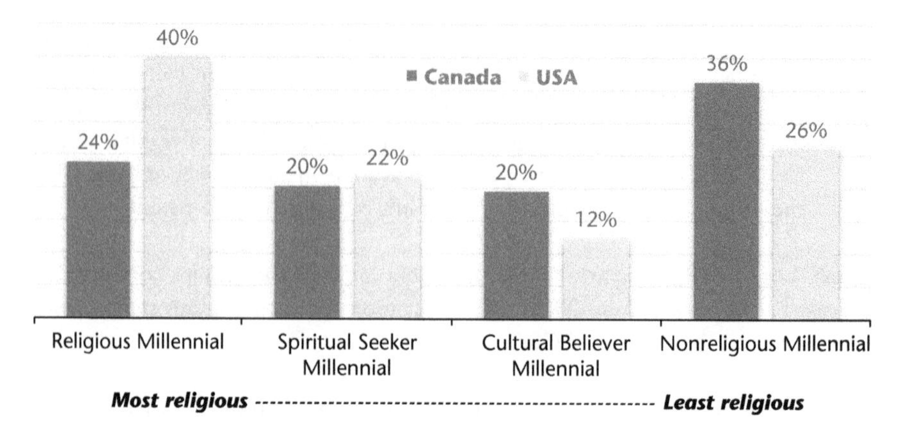

FIGURE 2.12 Proportional size of each latent class among Canadian and American Millennial respondents, MTS 2019

Figure 2.12 also contains the estimated size of each latent group in the United States and Canada. Young adult respondents from the 2019 MTS were classified into one latent class over the three others if they had a probability of 50% or more of falling into that given latent class. Based on this classification, Canada is still showing a more secular trend than the United States: nonreligious Millennials make up the largest proportion in Canada (36%), compared with religious Millennials in the United States (40%). Rates of cultural believers are also higher in Canada (20%), compared with the United States (12%). It is only the rates of spiritual seekers that are roughly the same in both countries: 20% in Canada and 22% in the United States.

***

To highlight some of the key takeaways from this chapter before we move on, we do see the two trends of greater religious diversity and greater decline of organized religion among Millennials. But to simply stop there would be to miss some important additional facts about religion and spirituality within this generation. Religious diversity, although more prevalent among Millennials than among generations past, still has its limits in terms of the size of non-Christian religious minorities and the public opinion acceptance of some of these minorities even among this younger adult generation.

And yes, a secular transition does appear to be underway with lower levels of many religious indicators among Millennials in both the United States and Canada. Yet, this secular transition is not affecting all religious or spiritual beliefs: the beliefs in life after death and in the supernatural power of deceased ancestors are doing relatively well among Millennials for example. Additionally, decline does not necessarily imply disappearance. Christian and other monotheistic beliefs are still held by a majority of this younger generation in both countries. There are also substantial minorities among Millennials who are either more traditionally religious, or who practice less conventional forms of spirituality removed from organized religion.

Some observers have gone further and wondered if digital religion and unchurched spirituality have replaced organized religion altogether among Millennials, and have become as prevalent among this generation as organized Christianity was in the past among older birth cohorts. I do not find this to be the case, but we are seeing digital religion and unchurched spirituality among an important proportion of Millennials (just not a majority), and thus I consider them important to study and understand in their own right.

Of course, there is much additional diversity within each latent class presented in this chapter, both demographically and regarding how Millennials approach religion, spirituality and secularity. We will explore much of this diversity along with key dynamics of each group in the chapters to come. The four latent classes introduced here provide the framework for the remaining chapters of this book, with each following chapter exploring one of these groups of Millennials in depth. We begin in the next chapter with the religious Millennial.

Notes

1 Most of the Canadian data in this chapter from the 2018 General Social Survey are taken from Cycle 33. However, the data in Table 2.12 are taken from Cycle 32, administered earlier in 2018, since the salience of beliefs measure is not available in Cycle 33.

2 A model of four latent classes was selected over three, since there are important distinctions between spiritual seeker and cultural believer Millennials, which we explore in some detail in this chapter and further in later chapters. In turn, a model with five latent classes did not improve model fit substantially, compared with the four latent classes model, and did not raise any clear important distinctions within each of the final four latent classes.

References

Ammerman, Nancy. 2014. *Sacred Stories, Spiritual Tribes: Finding Religion in Everyday Life.* New York, NY: Oxford University Press.

Beaman, Lori G. 2017. *Deep Equality in an Era of Religious Diversity.* New York, NY: Oxford University Press.

Bibby, Reginald W., Joel Thiessen, and Monetta Bailey. 2019. *The Millennial Mosaic: How Pluralism and Choice Are Shaping Canadian Youth and the Future of Canada.* Toronto, ON: Dundurn.

Clarke, Brian, and Stuart Macdonald. 2017. *Leaving Christianity: Changing Allegiances in Canada since 1945.* Montréal, QC: McGill-Queen's University Press.

Drescher, Elizabeth. 2016. *Choosing Our Religion: The Spiritual Lives of America's Nones.* New York, NY: Oxford University Press.

Frey, William H. 2018. *Diversity Explosion: How New Racial Demographics Are Remaking America.* Washington, DC: Brookings Institution Press.

Fuller, Robert. 2001. *Spiritual But Not Religious: Understanding Unchurched America.* New York, NY: Oxford University Press.

Heelas, Paul, and Linda Woodhead. 2005. *The Spiritual Revolution: Why Religion Is Giving Way to Spirituality*. Oxford, UK: Blackwell.

Houtman, Dick, and Stef Aupers. 2007. "The Spiritual Turn and the Decline of Tradition: The Spread of Post-Christian Spirituality in 14 Western Countries, 1981–2000." *Journal for the Scientific Study of Religion* 46 (3): 305–320. doi:10.1111/j.1468-5906.2007.00360.x

Meintel, Deirdre, and Géraldine Mossière. 2013. "In the Wake of the Quiet Revolution: From Secularization to Religious Cosmopolitanism." *Anthropologica*, 55 (1): 57–71.

Meunier, E.-Martin, and Sarah Wilkins-Laflamme. 2011. "Sécularisation, catholicisme et transformation du régime de religiosité au Québec. Étude comparative avec le catholicisme au Canada (1968–2007)." *Recherches Sociographiques* 52 (3): 683–729. doi:10.7202/1007655ar

Mossière, Géraldine. 2021. "Cosmopolitanism, Sociability and Assemblages of Symbolic Resources Among Youths Attracted by Islam." *Secular Studies* 3: 71–92. doi:10.1163/25892525-bja10016

Putnam, Robert, and David Campbell. 2010. *American Grace: How Religion Divides and Unites Us*. New York, NY: Simon and Schuster.

Sherkat, Darren E. 2014. *Changing Faith: The Dynamics and Consequences of Americans' Shifting Identities*. New York, NY: New York University Press.

Smith, Christian, Kyle Longest, Jonathan Hill, and Karl Christoffersen. 2014. *Young Catholic America: Emerging Adults In, Out of, and Gone from the Church*. New York, NY: Oxford University Press.

Smith, Christian, and Patricia Snell. 2009. *Souls in Transition: The Religious and Spiritual Lives of Emerging Adults*. New York, NY: Oxford University Press.

Taylor, Charles. 2007. *A Secular Age*. Cambridge, MA: The Belknap Press of Harvard University Press.

Thiessen, Joel. 2015. *The Meaning of Sunday: The Practice of Belief in a Secular Age*. Montréal, QC: McGill-Queen's University Press.

Thiessen, Joel, and Sarah Wilkins-Laflamme. 2020. *None of the Above: Nonreligious Identity in the U.S. and Canada*. New York, NY: New York University Press.

Voas, David. 2009. "The Rise and Fall of Fuzzy Fidelity in Europe." *European Sociological Review* 25 (2): 155–168. doi:10.1093/esr/jcn044

Watts, Galen. 2022. *The Spiritual Turn: The Religion of the Heart and the Making of Romantic Liberal Modernity*. New York, NY: Oxford University Press.

Young, Pamela Dickey, and Heather Shipley. 2020. *Identities under Construction: Religion, Gender, and Sexuality among Youth in Canada*. Kingston, ON: McGill-Queen's University Press.

3

THE RELIGIOUS MILLENNIAL

Being dedicated to one's faith is in many ways a different experience among Millennials now than among older generations from earlier decades and centuries. This chapter explores some of the key new social realities shaping the religious experiences of young adult Millennials today. Although proportionally smaller than among older living adults, the category of religious Millennial still represents a substantial part of this younger generation: an estimated 24% in Canada and 40% in the United States as we saw at the end of the last chapter. This is your group of young individuals who regularly populate churches, synagogues, temples, gurdwaras, mosques and other places of worship across the continent. This is your group of individuals who most often brings their faith into their homes with prayer, religious symbols, the reading of religious texts and other practices, as was done by most of their parents during these individuals' childhoods in the 1980s, 1990s and early 2000s. This is your group of individuals who actively keep their faith as a salient part of their lives while going through the tumultuous and transitional period of emerging adulthood often characterized by job insecurity, relationship uncertainty, geographical mobility, self-discovery and exposure to new worldviews.

Yet, unlike their parents' and grandparents' generation, digital religion has become a much more prominent (virtual) space for Millennials to learn about, develop, share and reinforce their faith, often complementing their in-person religious activities. Many religious Millennials are also much more left of the political spectrum on a large number of socio-political issues than their religious counterparts from older generations. This is currently leading to large upheavals within many local, regional and national religious organizations. These more progressive Millennial views at times clash and at times evolve with the more conservative views traditionally found within many religious groups. Finally, religious Millennials are an important minority within their generation, but a

DOI: 10.4324/9781003217695-3

minority nonetheless. This shapes their own identities as well as their interactions with others in ways never before seen among older generations where religious individuals often held a majority position in society. Later in this chapter, I will unpack each of these three key dynamics in detail, exploring macro statistical trends and micro interviewee experiences of these new realities. First though, it is worth taking a bit more space here to explore some of the characteristics and internal diversities of this category that is the religious Millennial.

In the 2019 Millennial Trends Survey (MTS) sample, the largest religious traditions found among religious Millennials are Catholics (37% among Canadian religious Millennials and 36% among U.S. religious Millennials), Protestants (22% among Canadian religious Millennials and 31% among U.S. religious Millennials), Muslims (11% among Canadian religious Millennials and 6% among U.S. religious Millennials) and Orthodox Christians (10% among Canadian religious Millennials and 6% among U.S. religious Millennials). Most (80%), but not all, received a religious or spiritual education at school, at home or at a place of worship at least once a week while growing up. This is in line with Smith and Snell's (2009, 211–256) findings on the importance of religious socialization from parents and during childhood and teenage years for keeping the faith later in life during emerging adulthood. Although not a representative sample by any means, the 23 religious Millennials from the Pacific Northwest focus groups and the Québec life history interviews all experienced a religious childhood and primary socialization from their parents.

What is striking from the comparison of some statistical trends in Table 3.1 between the religious Millennial subsample and the rest of the 18–35 years old respondents in the 2019 MTS is that, not only is this subsample way more religious (kinda figured, given the way the category was put together), but it also bucks some of the demographic differences that exist between religious and nonreligious

TABLE 3.1 Characteristics of religious Millennials

	Religious Millennials	*Rest of Millennials*
% weekly or more frequent childhood religious or spiritual education	80%	43%
% monthly or more frequent religious service attendance as adults	92%	9%
% weekly or more frequent prayer as adults	88%	16%
Mean age	26 years	26.2 years
% female	44%	51%
% non-White ethnic background/race	48%	26%
% university educated	31%	23%
% with less than $20,000 household income	19%	16%
% rural residents (pop. < 50,000)	24%	28%

Source: MTS 2019.

populations among older generations. A large number of general population studies in the United States and Canada have shown that men, the university educated and urban residents, tend to be much less religious on average (Baker and Smith 2015; Strawn 2019; Thiessen and Wilkins-Laflamme 2020). Yet, these demographic differences are not present among the younger 2019 MTS sample: the religious Millennial category actually has a slightly higher ratio of men to women than the rest of the sample, a higher ratio of university educated respondents to less educated respondents, and a fairly similar ratio of rural to urban residents. These reversed demographic distinctions pale in magnitude though compared with the main demographic effect observed in Table 3.1: that nearly half of the subsample of religious Millennials is from a non-White ethnic or racial background, compared with only 26% among the rest of the sample. These demographic differences between religious and other Millennials are present in both the U.S. and Canadian subsamples of the survey, and are notably the consequence of the growing religious pluralism (especially from immigration) and nonreligion trends (notably among White European settler populations) explored in the previous chapter.

Some observers expect to see the religious Millennial category expand to represent a larger proportion of this generation as Millennials age and move into a more financially and geographically stable phase of middle adulthood and family life. These observers see young and emerging adulthood as always having been a life period when individuals are less religious, only to return to their faith as individuals "settle down," have kids and think about the big questions tied to raising these kids and growing old. Although my present study will not have the final say on this, we will have to wait for future data in the coming decades, what I can say is that there is not much evidence to support this life cycle effect of a return to religion among older Millennials as they transition to middle adulthood in the current data I have access to. Religious Millennials represent a smaller proportion of young adults today than young adults in the past: for example, as we saw in Tables 2.7 and 2.8 in the last chapter, 44% of 20–29 years old from 1988 attended religious services at least once a month in the United States, compared with only 31% among the same age group in 2018. Consequently, there seems to be at least some more permanent generational declines of this religious category going on. Additionally, among older Millennials 30–35 years old who are transitioning out of emerging adulthood into middle adulthood, 23% and 49% respectively attend religious services at least once a month in Canada and the United States according to the 2019 MTS, compared with 29% and 46% among 18–24 years old in Canada and the United States. There has not been a huge increase in rates of regular religious service attendance among Millennials in their thirties: only a very slight (not statistically significant) increase in U.S. rates, and a decline in Canada.

These results are one indication then that a more permanent shift has happened among Millennials in that religious individuals of this generation will continue to represent only a minority moving forward. Like I mentioned earlier though, they represent a substantial minority nevertheless; one worthy of attention in their own right, especially when it comes to some of the new social dynamics impacting religious experiences among this group.

Digital Religion among Millennials[1]

With the arrival of communication technologies such as radio, television, and more recently the Internet and social media, scholars of religion as well as religious leaders have long debated the place of these technologies in the religious and spiritual lives of individuals. To what extent do the religious and spiritual uses of these technologies play a complementary role only to in-person activities and community for those who are already actively religious in-person? Or do these technologies also play an alternative role in terms of religion and spirituality for some, reaching new audiences that in-person activities cannot?

These questions can more recently be raised for the role of digital religion in the lives of Americans and Canadians, and are especially important for young adult Millennials. As discussed in Chapter 1, Millennials are the first truly digital natives in North America in that many were raised since childhood with the digital world at their fingertips (Prensky 2001). This includes all things under the umbrella concept of digital religion, defined by Campbell (2013, 1) as "... a new frame for articulating the evolution of religious practices online ..." and "... points to how digital media and spaces are shaping and being shaped by religious practice."

Surprisingly, very few existing studies have examined the empirical prevalence of different forms of digital religion among populations though, including younger populations, as well as the national differences in rates of these digital religious and spiritual practices. One key exception to this lack of research is the Pew Research Center report published in 2001 titled *CyberFaith: How Americans Pursue Religion Online* (Pew Research Center 2001). In this report, Pew found that an estimated 25% of Internet users did digital religion at some point in the United States, a group that Pew refers to as 'religion surfers' (how very early 2000s of them). These religion surfers were more likely to also be actively religious in-person, to be religious converts (practicing a different faith than the one they were raised in), and to be individuals who felt somewhat marginalized by their own religious group. However, these Pew data are now more than 20 years old, and a lot has changed since 2001 in the digital world and regarding the prevalence of the digital in our lives. The Pew data are also from a sample of U.S. adults of all ages in 2001, so with little data from Millennials and no specific focus on this generation. The Pew data also only come from one national context: the United States.

Another notable exception to the lack of existing research is a chapter in Wuthnow (2007, 201–213) on the virtual church among younger adults of Generation X. With 2000 and 2002 American GSS data, Wuthnow estimates that 20% of adults aged 21–45 visited religious websites in the 30 days prior to the survey, most to look for information about their own or other faiths.

This rate is low compared with other types of website activity, with news (just under 80% of younger adults visiting in the past 30 days), travel (just over 60%), work (60%) and education (just under 60%) websites being the most popular. Many younger adults in the GSS samples who did visit religious websites regularly were also those who attend religious services regularly in person, and tend to see the Internet as a supplement to their much more meaningful in-person practices.

Wuthnow's (2007) data are also about 20 years old now, and cover members of Generation X, not Millennials. These data also only come from the U.S. context, and so there is no international comparison with other countries to determine America's level of (non)exceptionalism in this case.

In the previous chapter, we saw that digital religious and spiritual practices measured in the 2019 MTS, including reading or watching online content (referred to from now on as digital content consumption) as well as posting on social media about religious or spiritual beliefs, values, ideas or practices, were more frequently found on average among our category of religious Millennials (see Figure 2.5 and Table 2.13 in Chapter 2). Figure 3.1 in turn contains the more detailed distribution of young adult respondents according to their self-declared frequency of religious or spiritual digital content consumption and social media posting for both Canada and the United States. Frequent digital religion practices are found among a substantial minority of the Millennial population: 29% of Canadian Millennial respondents consume religious or spiritual digital content at least once a month, and 41% do so in the United States. For a more active form of digital religion, 17% of Canadian young adult respondents post on social media about religion or spirituality at least once a month, and 32% do so in the United States. A majority in both countries consume religious or spiritual digital content at least once a year, although our survey data do not provide further information into the various reasons why respondents consume this content and what they end up doing with it. More on this in a bit.

To compare more directly with the 2001 Pew Research Center data, 67% of American MTS respondents who used the Internet at least once in the year prior to the 2019 MTS also consumed digital content on religion or spirituality at least once in that same year. The Pew Research Center had found that 25% of their Internet users of all adult ages were similar religion surfers back in 2001. The much higher rate found with the MTS data is striking, although it is at least in part most likely a product of greater Internet use in the general population in 2019 compared with 2001, the focus on young adult respondents who have much higher rates of Internet use in general, and more digital content on religion and spirituality available online in 2019 than in 2001.

Wuthnow (2007, 201–213) in turn found that 20% of American adults aged 21–45 visited religious websites in the 30 days prior to the 2000 and 2002 GSS. In the 2019 MTS among American adults aged 18–35, the rate who consumed digital content on religion or spirituality at least once a month in the year prior to the survey stood at 41%. As rates of more conventional religious practices, such

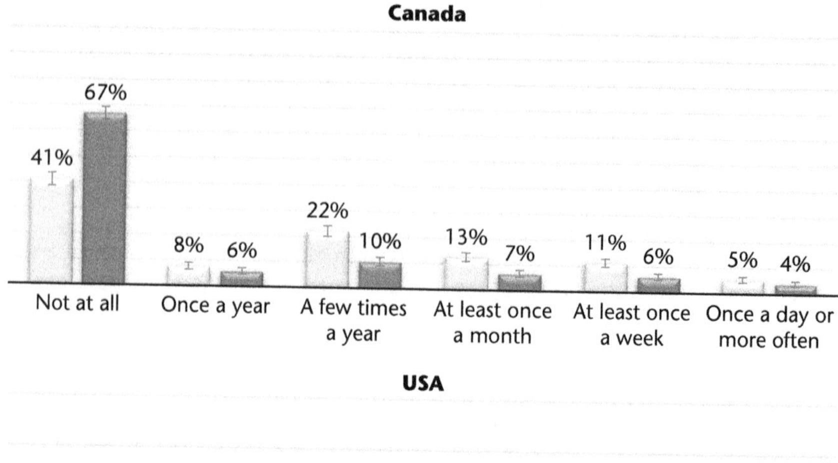

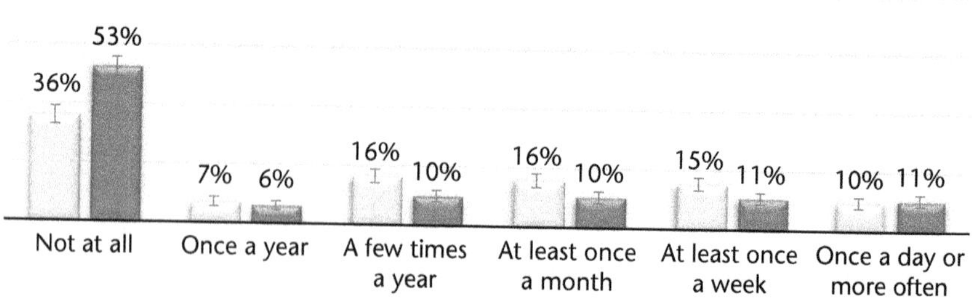

FIGURE 3.1 "In the past 12 months, how often on average did you do the following on the Internet? Read or watched online content on religious or spiritual beliefs, values, ideas or practices; posted on social media (Instagram, Snapchat, Twitter, Facebook, YouTube, Reddit, etc.) about religious or spiritual beliefs, values, views or practices," respondents 18–35 years old, United States and Canada, 2019, with CI 95%

as in-person religious service attendance, have fallen in more recent years among younger generations, the expansion of the Internet in our lives has meant that a larger proportion of Millennials are coming into somewhat regular contact with religion and spirituality online.

Another trend to note in these MTS data is the wider prevalence of digital religion practices among U.S. Millennials, compared with those in Canada. Fifty-nine percent of Canadian Millennial respondents consumed religious or spiritual digital content at least once in the year prior to the survey, compared with 64% in the United States. In turn, 33% of Canadian young adult respondents posted on social media about religion or spirituality at least once in the year prior to the survey, compared with 47% among U.S. young adults. These lower rates of digital religion practices among Canadian Millennials thus continue the trend of lower religiosity indicators in general when compared with the United States, such as lower rates of frequent religious service attendance in Canada, lower prayer rates, and lower rates of belief in God or a higher power, a trend which we saw throughout much of the data presented in the previous chapter.

If we focus now on those who consume religious or spiritual digital content at least once a month, for whom this religious or spiritual digital content consumption most likely plays a more important role in their lives, Figure 3.2 illustrates the extent to which this frequent religious and spiritual digital activity overlaps with two others among young adult respondents: monthly or more frequent religious service attendance, and monthly or more frequent unchurched spiritual activities.[2] The results illustrated in this graph show that most U.S. and Canadian Millennials who do digital religion at least once a month also do at least one in-person religious or spiritual activity monthly or more frequently. There are only 5% of young adult respondents (16% of monthly or more frequent digital content consumers) who only do monthly or more frequent religious or spiritual digital content consumption without also attending religious services at least once a month or practicing an unchurched spirituality at least once a month. Another 11% do both monthly or more frequent digital content consumption and religious service attendance; 6% do both monthly or more frequent digital content consumption and unchurched spiritual activities; and another 10% do all three types of activities at least once a month.

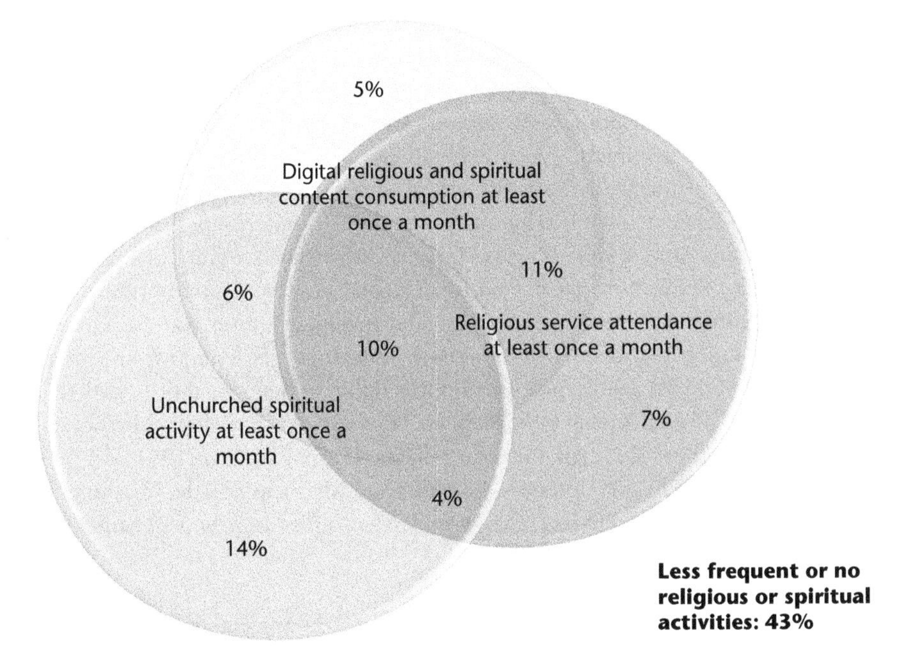

FIGURE 3.2 Overlap and rates of monthly or more frequent religious or spiritual activities, respondents 18–35 years old, United States and Canada, MTS 2019

In other words, 25% of Millennial respondents across both countries take part in less conventional spiritual or religious activities at least once a month, and 11% include a digital component to these activities. Another 25% pair these frequent less conventional religious and spiritual activities with monthly or more frequent religious service attendance, among whom almost all include a digital component. A further 7% only take part in more conventional religious service attendance at least once a month without other digital or unchurched religious and spiritual activities. So as the Pew Research Center (2001) and Wuthnow (2007, 201–213) also found, we see a lot of overlap between digital religious and spiritual content consumption and religious service attendance among respondents. This said, it is also important to note that there is a smaller minority of Millennials who seem to do digital religion away from organized religion.

Some readers may be surprised then that not all religious Millennials in the conventional sense, those who attend religious services or meetings at least once a month, also do digital religion. Other readers may instead be surprised that a minority of Millennials who do not attend religious services regularly still do digital religion. With our data, we do observe many complexities when it comes to the patterns of digital religious and spiritual practices. Yet, the following key trends also emerge. First, digital religion as measured here is definitely a phenomenon present among many Millennials, although it is also not present among all or a vast majority of this demographic. Second, social environment does seem to play an important role: in our data: digital religion practices are much more prevalent as a phenomenon in the generally more religious U.S. context, compared with the generally more secular Canadian context. Third, digital religion practices are often, but not always, tied to other in-person religious and spiritual activities among Millennials.

Fourth, there appears to be a distinction in nature to be made between the more passive form of digital religion that is digital content consumption, and the more active and outwardly visible form of digital religion that is social media posting. The more passive form of digital content consumption of religion or spirituality requires less effort and engagement on the part of the individual, and is more common in both countries. By contrast, the more active form of social media posting about religion and spirituality is tied to a smaller group of Millennials who seem to be willing to put their religion and spirituality out there for their followers to see. Jayden, born in 1994 and who sat down for a life history interview with Lynne Marks in Seattle, Washington in June 2018, has a sister like this who Jayden affectionately nicknames the "Instagram Christian":

> So she [Jayden's more spiritual sister] does like a lot of expression of spirituality and faith on, like, Instagram with her art. So she'll post, like, a picture of whatever she's drawn. It might be like a person, might be a statue. It's completely anything, and she'll post a Bible quote with it ....

These quantitative data for the most part dispel what I will call here the "digital-without-in-person religion" myth. This myth is similar to what Smith and Snell (2009, 251) refer to as the "internal-without-external religion" myth:

> … the widespread belief that, as teenagers grow into emerging adults, they tend to drop out of public, external expressions of faith—like religious service attendance and other religious group participation—but that their religious faith nevertheless remains highly valued and vital in their private, subjective, internal lives, as might be expressed in a high importance of faith or high frequency of personal prayer. The subjects of such a belief, in short, do not participate much in religious congregations or do much else socially that looks religious, but for them religious faith nonetheless is greatly valued and practiced in private.

The "digital-without-in-person religion" myth in turn believes that a large majority of young adults are accessing digital religion in private even when they are not practicing more conventional in-person religious activities. My data here show that a small minority do so, but for the most part it is conventionally religious Millennials who are also into digital religion. There is no widespread revolution going on among the vast majority of Millennials when it comes to digital religion and spirituality. Smith and Snell (2009, 252) also find little evidence for the "internal-without-external religion" myth:

> What we can say here, however, is that little evidence supports the idea that emerging adults who decline in regular external religious practice nonetheless retain over time high levels of subjectively important, privately committed, internal religious faith. Quite the contrary is indicated by our analysis. The emerging adults who do sustain strong subjective religion in their lives, it turns out, are those who also maintain strong external expressions of faith, including religious service attendance.

What is happening is that a large portion of religious Millennials are consuming and posting digital content on religion. Like with most other aspects of our lives, the digital has become an essential space for living one's faith, along with in-person religious activities. This has been heightened by the 2020–2021 COVID-19 pandemic lockdowns, which put a halt to many in-person religious group activities and moved many even more into digital spaces. The post-pandemic world may very well be where hybrid combinations of in-person and digital experiences of religion are the norm, bringing together what many missed about in-person activities during the lockdowns with what worked well and what has been developed in the remote online settings during the pandemic.

What are Millennials' motivations when doing digital religion? In the early days of wider public access to the Internet in the late 1980s and 1990s, most religion online had to do with information seeking on websites (hopefully with a healthy degree of caution), as well as staying in touch with and meeting new Internet users by e-mail and in chat rooms. As the possibilities of what individuals could do online developed, along with the enabling technologies, so did digital religion experiences: from virtual community sharing and support to online prayer and faith healing, to virtually participating in activities, festivities and rites, to downloading or streaming religious music, sermons and podcasts, to regularly posting ideas, views and advice on religion and spirituality to wider audiences using the sophisticated video filming and production technology on one's smartphone. Daniel, from the Québec life history interviews, uses a Bible app on his smartphone for example, rather than carrying around a hard copy. He explains in his interview that, instead of attending Bible study groups in person which are over an hour's drive away for him, he prefers to supplement his Bible readings with information and discussions he finds online. As another example, Vanessa, born in 1984 and also from the Québec life history interviews, says she occasionally streams the Pope's sermons online, rather than attending Mass in person.

It would be easy to assume that digital religion is a simple replacement for gathering information about a faith tradition in person with religious leaders, attending religious community activities and rites in person, and sharing one's thoughts and opinions about faith with others in person. Digital religion would then mainly be meant for seekers just getting started out in religion, for those who cannot or prefer not to do all such activities in-person, or who want to do more of these activities even when they are not offered in person. Yet, existing research shows us that digital religion is not always just a reproduction online of what individuals experience in-person at places of worship. In other words, digital religion is not just a different way of accessing the same religious content and community that is available offline. The nature of digital religion is often different from analog religion, and mediates and impacts in new ways Millennials' religious experiences.

There is of course the obvious difference of digital religion: individuals just have access to a whole lot more of it online than what they can often find in-person in their local area. More information on a faith tradition from more viewpoints, information on more faith traditions, debates about beliefs and rituals, virtual tours of holy sites from around the world, streamed religious services, lectures and webinars from around the world, more people to virtually gather with, pray with, chat with and share experiences with, and so much more.

As well as giving their religious experiences and interests a more global focus, this online environment also facilitates religious Millennials to be bricoleurs, tinkerers and to adopt a more consumer-based and interactive approach to their religion, as different existing studies have named the phenomenon (Bibby, Thiessen, and Bailey 2019; Dawson and Cowan 2004; Wuthnow 2007). Although this has always been a phenomenon present to a certain extent over the centuries, in the digital age individuals are now free in many countries to explore, experiment with as well as pick and choose from a wide variety of available online resources with the goal of building a system of beliefs and rituals that suits their own needs and that they perceive as authentic to their own identities

(Campbell 2013; Dawson and Cowan 2004). Not all individuals choose to do so, many remaining removed from digital religion or who may not have the resources and opportunities to access it, but many other religious Millennials do. These individuals can then also find online networked communities of like-minded individuals to build and share these ideas, experiences and rituals with through the intermediary of new media. This can be done in a more anonymous environment somewhat removed from the social pressures of religious authorities and one's peers, although not completely removed from their influence either since the online content and comments often do come from specific people and groups.

Although the online world is often portrayed still as a wild west of complete freedom and anonymity for the individual if they so choose (think of the common media portrayal of a shadowy anonymous figure hooked to a screen and typing away at a computer in a dark, assumed-to-be-basement room), in reality many individuals choose instead to share a lot of information about themselves online, and there are still important gatekeepers to much of the available digital religion content. For some of this content, the generators and gatekeepers are from more conventional religious organizations. Even for the more audience-generated content, it is often a smaller number of influencers who play a disproportionate role in this content creation, some of which is placed behind a membership or paywall, and/or is suited to specific (and pricey) tech.

The online world has thus created a shift in power and authority in some instances, but most definitely not their disappearance. In fact, a new source of religious authority comes from the capacity for religious leaders to harness and master the digital world and go viral in the process. This said, the possibility to choose, form, redefine and express one's own religious identity has challenged the role of traditional religious communities in the formation and control of religious identities (Hellend 2004, 30, 33), and led in many instances to more personalized forms of religious experience controlled and mediated first and foremost by the individual themselves (Cheong 2013; Knowles 2013; Turner 2007).

These new digital realities for religion also do not stay isolated in the online world. They can change expectations, ways of doing and power structures in the in-person world as well, potentially leading to tensions and struggles at times with more conventional or traditional forms of religion. More and more, the digital and in-person worlds have a reciprocal relationship that is shifting the way religious Millennials do religion both online and offline. This reciprocal relationship is part of the very definition that Campbell (2013, 4) provides for digital religion:

> We can think of digital religion as a bridge that connects and extends online religious practices and spaces into offline religious contexts, and vice versa. This merging of new and established notions of religious practice means digital religion is imprinted by both the traits of online culture (such as

> interactivity, convergence, and audience-generated content) and traditional religion (such as patterns of belief and ritual tied to historically grounded communities).

Faith and belief becoming more focused on personal experiences, and the authority to choose and adhere to specific religious beliefs and practices becoming more the domain of each individual, are trends that have been affecting religion and spirituality since especially the 1960s in Western cultures (Berger 1979; Heelas and Woodhead 2005; Taylor 1991). Nonetheless, digital religion has in many ways further facilitated and accelerated these shifts among religious individuals, especially among religious young adults. The growing presence and influence of digital religion is a key dynamic of social and technological change impacting religious members of the Millennial generation.

Yet, the digital is not the only aspect of social change affecting this subpopulation. Just as religious Millennials are not isolated from the developments of the wider digital age, they are also not immune to wider political shifts among their generation. Many studies have shown over the years that Millennials on average are much more left-leaning and progressive along the political spectrum than older adults (Bibby, Thiessen, and Bailey 2019; Pew Research Center 2010): for example, Millennials are on average much more pro-choice, pro-environment, pro-LGBTQ+, pro-immigration, pro-socialism, pro-BIPOC and pro-women in their issue stances. These left-leaning attitudes are not only the domain of the nonreligious. This political shift also extends to a certain degree to more religious members of the generation.

Headed Left: Moving along the Political Spectrum

There exists a long-standing religiosity effect on political conservatism that can be found within most Western liberal democracies: more religious individuals tend to be more conservative in their attitudes and political choices. Socialization and the social environment in which individuals find themselves are key. Those who are more actively involved with a religious group as children and in their adult years, both in person and digitally, are more likely to be regularly exposed to more right-leaning values within congregations and faith groups, their family, the faith-based schools, colleges and universities they are more likely to attend, and their social network of friends and acquaintances who are more likely to share their own religious identities and beliefs (Adkins et al. 2013; Nicolet and Tresch 2009; O'Neill 2001; Putnam and Campbell 2010; Raymond 2011; Reimer 2003; Smidt et al. 2010; van der Brug, Hobolt, and de Vreese 2009). To be clear, however, not all organized religious groups have more right-leaning teachings and values on sexuality, reproductive rights, family values, gender roles and the roles and responsibilities of government in society for example; but on average more do than what can be found in general Western popular cultures and societies.

The results illustrated in Figure 3.3 are another example of this effect among Millennials. A reminder from the last chapter that respondents in the 2019 MTS

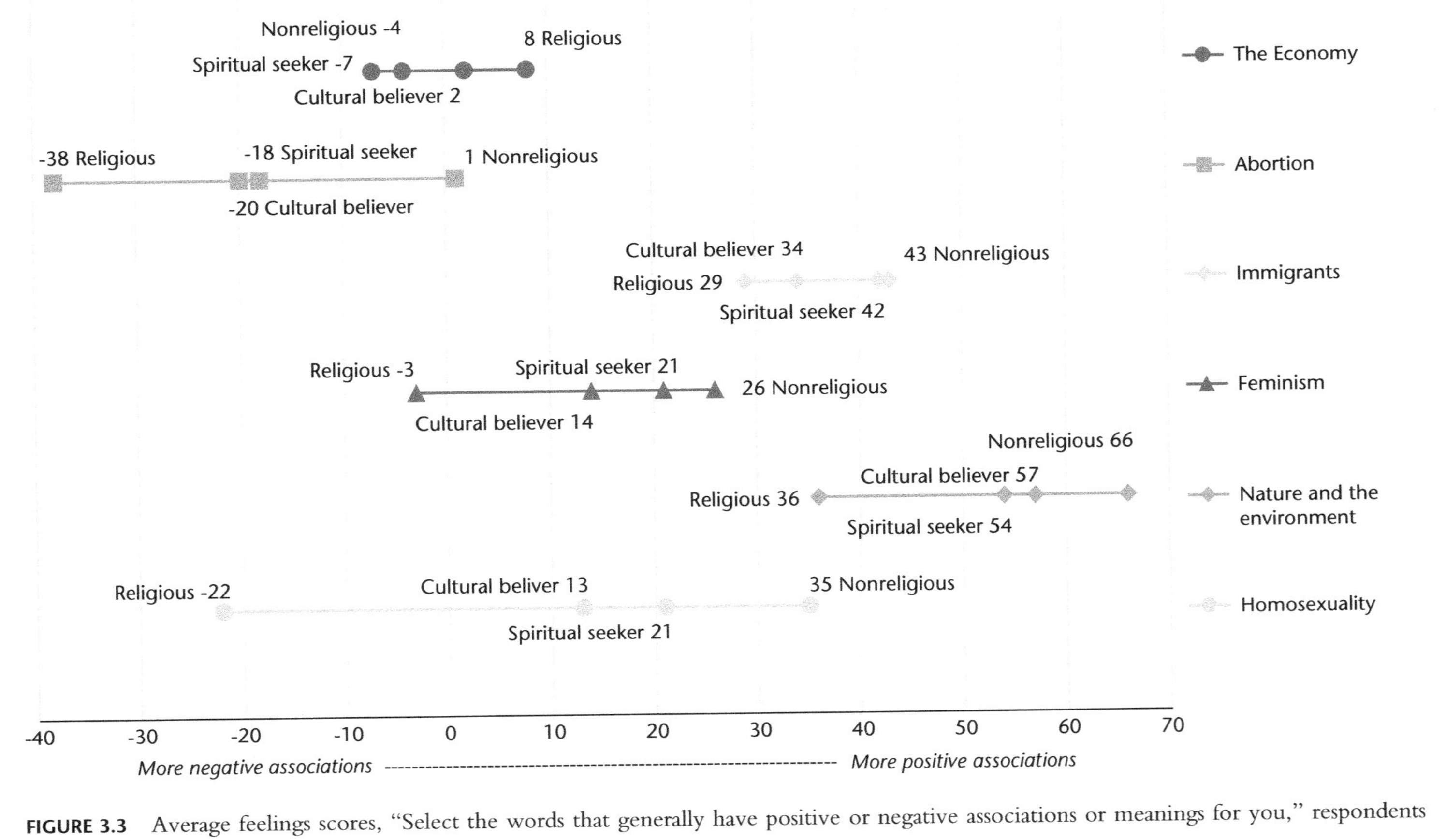

FIGURE 3.3 Average feelings scores, "Select the words that generally have positive or negative associations or meanings for you," respondents 18–35 years old, MTS 2019

were presented with a list of words in random order and asked to select which of these words have positive associations or meanings for them, and which have negative associations or meanings. I then assigned a score of +1 for each 1% of respondents who selected a word for positive associations; a −1 for each 1% of respondents who selected the same word for negative associations; and 0 for each 1% of respondents who did not select the given word at all. These points were then tallied to create each word's average feeling score among the four latent classes of MTS respondents: religious, spiritual seeker, cultural believer and nonreligious Millennials. These scores are illustrated in Figure 3.3 for the words "the economy," "abortion," "immigrants," "feminism," "nature and the environment" and "homosexuality." For example, among religious Millennials in both Canada and the United States, 31% of MTS respondents indicated negative associations for "homosexuality" (−31), 60% did not select this word for positive or negative associations (0) and 9% had positive associations with "homosexuality" (+9), which gives a total feeling score of −22 for "homosexuality" among religious Millennials.

These results in Figure 3.3 show that for all six words at study here, religious Millennials score more in a politically conservative direction than any of the other latent classes of respondents of the same age group. Religious Millennials have the highest feeling scores (more positive associations) for the economy; and the lowest feeling scores (more negative associations) for abortion, immigrants, feminism, nature and the environment and homosexuality.

Yet, when we add generational comparisons to the mix, a more complex picture emerges. Case in point: the results illustrated in Figure 3.4 from 2020 American National Election Study data, a survey series run during each presidential election since 1948. We can first see in Figure 3.4 that Millennials who attend religious services at least once a month remain more conservative on the issues of abortion, immigration, the environment, women in politics and gays and lesbians than their less religious generational counterparts. For example, only an estimated 32% of more religious Millennials support legal access to abortion, compared with 65% of Millennials who attend religious services less than once a month. Yet, compared with other more religious members of older generations, Figure 3.4 also shows that religious Millennials in the United States in 2020 are more progressive on the five measured socio-political issues. Support for legal access to abortion may only stand at 32% among more religious Millennials, but this is still a higher rate than the 21%, 27% and 25% among religious adults of the Silent, Boomer and Gen X generations, respectively. Support for immigration as well as for gays and lesbians also reaches its highest among Millennials when looking at the more religious population. Support for the environment is similar among religious Boomers and Millennials, which in turn is slightly higher than support found among religious members of the Silent generation and Gen X. Support for women in politics is highest among religious members of the Silent generation and Millennials, slightly higher than among religious Boomers and Gen Xers.

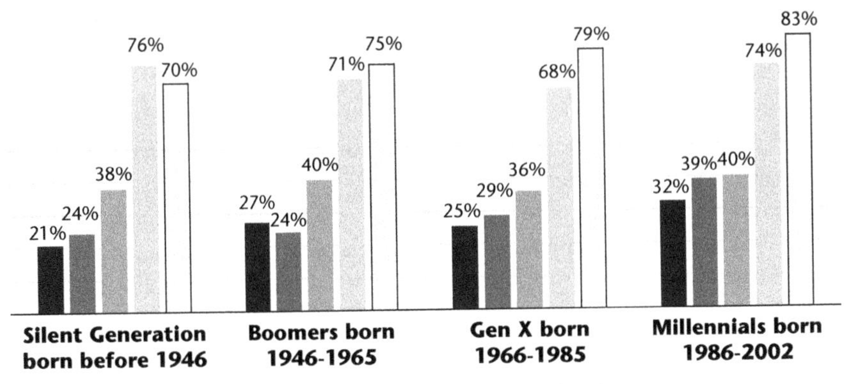

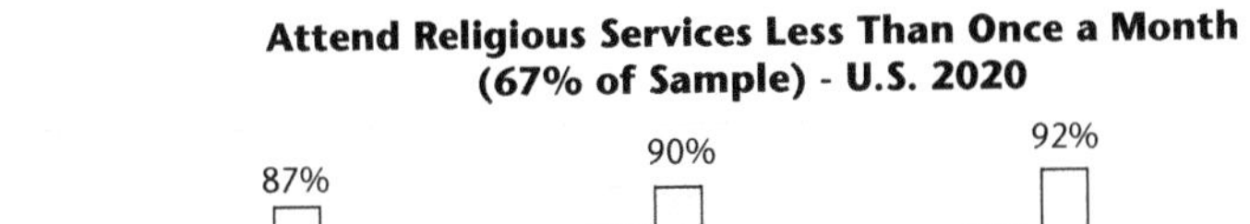

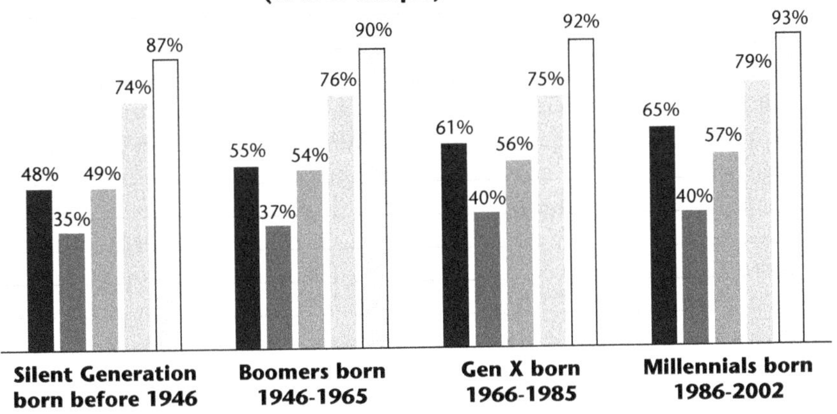

FIGURE 3.4 Issue stance, religious and rest of population, by generation, American National Election Study 2020

There is a generational shift headed left along the political spectrum in the United States, and it is also happening among the more religious in the country. This can be and has been a source of generational conflict among many congregations and faith groups in the country in recent years, especially among those groups that espouse more socially conservative teachings. More and more religious Millennials are pushing back against such socially conservative stances, by either trying to effect change within their own faith group as they begin to occupy leadership roles, or by leaving their original more conservative congregation for a more progressive one, or in some cases by becoming disillusioned with faith groups and disaffiliating altogether. More on this last trend in Chapter 6. Rachel, a reformed Jew born in 1992 who took part in a Portland, Oregon focus group, states:

> I think with the gender, and spirituality or sexuality and religion, it will be interesting to see where we're at 60 years from now because the conversations that we're having today are drastically different than even 10–15 years ago. I think Millennials have a great role to play in moving that forward because we're going to be the people standing up and leading these congregations and these communities. It will be interesting to see where we end up.

Michelle, a practicing Episcopalian born in 1999 who took part in a Seattle, Washington focus group, describes her journey to her present denomination:

> I did realize they [Episcopalian Church] were the White Anglo-Saxon Protestant church, but I also saw conscious efforts being made that I didn't see in my previous church. I wanted more care and attention to present social action that I hadn't seen before, which is part of the reason why I chose the denomination.

The situation in Canada shares some commonalities with the American context in this regard. Yet, populations north of the 49th parallel are also characterized by some key differences compared with the United States. Canadians of all ages are more left-leaning and progressive on most socio-political issues than their American counterparts. For example, as illustrated in Figure 3.5 with data from the Canadian Election Study run during the 2019 federal election, support for legal access to abortion reaches a higher rate of 54% among more religious members of the Silent generation, and a high of 86% among less religious Boomers.

However, since left-leaning and progressive issue stances are so common among older Canadians, including among older religious Canadians, Millennials are actually not the most progressive generation on many of the issues measured in Figure 3.5 in Canada. Millennials overall actually score a bit lower compared with some older adults in the country on support for legal access to abortion. On other issues, they have similar rates of support as members of older generations, including for immigration (similar to Boomers and Gen X), and women in politics (similar to all older living generations). It is only for support for the environment as well as for gays and lesbians that Millennials score higher than their older counterparts. Most of these generational trends can be found among both more and less religious Canadian Millennials. One exception though is that religious Millennials show a bit less support for gays and lesbians than religious members of older generations.

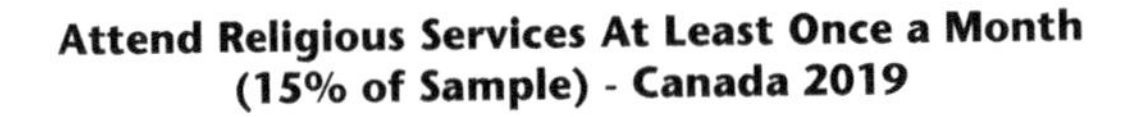

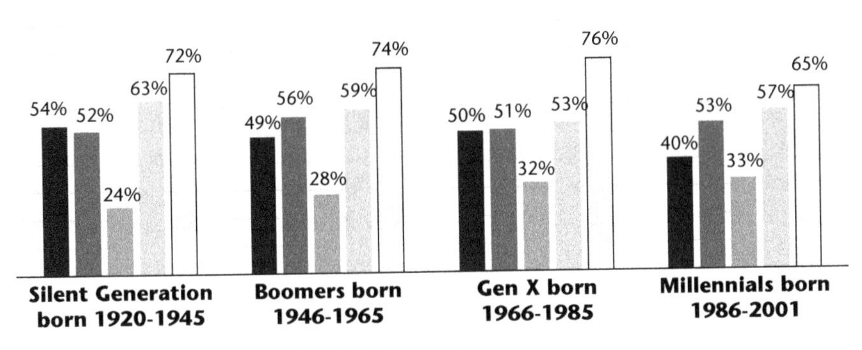

■ In favour of keeping current legal abortion policy
■ Disagree or strongly disagree that immigrants take away jobs
■ Jobs should not come before the environment
Agree or strongly agree that women's interests would be better represented if more women were elected to parliement
□ Like-really like gays and lesbians

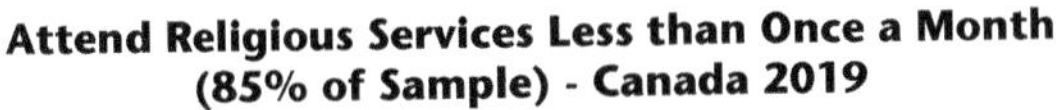

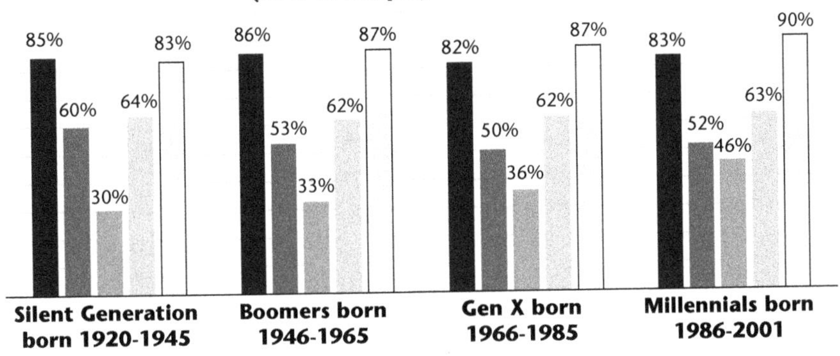

FIGURE 3.5 Issue stance, religious and rest of population, by generation, Canadian Election Study 2019

We may be seeing the impact of the cultural generation gap play out more in Canada on these socio-political issues. Since rates of first- and second-generation immigration from parts of the world which are characterized by more socially conservative stances are higher among Canadian Millennials than among many older generations, this impacts average socio-political attitudes among Millennials to a greater degree. Additionally, since religious Millennials are more concentrated in Canada among first- and second-generation immigrants from non-Western countries, more so than for older generations or compared with religious Americans, this slightly more conservative bend plays out even more among religious Millennials in Canada. Nevertheless, it is worth saying again that, despite these slightly more conservative trends on some socio-political issues among Canadian Millennials, their issue stances are still more left-leaning and progressive on the issues of abortion and immigration compared with their American counterparts of the same age; similar on support for the environment; and only slightly more conservative on women in politics. Although average feeling scores for gays and lesbians are slightly lower among Canadian Millennials than among American emerging adults, support for same-sex marriage more specifically is higher in Canada (and legal in all provinces and territories) compared with the United States.

Experiencing the Cross-Pressures

Faced with a Millennial generation defined especially by their progressive attitudes as well as by their secularity, there is a certain pressure on those of the same age who do not necessarily fit this mold. Among older birth cohorts and in earlier periods when religiosity was more the norm among individuals, someone who was active in their faith usually took for granted this status and may not have thought much about it. Members of a majority often do not have to confront situations in which their majority beliefs and behaviors are challenged or thrown into question. Whereas now the religious Millennial must often justify their more exceptional behavior to other less religious members of their age group, as well as to themselves; and this, especially when they find themselves in the more secular social milieus common among their generation (especially in Canada, but also in the United States). Often (but not always) faced with the everyday possibility of not being religious if they did not want to be, more religious Millennials are perhaps more aware of the reasons why faith is so important to them compared with many members of older generations. This more aware, defensive and minority stance when faced with a largely secular generation and society shapes in some ways the religious experiences of the individual.

Nicole, born in 1993, an active member of their Jewish community and who took part in one of the Portland, Oregon focus groups, discusses how they feel as part of the minority among their generation, not just as a Jew, but also as someone who is more religious: "… the first step for me, anywhere new that I go, is: where are the Jews? Where is the synagogue. I'd say that I'm not a typical Millennial, in that I joined a synagogue and I'm very part of the institutional …." Cody, an Evangelical Christian born in 1995 who was a research participant from one of the Vancouver, British Columbia focus groups, states:

> I tend to … because identifying, telling other people that I am a Christian is so weighted. I tend to tell them after I've really met them, or at least have

> a brief conversation, or if it's relevant essentially. I don't think I would deny it, but it's because it's so weighted, I feel like that's, it's weighted.

William, a practicing Catholic born in 1984 and interviewed in Laval, Québec in June 2018, recollects:

> It was more in high school when I started to realize and feel that there was a difference between what I thought and what others could think and believe. … it's when I was in high school that I understood, and others took joy in making me understand, that I was not the same as them, that I did not live in the same way as them, that I had not been raised the same as them. … there were insults surrounding it, until I went quiet about it. … Now I don't say anything to anyone about it [his faith]. I hide it, I keep it for myself, my family, and my friends who are in it [the Church]. … it becomes something that's very private, very personal, and that I don't talk about. Sometimes I would even go so far as to, I'm not proud of this, but I would go so far as to deny it [his faith] in front of certain people when I didn't want to be ostracized. … we [his siblings and him] were very conscious that, when we were at church we were often the only people there under the age of 30.

Kamal, a Muslim from Vancouver, born in 1989 and who we met earlier in Chapter 2, takes the opposite approach to William by not staying quiet about his faith, both by choice and also perhaps because as a racial minority he cannot as easily hide within a White secular majority. Kamal says:

> I recognize the privilege that I have as someone who is English-speaking, male, like I can speak about Islam in a way that many people can't. … I think for me it's using my privilege to, you know, exert my Islamic identity in a public space to change the cultural perception of what it is to be a Muslim and how that's perceived. So it's like a deeply political project at the same time.

Adam, a practicing Catholic born in 1983 and interviewed in Montréal in August 2018, answers the following when asked if having atheist and agnostic friends influences the way he practices his faith:

Interviewer: OK. And those in your entourage who are atheist or agnostic: does that influence the way you practice your religion? The way you live your religion?

Adam: Of course! Because it's not, even in life, some say that I just want to be marginal. Maybe if I had lived in the 1940s–1950s I would have been Marxist, communist. So yes, it could be. Yes, it definitely plays a role. And I think that it's for the better. Not for the worst, but for the better … yes.

> In what capacity, I don't know! No idea! Maybe it forces me to be more careful, to put things in brackets.

Even the less or nonreligious research participants are aware of some of the cross-pressures that religious individuals in their entourage have to grapple with. Jamie, a nonreligious individual born in 1996 from one of the Victoria, British Columbia focus groups, recollects: "… one friend's experience would be they had a hard time even sharing that they were religious, or being very open about that. And then hiding a lot of their values or the reasons for their values." Beatrice, who was once conventionally religious but now falls more into the spiritual seeker category and who was interviewed over the phone in Mukilteo, Washington in June 2018, remembers things she witnessed during her teenage years:

> I'm just going to take my experience from my high school, because we had a, like, kind of a organization group club called One Voice. Which is like a choir kind of meeting group, where people who were of Christianity or, I think it catered mostly to Christianity. And they would get together, have a good time, sing, blah blah blah. And then there's also Young Life, which is a program that, we had, like, a center of outreach at our school. And they do the Christian, like nature walks, or yeah. It's like just another Christian organization. And I, because I had a lot of different people that I connected with during my school career, I heard a lot of, I don't remember specifics, but there were kind of derogatory terms and kind of insulting the kids, because they were very, they viewed them as, like, do-gooders. Kind of brownnosers. People who just kind of wanted to, like, be the teacher's pet. Or, yeah, just, there was a lot of negative stereotyping about the Christian, people of Christian faith. And that also they were, like, Jesus freaks, or like Bible thumpers, or, I can't remember many of the terms, but … There's definitely a negative stigma.

Martine, born in 1992, self-defines as nonreligious and was interviewed in Saint-Augustin, Québec in August 2018, relates a recent experience with two of her friends:

> … recently two people close to me had a sort of 'coming out' experience of being religious … one of them told me 'ah I don't talk a lot about it, but you know I'm Catholic and I have a very developed spirituality and it's not something I'm comfortable saying most of the time.'

Emilie, born in 1990 and a practicing Catholic, sees only a core of remaining Catholics within the Québec Church:

> My vision of the Church in Québec, I see it as … we're in survival mode. The Church is no longer what it once was. … There remains the cream of the crop. Those who are still in the Church, those who want to be, they really believe and we move forward, we try.

William, another practicing Catholic from Québec who we heard from earlier, also feels the same way and sees a positive element to this:

> But there is still, the thing that's positive is that, in the old days I think there were lots of people in the churches who were there because it payed, because it gave them access to lots of things, and all the abuses they experienced from that, and stuff. Then slowly that disappeared, slowly I think there's been a return to what's essential. What's essential in religion is the heart, it's the practice, it's not to say 'we're 350 at Mass this weekend.' Even if there are only four people, those four people are there for the real or deep reason.

Taylor (2007, 539–593) implies that the cross-pressures of the other side are equally felt in our secular age by believers and nonbelievers alike; always aware of the uncertainty surrounding their own identity and worldview when faced with others in our diverse societies. This may be true in certain social contexts. Yet, I argue here instead that the cross-pressure is often felt more by the religious Millennial than by the nonreligious Millennial. As we will see in more detail in Chapter 6, indifference toward religion is the name of the game for many nonreligious Millennials, because they find themselves in a social context that often allows for this indifference. This is of course not a blanket reality across all of Canada and the United States. There are some social milieus where being nonreligious still comes with a large social penalty in the two countries. Nevertheless, Millennials are a transitional generation where these more religious social milieus are becoming more and more rarified. Whereas scholars such as Charles Taylor, as well as Beaman (2017) and Habermas (2010), hope for more accepting, plural and deep equality social settings as the transition to a (post)secular age and society unfolds; social settings where various religious traditions and nonreligion can coexist peacefully and everyone can be very accepting of difference; reality does not always meet this ideal. Governments aiming for a secular State may bring in policy that unduly affects religious minorities, such as the province of Québec's 2019 Bill 21 which bans the wearing of religious symbols and clothing for many public employees, including teachers. Religious Millennials, now a minority within their generation, may receive acceptance by many, but may also be confronted more and more by a nonreligious majority who does not understand why organized religion is still a thing for some.

***

Yet, despite experiencing these secular cross-pressures, along with the pressures of emerging adulthood in general, religious Millennials choose to remain religious. For many religious Millennials, religion becomes a key aspect of identity differentiation from the masses, and community building with similar-valued individuals. Faith becomes an important, albeit not exclusive, source of identity construction in North American societies, societies which now highly value and promote perceived individual distinctiveness and authenticity.

Andrea, born in 1983 and a practicing Jew from one of the Portland, Oregon focus groups, says:

> Judaism had been in my life forever off and on, but then throughout my life it was the thing that spoke to me the most and that made the most sense for me, and that made me feel very grounded, but with the freedom to still have that autonomy that I find so very important ….

Kyle, a practicing Christian born in 1990 and who also took part in one of the Portland, Oregon focus groups, states: "The church from my experience has been a place to come and figure out: 'who am I.' Asking these questions like 'what is my purpose?' And going to a church and different leaders and navigating those questions." Lindsey, born in 1993 and who took part in one of the Victoria, British Columbia focus groups, reflects:

> You wanted to know what 'religious,' what that term means to me? So personally, the term 'being religious' is partially about identity, that I identify as a Christian. And that there's a sense of—there's a history there. I identify with the Christian story and the Judeo-Christian story, what it means to be carrying that tradition with you, on your back as it were. It also, for me, comes with a sense of responsibility. That there's a—by choosing to identify that way, I have to then intentionally push back at what Christian-ness is. And try to own that.

William, who we heard from a couple of times earlier in this chapter, started his interview by saying:

> God and everything surrounding Him occupies an everyday place in my choices, in my way of being, in my way of living, in my way of spending my time, let's say in my way of occupying my time during the day. It's also significant that I mention Catholic and not just spiritual, because it means for me that my belonging really goes to the Catholic Church, meaning the life of the Church, meaning essentially the sacraments and the religious practice within the Church, but also within a historical tradition. So, that includes saints, authors, etc. So, it means that I draw nourishment from that: from both the life of the Church and from its tradition, and that I make both part of my daily life.

Jessica, a practicing Jew born in 1993 and from one of the Portland, Oregon focus groups, simply says: "The day I got here after officially moving here, I went and met with young Jewish people. I was super comfortable, and I was like, 'Okay, I have friends,' basically."

It is a brave new world out there for religious Millennials. Young adults who do more conventional organized religion now form a smaller proportion of their generation than the religiously active among older birth cohorts. Religious Millennials are still very much present though. For many of them, digital religion plays an important complementary role to the in-person practicing of their faith. Many religious Millennials also find themselves torn between a more conservative setting and older members of their faith group, and their own more left-leaning values from their younger generation. Many have also had to carve out their place as religious Millennials within a wider, more secular generation.

Many Millennials find religion worthwhile within the sea of available religious, spiritual and secular options competing for their time and attention. The next chapter looks at a different group, one that leans more toward less conventional, de-institutionalized spiritual beliefs and activities to express and explore their faith: the spiritual seeker Millennial.

Notes

1 The statistical results from this section were originally part of my *Review of Religious Research* article "Digital Religion Among U.S. and Canadian Millennial Adults" (Wilkins-Laflamme 2021).

2 See Figure A.1 in Appendix A for a similar graph for monthly or more frequent social media posting about religion and spirituality. Percentages are quite similar to those in Figure 3.2.

References

Adkins, Todd, Geoffrey C. Layman, David E. Campbell, and John C. Green. 2013. "Religious Group Cues and Citizen Policy Attitudes in the United States." *Politics and Religion* 6: 235–263. doi:10.1017/S1755048312000545

Baker, Joseph O'Brian, and Buster G. Smith. 2015. *American Secularism: Cultural Contours of Nonreligious Belief Systems*. New York, NY: New York University Press.

Beaman, Lori G. 2017. *Deep Equality in an Era of Religious Diversity*. New York, NY: Oxford University Press.

Berger, Peter. 1979. *The Heretical Imperative: Contemporary Possibilities of Religious Affirmation*. New York, NY: Doubleday.

Bibby, Reginald W., Joel Thiessen, and Monetta Bailey. 2019. *The Millennial Mosaic: How Pluralism and Choice Are Shaping Canadian Youth and the Future of Canada*. Toronto, ON: Dundurn.

Campbell, Heidi A., ed. 2013. *Digital Religion. Understanding Religious Practice in New Media Worlds*. New York, NY: Routledge.

Cheong, Pauline Hope. 2013. "Authority." In *Digital Religion. Understanding Religious Practice in New Media Worlds*, edited by Heidi A. Campbell, 72–87. New York, NY: Routledge.

Dawson, Lorne, and Doug Cowan, eds. 2004. *Religion Online: Finding Faith on the Internet*. New York, NY: Routledge.

Habermas, Jürgen. 2010. *An Awareness of What is Missing: Faith and Reason in a Post-Secular Age*. Cambridge, UK: Polity.

Heelas, Paul, and Linda Woodhead. 2005. *The Spiritual Revolution: Why Religion Is Giving Way to Spirituality*. Oxford, UK: Blackwell.

Hellend, Chris. 2004. "Popular Religion and the Internet: A Match Made in (Cyber) Heaven." In *Religion Online: Finding Faith on the Internet*, edited by Lorne Dawson and Doug Cowan, 23–35. New York, NY: Routledge.

Knowles, Steven. 2013. "Rapture Ready and the World Wide Web: Religious Authority on the Internet." *Journal of Media and Religion* 12 (3): 128–143. doi:10.1080/15348423.2013.820527

Nicolet, Sarah, and Anke Tresch. 2009. "Changing Religiosity, Changing Politics? The Influence of 'Belonging' and 'Believing' on Political Attitudes in Switzerland." *Politics and Religion* 2 (1): 76–99. doi:10.1017/S1755048309000042

O'Neill, Brenda. 2001. "A Simple Difference of Opinion? Religious Beliefs and Gender Gaps in Public Opinion in Canada." *Canadian Journal of Political Science* 34: 275–298. doi:10.1017/S0008423901777906

Pew Research Center. 2001. *CyberFaith: How Americans Pursue Religion Online*. Accessed March 24, 2021. https://www.pewresearch.org/internet/2001/12/23/cyberfaith-how-americans-pursue-religion-online/

Pew Research Center. 2010. *Millennials: A Portrait of Generation Next. Confident. Connected. Open to Change*. Accessed December 2, 2020. https://www.pewsocialtrends.org/2010/02/24/millennials-confident-connected-open-to-change/

Prensky, Marc. 2001. "Digital Natives, Digital Immigrants Part 1." *On the Horizon* 9 (5): 1–6.

Putnam, Robert, and David Campbell. 2010. *American Grace: How Religion Divides and Unites Us*. New York, NY: Simon and Schuster.

Raymond, Christopher. 2011. "The Continued Salience of Religious Voting in the United States, Germany, and Great Britain." *Electoral Studies* 30: 125–135. doi:10.1016/j.electstud.2010.10.001

Reimer, Sam. 2003. *Evangelicals and the Continental Divide: The Evangelical Subculture in Canada and the United States*. Montréal, QC: McGill-Queen's University Press.

Smidt, Corwin E., Kevin den Dulk, Bryan Froehle, James Penning, Stephen Monsma, and Douglas Koopman. 2010. *The Disappearing God Gap? Religion in the 2008 Presidential Election*. New York, NY: Oxford University Press.

Smith, Christian, and Patricia Snell. 2009. *Souls in Transition: The Religious and Spiritual Lives of Emerging Adults*. New York, NY: Oxford University Press.

Strawn, Kelley D. 2019. "What's Behind the 'Nones-sense'? Change Over Time in Factors Predicting Likelihood of Religious Nonaffiliation in the United States." *Journal for the Scientific Study of Religion* 58 (3): 707–724. doi:10.1111/jssr.12609

Taylor, Charles. 1991. *The Ethics of Authenticity*. Cambridge, MA: Harvard University Press.

Taylor, Charles. 2007. *A Secular Age*. Cambridge, MA: The Belknap Press of Harvard University Press.

Thiessen, Joel, and Sarah Wilkins-Laflamme. 2020. *None of the Above: Nonreligious Identity in the U.S. and Canada*. New York, NY: New York University Press.

Turner, Bryan. 2007. "Religious Authority and the New Media." *Theory Culture & Society* 24 (2): 117–134. doi:10.1177/0263276407075001

van der Brug, Wouter, Sara B. Hobolt, and Claes H. de Vreese. 2009. "Religion and Party Choice in Europe." *West European Politics* 32: 1266–1283. doi:10.1080/01402380903230694

Wilkins-Laflamme, Sarah. 2021. "Digital Religion Among US and Canadian Millennial Adults." *Review of Religious Research*. doi:10.1007/s13644-021-00463-0

Wuthnow, Robert. 2007. *After the Baby Boomers: How Twenty- and Thirty-Somethings Are Shaping the Future of American Religion*. Princeton, NJ: Princeton University Press.

4

THE SPIRITUAL SEEKER MILLENNIAL

Many individuals who I have been classifying as religious Millennials in the last couple of chapters according to my latent class analysis first introduced in Chapter 2 would probably prefer to define themselves more as spiritual persons. Laura, a practicing Christian born in 1987 and who took part in one of the focus groups conducted in Victoria, British Columbia in May 2018, says to this effect: "… I think we're such spiritual beings, that everything we do has to be part of our spiritual practice." Daniel, another practicing Christian born in 1993 from Montréal, similarly says:

> … in the end, the principle that comes from religion is spirituality. I learnt that, as long as I have a certain spirituality, whether going to church or not, I still have a feeling inside of me of accomplishment. … I'm more anchored to myself.

The terms "religion" and "religious" seem to have a negative connotation for many today, compared with the words "spiritual" and "spirituality." Religion is often associated with the negative historical and contemporary baggage of institutional and oppressive doctrine, authority and abuse of power. Whereas spirituality seems to be associated with personal freedom, exploration, self-reliance, choice, self-development and authenticity, these being highly prized values in current Western cultures that experienced a "massive subjective turn" since the 1960s (Taylor 1991). Many interviewees from other existing American and Canadian studies, such as from Ammerman (2014), Drescher (2016) and Thiessen and Wilkins-Laflamme (2020), use the language of "spirituality" to imply inclusive, experiential and subjective qualities and identity boundaries. In the 2019 MTS, "spirituality" has much higher average feeling scores among all four

DOI: 10.4324/9781003217695-4

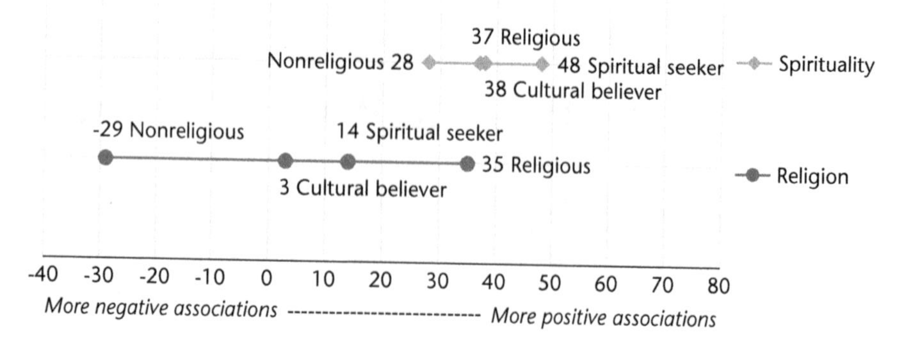

FIGURE 4.1 Average feelings scores, "Select the words that generally have positive or negative associations or meanings for you," respondents 18–35 years old, MTS 2019

categories of Millennials—the religious, spiritual seeker, cultural believer and nonreligious—compared with "religion" (Figure 4.1).

There are a number of similarities between the categories of religious and spiritual seeker Millennials in this book's study. Many religious Millennials will take part in both more conventional religious practices as well as unchurched spiritual activities: a quarter of religious Millennials practice meditation, mindfulness, outdoor nature or other spiritual activities away from conventional religious groups at least once a year. Many spiritual seeker Millennials, defined especially by their spiritual identities and unchurched spiritual activities, will in turn also take part in more conventional religious practices, albeit usually less often than their religious counterparts: only 18% of spiritual seekers attend religious services monthly or more frequently, but 87% of them attend religious services at least once a year.

This said, representing about a fifth of both Canadian and U.S. MTS respondents, spiritual seeker Millennials are also distinct from their religious counterparts in a few important ways. They score higher on all things spiritual: higher rates of unchurched spiritual activities, more positive feeling scores for the word "spirituality," higher rates of identification as "spiritual with no religion," and higher rates of believing that we are all part of a mysterious and connected natural world and universe without a specific belief in God or higher power. Spiritual seekers also score lower than religious Millennials on more conventional indicators of religiosity, such as frequency of religious service attendance, affiliation with a religious tradition, frequency of reading religious or spiritual materials (digitally or on paper) and so forth. Spiritual seekers are also characterized by a slightly larger proportion of female respondents and those with higher household incomes, compared with religious Millennials, and slightly lower rates of non-White racial and ethnic diversity as well as university education.

Compared with all other MTS respondents, not just religious Millennials, spiritual seekers nevertheless have a slightly larger proportion of non-White racial

TABLE 4.1 Characteristics of spiritual seeker Millennials

	Spiritual seeker Millennials	*Rest of Millennials*
% weekly or more frequent childhood religious or spiritual education	52%	54%
% monthly or more frequent religious service attendance as adults	18%	37%
% weekly or more frequent prayer as adults	25%	39%
% monthly or more frequent unchurched spiritual activities as adults	34%	25%
Mean age	25.9 years	26.2 years
% female	49%	49%
% non-White ethnic background/race	37%	31%
% university educated	25%	25%
% with less than $20,000 household income	16%	17%
% rural residents (pop. < 50,000)	24%	28%

Source: MTS 2019.

and ethnic minorities among their ranks, a slightly higher proportion of urban residents, and average levels of childhood religious or spiritual education (Table 4.1). Most still do identify with a religious tradition, with 40% of Canadian spiritual seeker Millennials and 35% of U.S. spiritual seeker Millennials identifying as Catholic; 9% in Canada and 8% in the United States identifying as Protestant; 6% in Canada and 7% in the United States identifying as Hindu; 6% in both Canada and the United States identifying as agnostic; and 8% in Canada and 9% in the United States identifying as spiritual with no religion.

This fourth chapter delves deeper into the world of the spiritual seeker Millennial by first exploring the conceptual distinction often made between the religious and the spiritual, which allows us to explore these two phenomena separately even though in practice we often find them both present and complementary to each other. Then, although there are many milieus where spirituality plays out, including in the home, at work, in relationships, in the world of art, in health, as well as within political activism, we focus more specifically in this chapter on an important and fundamental source for spirituality among Millennials: outdoor spaces and the natural environment.

Conceptually Distinct, but Empirically Entwined

Most scholars in the fields of sociology of religion and religious studies now make a conceptual distinction between religion, referring to organized religious groups and traditions as well as related religious practices, and spirituality matters removed from conventional religion. Spiritual But Not Religious (SBNR), a label first developed by Fuller (2001) in his book *Spiritual but Not Religious: Understanding Unchurched America*, has become a popular term to describe those individuals who are concerned with spiritual matters but choose to pursue them away from organized religion, or in other words are unchurched (Ammerman 2014; Drescher 2016; Heelas and Woodhead 2005; Roof 1999; Wuthnow 1998).

As Joel Thiessen and I explored in our 2020 book on nonreligious identities (Thiessen and Wilkins-Laflamme 2020), "spiritual" refers to the private realm of individual seeking and bricolaging of various beliefs and practices, often centered on a holistic this-worldly view of an interconnected universe and energies, and the transcendent, which can be experienced in the body and the self once a level of heightened consciousness and authenticity are achieved. "Religious" on the other hand is associated with membership and behavior linked to a religious institution or organized religious group. Ammerman (2014) points out that these two terms can be used as boundary markers against one another: "spirituality" denotes personal experience and authority over and against institutional, formal, dogmatic and authoritarian forms of religious life.

This conceptual distinction between "religion" and "spirituality" emerged and sharpened especially as many researchers began to argue from the 1990s onward that what defines religion today is not so much its decline, but rather its shift to more personalized and individualized forms of spirituality, also known as self-spirituality, among large segments of Western populations (Ammerman 2014; Aupers and Houtman 2010; Davie 1994; Drescher 2016; Fuller 2001; Heelas and Woodhead 2005; Watts 2022). Organized religion may be on the decline across birth cohorts in Western democracies, like with membership and participation in many different types of organizations for that matter (Putnam 2000), but religion conceived of more broadly is thriving in new individualized and spiritualized forms. Faced with advanced modernity's alienating dynamics of neo-liberal capitalism and extreme individualism, individuals turn to new forms of spirituality which sacralize the self and provide new sources of comfort, wellness and meaning in the modern age.

Rather than narrowly defining and measuring religion against conventional institutional markers, such as church attendance or communal-oriented religious activities, those scholars who adopt a more individual spiritualization framework stress ongoing self-spirituality among individuals. Spiritual needs are seen within this framework as core to human existence, rather than simply learnt in certain times and places; fundamental spiritual needs that may be answered in new ways in contemporary societies. More and more individuals draw on a number of identity constructs, beliefs, rituals and practices from a variety of sources, some of these sources linked to religious groups and some of them not, individuals sometimes by themselves and sometimes with the support of like-minded networked communities, to build and maintain their own personalized faith systems within their social environments (Hervieu-Léger 1999).

As mentioned in Chapter 1, Luckmann (1967) famously refers to this phenomenon as "invisible religion," Heelas and Woodhead (2005) as the "spiritual revolution" and Watts (2022) as the "religion of the heart." Houtman and Aupers (2007, 305) argue their cross-national findings from Europe provide evidence for a surge in post-Christian types of spirituality, and "… confirm the theory of de-traditionalization, according to which a weakening of the grip of tradition on individual selves stimulates a spiritual turn to the deeper layers of the self." Although this form of self-spirituality is now also common among active members of religious groups, and is shaping these groups in new ways, it is also found outside of conventional religious traditions.

Its eclectic nature means that scholars within this individual spiritualization framework are constantly grappling not only with what to call this phenomenon, but also how to define it and what to include within the confines of its concepts. Initially, spiritualities away from conventional religion would usually refer to those aspects of Eastern religions, pagan rituals and traditional Indigenous ways of life that some (especially White middle-class) members of the Boomer generation imported, appropriated and popularized within Western cultures notably in the 1960s and 1970s hippie counter-culture movement: specifically New Age (energies, alternative healing therapies, spiritual environmentalism, holism, etc.), astrology, yoga, meditation, mindfulness and so forth. Now, however, the concept of spirituality as distinct from religion is conceived of more broadly. Most researchers in the individual spiritualization framework agree that there are elements common to spiritual endeavors; even a broad shared doctrine among these spiritualities. This would include any search for one's "authentic" self, valuing personal authenticity above conformity to external religious norms and authorities, and relocating the sacred from the external and transcendent to the internal and immanent (Aupers and Houtman 2010; Taylor 2007).

Such forms of spirituality would seem at first glance to be especially well suited for the Millennial mindset, with an emphasis on personal authenticity, self-development, independence, freedom and self-reliance (Watts 2016). Self-spiritualities may tie in well with emerging adulthood when self-focus and identity formation play a prominent role in an individual's development (Arnett 2015; Young and Shipley 2020). Possible in a context of growing pluralism where a "you-do-you" mentality prevails, these self-spiritualities pair well with a generational social location strongly impacted by individualism. These self-spiritualities may also provide a sense of self-mastery and control as well as a source for new social capital in the face of economic precarity and inequality. Since they are not tied to one specific geographic location, in contrast to a local congregation, for example, these self-spiritualities seem to be well suited for an emerging adulthood often defined by mobility and transition.

This said, as we saw in Chapter 2, it is not just more conventional measures of religiosity that are on the decline among the Millennial generation in the United States and Canada; other broader indicators of individualized spiritualities are also on a downward trend. These indicators include frequency of prayer and other spiritual practices on one's own as well as salience of spiritual beliefs in one's life. There has not been a "spiritual revolution" among Millennials in the sense that a majority have adopted signs of these spiritualities as far as we can measure them. Only 21% of U.S. adults of all ages and 24% of 18–35 years old self-select as "not following a religion but being a spiritual person" when given the four following options in the 2018 International Social Survey Programme (ISSP): "following a religion and being a spiritual person"; "following a religion and not being a spiritual person"; "not following a religion and not being a spiritual person"; and "not following a religion but being a spiritual person." In Canada, 39% of adult respondents of all ages from the Angus Reid Institute (2015), and 38% of 18–34 years old, self-select into the same SBNR category when provided with the four following options: "religious and spiritual"; "religious, but not spiritual"; "neither religious nor spiritual"; and "spiritual, but not religious." This represents a substantial minority, but not a vast majority, of young adults.

Additionally, many who self-select as SBNR can actually be classified as more conventionally religious when we look at how they score on other measures. Eleven percent of the "not following a religion but being a spiritual person" U.S. 18–35 years old respondents of the 2018 ISSP also say they attend religious services at least once a month. In other words, only an estimated 21% of young adults in the United States identify as spiritual persons and attend religious services less frequently, and so can be considered truly SBNR by the scholarly definition of the concept. In turn, 18% of those who say they are inclined to embrace religion in Canada also define themselves as SBNR (Angus Reid Institute 2015), and so make up part of that category in the country.

There are many signs of less conventional spiritual activities present among Millennials in the 2019 MTS data. Figure 4.2 illustrates for example the frequency with which MTS 2019 respondents practiced an unchurched spiritual activity, among the 29% who identified taking part in at least one unchurched spiritual

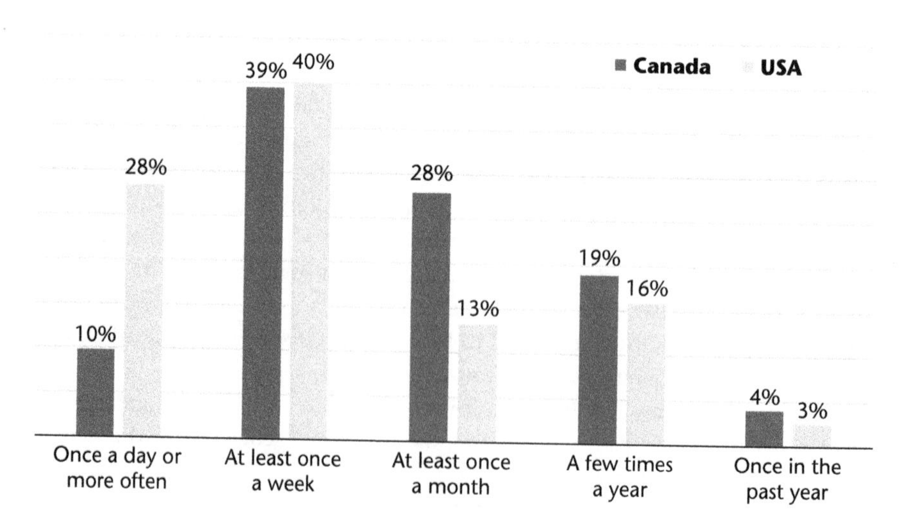

FIGURE 4.2 Frequency of spiritual activity, among the 29% of respondents 18–35 years old who practice unchurched spiritual activities, MTS 2019

activity in the year prior to the survey. It is interesting to note in this figure that, although Canadian young adult respondents are slightly more likely to take part in an unchurched spiritual activity over the course of a year, U.S. young adult respondents who do practice these activities do so with more frequency.

In Chapters 1 and 2, we met both Stephanie and Nicholas from the West coast focus groups who shared their spiritual experiences. Many more Millennials from the Pacific Northwest focus groups shared their own spiritual experiences and activities as well as the personal rewards they derived from them. Beatrice, born in 1996 and who we met in the last chapter, describes her spirituality:

> I'm very, like, connected, I call it, I'm connected to my higher self. And like the inner voice. And that's kind of what guides me. And I'm very much, I'm an artist, so I connect to my intuition and kind of the quiet stillness that is within. So I definitely have a lot, and I draw everyday as a part of, kind of, meditation. And to, like, focus on the values that I find important. That I've learned from spirituality. And like, I try and cultivate that and take that out into my job and my school. And when I'm like, you know, if I'm not feeling well I definitely use spiritual, like, connection and recognition of the divine and my, like, place in the bigger picture. So I definitely, definitely have a spiritual mindset, for sure. ... the word I have found recently through research is pantheistic, where they take the natural world and the human conscious experience as kind of being equivalent to divinity and not necessarily having a guy in the sky kind of removed god. But it's the, what we're in right now is the conscious experience of the sacred. So pantheistic would be my word.

Avril, born in 1994 from Montréal, Québec and self-defined as an atheist who doesn't believe in God but does believe in life after death, speaks to her deceased grandmother from time to time, and defines this as a spiritual activity. Three of the Millennial interviewees I came across in the Pacific Northwest and Québec studies identified their own experiences of hallucinogenic drugs as spiritual. As a final example here among many I could have chosen from, Ken, born in 1993 from Montréal, Québec, practices meditation for about an hour each day by sitting on his meditation cushion, listening to music, and focusing on the now and on the self. Such unchurched spiritual activities and experiences are especially present among the roughly one-fifth of 2019 MTS respondents classified as spiritual seekers according to my latent class analysis: an important category, but just not a majoritarian one among Millennials.

Additionally, in practice less conventional spiritual activities often go hand in hand with more conventional religious ones for many individuals. Michelle, who we met in the last chapter, says:

> I am definitely very spiritual in the sense that I pray frequently, I think my prayers are heard, I do believe a lot of the weird cosmic stuff in the Bible,

> I genuinely genuinely do. … But I think, my religiosity and my religiousness as I know it now in the sense of liturgy and communities, helps that happen a bit more for me. I don't know if that's my personal personality, but I feel through the religiosity I am able to be more spiritual, which is I suppose the success of Christianity. So yes, I can understand them [religion and spirituality] as distinct things, I am trying to work to a point where I don't.

As another example, Fiona, born in 1990 and who took part in one of the focus groups in Seattle, Washington, reflects:

> I think I am still learning what it means to be Catholic and so there's a lot spirituality-wise. Maybe it's my spirituality that drives me to continue to be religious or something like that, but I don't, I wouldn't necessarily divide that [religion and spirituality] for myself and I think to me being Catholic has this full sense of who I am, what I do, what's important to me, what I believe in, all of that, so.

Ammerman (2014) stresses that religion and spirituality are not mutually exclusive terms. They overlap in many ways such that where you find religion you tend to find spirituality and vice versa. Beyer, Cummins, and Craig (2019) and Young and Shipley (2020) find for example that affiliation as SBNR and to many religious traditions often overlap among their young adult research participants. Bruce (2017, 138–143) argues that it is especially those who were exposed to organized religion as children that go on to hold beliefs and individualized forms of spirituality as adults, even if many are removed from organized religion in adult life in Western contexts. Less widespread religious socialization during childhood may be a key reason then why we only see a minority of Millennials interested in alternative spirituality matters during their young adult years.

The 2019 MTS measure for monthly or more frequent unchurched spiritual activity also shows statistically significant moderate positive correlations with many of the more conventional religiosity measures (Table 4.2), indicating that a number of individuals practice both types of activities. Although I treat the religious Millennial and the spiritual seeker Millennial categories as distinct in this study, and they are distinct in some key ways as we have seen previously, many individuals nevertheless combine both the religious and the spiritual in their everyday lives.

Nature and the Outdoors as Spiritual Resources

Natural and outdoor spaces are important for most individuals, regardless of their age. In the 2018 GSS, 67% of U.S. adult respondents said they somewhat or strongly agreed that "Usually, I spend time in natural environments, such as public parks, gardens or trails, at least once a week." This rate is fairly stable across generations, with 54% among the Silent Generation, 67% among Boomers, 69%

TABLE 4.2 Correlation matrix with spirituality and religiosity measures, MTS 2019

	Unchurched spiritual activity at least once a month	*Frequency of prayer*	*Frequency of religious service attendance*	*Frequency of reading religious or spiritual materials*	*Frequency of digital religious or spiritual content consumption*	*Frequency of social media posting on religion or spirituality*	*Frequency of celebrating rites of passage with religious group*
Unchurched spiritual activity at least once a month	1						
Frequency of prayer	**0.251*****	1					
Frequency of religious service attendance	**0.193*****	0.749***	1				
Frequency of reading religious or spiritual materials	**0.227*****	0.745***	0.801***	1			
Frequency of digital religious or spiritual content consumption	**0.263*****	0.522***	0.568***	0.627***	1		
Frequency of social media posting on religion or spirituality	**0.166*****	0.447***	0.494***	0.514***	0.565***	1	
Frequency of celebrating rites of passage with religious group	**0.205*****	0.488***	0.500***	0.474***	0.420***	0.352***	1

*** $= p \leq 0.001$.
$N = 2{,}454$. Spearman correlation coefficients.

among Gen X and 67% among Millennials. In Canada, an estimated 74% of adults took part in outdoor activities such as fishing, hunting, trapping, foraging, snowmobiling, off-road vehicle use, tent camping, canoe, kayaking, hiking, backpacking, snowshoeing, cross-country skiing, wildlife viewing, photography outside the home, mountain biking, motorboating and jet skiing at least once in the 12 months prior to the 2016 Statistics Canada GSS. This rate reached 45% among Silent Generation Canadians, 71% among Boomers, 81% among Gen X and 82% among Millennials.

Love of nature also came up frequently in the West coast interviews and focus groups, as well as in the Québec life histories. Stephanie from Seattle, who we first met in Chapter 1, explains:

> Reduction in distraction is a huge part of being in nature for me. But I guess it also represents an opportunity to strip down to a more basic form of myself and let my mind wander, or focus on what is in front of me. Whereas in the average, everyday existence, you know, there's advertisements here, and people talking here, and bus going down the street there, and it's like all I can do to focus on what I'm trying to get done. But practicing more of just being is definitely a big value that I get out of being in nature.

Martine, born in 1992 and from Saint-Augustin, Québec, is careful not to incur what she refers to as negative Karma from the environment: she does not eat meat, does not own a car and only purchases used goods when possible. Claudie, born in 1994 and from Québec City, simply states, "I just feel good outside."

There are lots of reasons why individuals partake in outdoor nature activities: exercise and physical health, relaxation and mental wellbeing, social and pet time to enjoy with fido, friends and family, the affordability of some outdoor activities (such as taking a walk in a free-and-easy-to-access park), curiosity and exploration, and many other reasons still. Spirituality also plays a role for many when it comes to these outdoor activities. Thirteen percent of the Canadian 2019 MTS subsample and 7% of the American subsample identify outdoor nature activities as a spiritual activity that they have taken part in at least once in the year prior to the survey, a spiritual activity defined in the survey as "a profound and usually positive experience that helps individuals find their authentic self, as well as connects them to a mysterious, universal, and overarching reality." In another survey I ran back in 2017, 49% of Millennial respondents from the Pacific Northwest regions of British Columbia, Washington State and Oregon who do outdoor nature activities at least once a year define these activities as spiritual experiences.[1]

Samuel, a Millennial from one of the Victoria B.C. focus groups, describes his spiritual experiences in the outdoors:

> … I've had spiritual feelings while out surfing, or just being on beaches. … I feel like being kind of immersed in nature in that way, physically being in the ocean, being present there, like, witnessing all of these natural powers,

> whether or not it's animals or waves coming at you or whatever, and just like seeing the landscape from out there has a very kind of awe-inspiring effect on you. To me, when I think about describing it, it feels profound, it feels spiritual, it feels significant.

Laura, who we first met earlier in this chapter, says:

> I live close to a beach, so … the feeling, the being at a beach and engaging in, like, inner conversation with God or just quiet, and stillness, and quieting the inner-self, I find so much more powerful by the ocean, or even in just nature. … I seek out what it is what I get there, … I just find something so powerful, so spiritual about it [nature]. … It's so true. It's so beautiful. And I think of something timeless about nature and about the landscape and my, if I think about faith, part of what it means to me is it interacts with where I came from. … and I think sometimes nature reminds me of going back to like what, just the basics of what's there.

Max, born in 1995 and from Montréal, Québec, conveys in his interview a sense of gratefulness at moments in nature, and describes them as spiritual. Avril, who we met earlier in this chapter, indicated at one point in her interview that she wants a green burial when she dies, to support the growth of a new tree.

Within the context of these interviews in both the Pacific Northwest and in Québec, the natural world and spiritual experiences within it are often contrasted with experiences of conventional religious groups. Morrill (2022, 236–237), using some of the same interviewee data from the Cascadia project as in this book, puts it best:

> For these interviewees who found some aspect of their spirituality in nature, nature created an experiential moment, one that is not defined by institutional structures, either architectural or theological. Interviewees identified their experiences in nature as being spiritual in a way that placed these experiences in opposition to more traditional expressions of religion. Indeed, … they seemed to find spiritual truth in nature because it is not constrained by institutional experiences and expectations. These experiences in nature seem to be quite individual and, on the surface, unmarked by communal, social, or cultural dimensions and, again, this seems, for those interviewed, to undergird the authenticity of their encounters.

How interviewees refer to spiritual experiences in nature fits into the larger massive subjective and self-spirituality turn discussed earlier in this book and chapter. Individual "authentic" experiences of connection and wellbeing are currently highly valued in our Western societies, and are mapped onto personal experiences of nature, defining these experiences and often elevating them to spiritual for many individuals.

A number of concepts have been coined by various scholars to try and identify and flesh out these spiritual experiences of the natural world. There is Albanese's (1990) concept of *nature religion* that refers to privileging the symbol of nature and finding within it the key to mastery and empowerment; religious impulses regarding nature that can be found within faith traditions as varied as Indigenous spiritualities to Puritan Calvinism, as well as beliefs, behaviors and values tied to nature within some political movements such as among Green parties. There is also Taylor's (2010) concept of *dark green religion* that encompasses spirituality entwined with environmental concern and the perception of nature as sacred and due reverent care.

Bramadat (2022) more recently coined a new related term in the context of the Pacific Northwest region of North America: *reverential naturalism.* Reverential naturalism for Bramadat:

> ... favours an orientation that is both accepting of scientific approaches to nature and inclined to perceive and imagine the natural world in ways that are redolent (from the Latin *olere,* "to smell") of mysticism, panentheism, animism, pantheism, and inclusive forms of theism. Reverential naturalism may be considered a metanarrative—with concomitant attitudes, assumptions, habits, and practices with respect to a breathtaking natural world—that animated the individual stories and perspectives of almost all the people we met during our research. (Bramadat 2022, 24)

Part of this concept covers some individuals' specific spiritual experiences with nature, or in other words the sublime or ecstatic dimension of nature for humans:

> ... experienced as beautiful (in the conventional sense of being harmonious, well-balanced, pleasing, picturesque, attractive) but also mystical and terrifying ... the land and sea are framed as extremely vulnerable and imbued with an indefatigable capacity to humble, nurture, and inspire humans. (Bramadat 2022, 30, 33; see also Shaw 2006 and Shibley 2011)

Whereas Taylor's dark green religion focuses on these spiritual experiences of interconnectedness with nature among more niche populations, such as within environmental movements and California surfer culture, Bramadat sees them more broadly throughout mainstream culture and among a large proportion of the population—albeit at times in more diluted forms. Yet, reverential naturalism also goes beyond this. It refers to a regional metanarrative that:

> ... permeates what we might call the dominant cultural rhetoric of the region ... an overarching meaning-conveying narrative according to which deference to and, for many, veneration of nature is framed as a distinctive, even definitive, feature of what it means to live well [in the Pacific Northwest]. (Bramadat 2022, 24, 25)

In a region characterized by the exceptional beauty of the Cascade mountains, Pacific Coast, and wild boreal and temperate rainforests, and by relatively easy access to many regional and national public parks as well as other natural spaces, a dominant cultural narrative and source of common identity have emerged in the Pacific Northwest in which nature and outdoor activities are seen as the primary source of human rejuvenation, balance, happiness, physical and mental wellbeing, as well as individual spiritual journeys.

This metanarrative of reverential naturalism is distinct from, although in some ways also inspired by, Indigenous spiritualities in the region. Indigenous spiritualities refer more specifically to the much longer history and contemporary realities of traditional ways of life among First Nations, Inuit and Métis peoples traversed by spirit beings, personal and community healing, ceremony, the teaching of Elders, the Medicine Circle, intimate relationships with nature and the journey of learning to live in the world put in place by the Creator (Crawford O'Brien 2022; Fiola 2015; Stonechild 2016).

Reverential naturalism on the other hand is more of a spiritual experience of nature found especially among White middle- to upper-class European-settler urban populations. Although the scholarly concept of reverential naturalism is fairly new, the phenomenon it refers to in the Pacific Northwest is not. Morrill (2022) shows that it has a history in the region, with many similar references to the sublime and awe-inspiring dimensions of nature found throughout European settler poetry and diaries from the 19th century as well as throughout family history interviews in the region. Morrill also points out that reverential naturalism was actually formed in the 19th century to the detriment of local Indigenous populations, with the White economic elite invested in keeping economic, social and cultural power in the hands of Euro-Americans and Canadians who were arriving in the Pacific Northwest to enjoy and exploit its natural resources and land taken from Indigenous peoples. Some of these practices of cultural genocide and land theft continue to this day, with some of those seeking their own reverential naturalism dreams ignoring and invading remaining Indigenous lands and culture. This said, many within the reverential naturalism frame also take inspiration from Indigenous spiritualities. Sunny, a resident of Vancouver Island in her late thirties from a British family background and participant in the Cascadia oral history interviews in 2018, says: "I think teachings around the interconnected nature of everything as one, which are really core teachings in a lot of Indigenous contexts, is one that really just makes a whole lot of sense to me, it really does."

Despite its history in the region that dates back to the 19th century, this metanarrative of reverential naturalism seems to be especially prevalent now in contemporary Pacific Northwest society, perhaps as a way to distinguish the region in the minds of its residents when faced with an ever more widespread, homogenized and dominant Anglo-American national and globalized culture. With actual regional differences in linguistic dialects, popular culture (music, films, theatre, art, etc.), lifestyle and food declining in recent decades, perhaps a region's metanarrative becomes more important for individuals to keep some form of identity differentiation, even if mostly symbolic, from the rest of the country or continent.

There is also an economic dimension feeding the metanarrative of reverential naturalism in the region. Historically, railroad companies in the late 19th century promoted the exceptional natural resources of the region to potential white Euro-American and Canadian settlers as key to profit-making and recreation (Findlay 1997; Morrill 2022). More recently, outdoor equipment, cottage development, eco-tourism and other such companies in the Pacific Northwest are some of the big promoters of the idealized images of happy, beautiful, physically fit (and usually White) people having their "authentic" experiences within a stunning natural (and usually devoid of other human beings) landscape—with all the latest gear or course (for those who can afford it); images that can be found plastered on these companies' store windows, websites, ad campaigns and social media. They act as an important source of socialization for individuals into the common identity of reverential naturalism in the region, along with other sources of socialization into this identity such as family traditions tied to nature experiences.

The current prevalence of the reverential naturalism metanarrative in the Pacific Northwest also seems to be tied to the relative weak presence of conventional religion in the area. British Columbia in Canada as well as the states of Washington and Oregon in the United States have some of the lowest measures of conventional religious behavior, believing and belonging on the continent; measures that have been on the decline for many generations now (Bramadat, Killen, and Wilkins-Laflamme 2022; Wilkins-Laflamme 2017). For example, those who say they have no religion when asked about their religious affiliation make up an estimated 32% of Washington's and Oregon's general adult populations according to the 2014 Pew Religious Landscape Study (Pew Research Center 2014), and 47% in British Columbia according to the 2018 GSS. Historically, a frontier mentality focused on mobility and resource extraction, political contestation between Indigenous, British and American groups, a physical and psychological distance from the rest of the continent, and a desire to be free of the Establishment in all its forms ensured that organized Christianity did not get as strong a foothold in the region in the 19th century as elsewhere in the United States and Canada (Barman 2008; Block 2017; Bunting 1997; Marks 2017; O'Connell 2003; Robbins 2001; Todd 2008). In fact, some argue that what defined northwestern exceptionalism in matters of religion was most notably the "irreligious experience" of many of its European settler residents (Block 2005, 2010; Marks 2007). The Pacific Northwest was to a certain extent "born secular" (Marks 2007), characterized by lower rates of regular church attendance among its population that date back to the 19th century. Religion never became as institutionalized during the mid-19th to mid-20th centuries among a majority of its population as it did in more eastern, central and southern parts of the continent. Additionally, the large waves of East Asian immigration to the region, among whom saying one had no religion was much more common, contributed to making nonreligion even more socially acceptable on the whole. Without one or a few dominant religious traditions to write the regional metanarrative, this opened up the space for reverential naturalism tied to the incredible natural beauty of the regional landscapes to dominate instead among religious, spiritual and nonreligious individuals alike.

Nevertheless, although prevalent in the Pacific Northwest, reverential naturalism can also be found elsewhere in the United States and Canada among at least some other regions, individuals and groups. Whether it be experiences of the big sky on the Prairies, the heights of the Rockies out West, the fury of the Atlantic Ocean out East, the aurora borealis on a cold clear northern night, the bizarre and beautiful rock formations of the deserts, or so many other picturesque and awe-inspiring natural features of the continent, many may see their spiritual experiences of this nature as a key part of their identity, even if the larger cultural metanarrative of reverential naturalism may not be as prevalent elsewhere as it currently is in the Pacific Northwest.

This reverential naturalism could also be understood as a form of substantive or positive nonreligion. Rather than defining less conventionally religious individuals, including spiritual seekers, by what they are not (religious), more and more researchers from the subfield of nonreligion and secularity studies are arguing that we should be focusing instead on these individuals' actual (and alternative to religion) identities, worldviews and behaviors (Cragun and McCaffree 2021; Lee 2015). More on this is given in Chapter 6. Cragun and Pasca (2021) show for example that nature and outdoor activities can be an important source for many when they define who they are, what they value and what they do and enjoy in life.

Millennials as Reverential Naturalism Forerunners?

Reverential naturalism being more pervasive in a less religious region like the Pacific Northwest and being understood as a substantive form of nonreligion in turn raises the question of whether it is also more widespread among a less conventionally religious generation such as among Millennials. The Pacific Northwest may be the North American region at the forefront of the reverential naturalism narrative, but are Millennials in turn at this narrative's generational forefront? Spiritual experiences of the natural world within the wider umbrella of reverential naturalism come up time and again in interviews with Millennials, both within and outside the Pacific Northwest as earlier examples of interviewee quotes in this chapter demonstrated.

Are many Millennials primed for reverential naturalism in a way? More of them have less conventional religion in their lives, which opens up space for alternative identity constructions and life narratives in their worlds—one nonreligious alternative being reverential naturalism. As discussed in Chapter 1, the environmental crisis is also one of the key concerns that Millennials have about the present day and the future, and this green shift in mentalities may further open up more Millennials to having different and more spiritual experiences of nature.

A nurturing, awe-inspired and reverential frame of mind toward nature, rather than one of more traditional Christian domination and stewardship, for example, may very well be more conducive to reverential naturalism experiences and identity formation.

Additionally, living in more urban settings, as the vast majority of Millennials now do, where direct daily contact with the wild is rarer, may actually be more conducive to reverential naturalism in some ways. Millennials can experience the positives of nature as special out-of-the-ordinary activities and holidays, without experiencing necessarily the more mundane or even negative realities of living in nature, such as your well pipes freezing in the winter, wild animals regularly wreaking havoc in your garden and garbage can, beaver dams breaking and washing out roads, lack of cell phone reception and high-speed wifi, bug season, potentially harmful plants and animals, crop destruction due to pests, drought, forest fires, flooding and landslides, etc. The wild and nature are put on a pedestal of sorts by many Millennials precisely because they only experience them on special occasions. This may allow for more spiritual, outside-the-normal experiences of the natural environment, because nature is no longer a normal part of everyday life for these urban populations. As mentioned earlier, there is also a whole branch of consumer capitalism in our societies focused on getting Millennials to spend their money in search of these reverential naturalism experiences, often through costly trips to nature and quite expensive elaborate outdoor activities and sports.

The COVID-19 pandemic has added another dimension to the potentially growing prevalence of reverential naturalism among individuals, including among Millennials. Throughout the pandemic, outdoor spaces have come to be seen as safer spaces with much lower risks of viral transmission. Nature and the outdoors represent freedom in a way for many individuals, more so than before the pandemic; freedom, even if temporary, from many of the pandemic's hardships and restrictions. Although the natural environment has long been an important space for many individuals to relax and recharge their mental health, this became even more crucial during the taxing times of COVID-19 lockdowns. With international travel being severely restricted and most indoor activities off limits, camping, hiking, cycling, skiing, boating and other outdoor nature activities that remained available saw a surge in popularity. I have been an avid cross-country skier since I was a kid, but I never saw as many people out on the trails as I did during the winter of 2020–2021. With the surge in popularity and renewed appreciation for the outdoors during the pandemic may also come a surge and renewal for spiritual experiences of the natural world among many.

It is not easy to say if reverential naturalism is more of a thing among Millennials than among older generations. The concept is still new and fluid, and the realities it refers to regarding human experiences of the natural world are not always easy to pin down with numbers and words. Further research and theorizing in future studies are needed. However, there seem to be many factors in reverential naturalism's favor among the Millennial generation, and not just in the

Pacific Northwest. And this, especially among the group of Millennials I classify as spiritual seekers: a group which for the most part has received some form of religious or spiritual socialization during childhood, who are primed with a mindset to think in terms of spirituality, but who often come into less frequent contact with organized religion. Nature and the outdoors may offer this group especially, as well as a significant portion of Millennials overall, an alternative space for spiritual innovation.

***

Spirituality away from organized religion, such as spiritual experiences within nature explored in depth in this chapter, is definitely a phenomenon present among many Millennials. This said, it also does not appear to be the default approach that a majority of Millennials are turning toward in their late teens, twenties and early thirties. This is why, in contrast to scholars within the individual spiritualization framework discussed earlier, I do not refer to this phenomenon as a spiritual revolution. An important phenomenon among Millennials, yes. A daily reality for a majority of Millennials, no. Other studies in fact point to SBNR as being a more prevalent trend among the Boomer generation (Bruce 2017; Mossière 2021); a generation who for the most part received a religious socialization during their childhood, attended religious services regularly with their parents, who were taught the importance of spiritual matters, but who moved away in large numbers from taking part in regular activities tied to organized religion in their adult years.

Some Millennials are into spiritual matters on a regular basis; some also pair this with more frequent conventional religious activities, and so are classified as religious Millennials in this study. Others who do spirituality only come into infrequent contact with organized religion, and so are classified as spiritual seeker Millennials here. Although a substantial minority important to study, these spiritual seeker Millennials nevertheless remain one of the smaller categories in my analyses. They have not fully replaced the intergenerational declines of more conventional religion that we have seen over the past decades, especially in Canada, but also more and more in the United States.

We now turn to our next category: the cultural believer Millennial. Removed from most forms of religious and spiritual behavior, this is a group that nevertheless remains tied to a cultural religious identity and some core related beliefs. Often lumped together with the nonreligious in previous studies with little afterthought, there are in fact some important distinctions to make between these two types of individuals. Religious identity plays an important cultural and family heritage role for the cultural believer Millennial, giving them a sense of belonging and place in the world. It can also in turn affect their attitudes toward others considered as outsiders or members of out-groups, such as religious minorities and immigrants. An intergenerational transitional bridge category in many ways between the religious and spiritual on the one side, and the nonreligious on the other, the cultural believer Millennial is a fascinating group worthy of our attention in the next chapter.

Note

1 The Pacific Northwest Social Survey (PNSS) was part of the research project *Religion, Spirituality, Secularity and Society in the Pacific Northwest*, led by principal investigator Paul Bramadat at the University of Victoria's Centre for Studies in Religion and Society. The 1,510 adult respondents from British Columbia as well as the states of Washington and Oregon formed the core survey sample. Special thanks to the Survey Research Centre at the University of Waterloo (https://uwaterloo.ca/survey-research-centre/) as well as the project's research coordinator Chelsea Horton at the University of Victoria for their key roles in the survey data collection and cleaning. For more details about the PNSS, visit https://uwspace.uwaterloo.ca/handle/10012/13406

References

Albanese, Catherine L. 1990. *Nature Religion in America: From the Algonkian Indians to the New Age*. Chicago, IL: University of Chicago Press.

Ammerman, Nancy. 2014. *Sacred Stories, Spiritual Tribes: Finding Religion in Everyday Life*. New York, NY: Oxford University Press.

Angus Reid Institute. 2015. *Religion and Faith in Canada Today: Strong Belief, Ambivalence and Rejection Define Our Views*. Accessed June 17, 2016. http://angusreid.org

Arnett, Jeffrey Jensen. 2015. *Emerging Adulthood: The Winding Road from the Late Teens through the Twenties*. New York, NY: Oxford University Press.

Aupers, Stef and Dick Houtman, eds. 2010. *Religions of Modernity: Relocating the Sacred to the Self and the Digital*. Leiden, Netherlands: Brill.

Barman, Jean. 2008. *British Columbia: Spirit of the People*. Madeira Park, BC: Harbour.

Beyer, Peter, Alyshea Cummins, and Scott Craig. 2019. "Religious/Spiritual Identity among Younger Adults in Canada: A Complex Portrait." In *Young People and the Diversity of (Non)Religious Identities in International Perspective*, edited by Elizabeth Arweck and Heather hipley, 15–31. Switzerland: Springer.

Block, Tina. 2005. "'Going to Church Just Never Even Occurred to Me': Women and Secularism in the Pacific Northwest, 1950–1975." *Pacific Northwest Quarterly* 96 (2): 61–68.

Block, Tina. 2010. "Religion, Irreligion, and the Difference Place Makes: The Case of the Postwar Pacific Northwest." *Social History* 43: 1–30. doi:10.1353/his.2010.0005

Block, Tina. 2017. *The Secular Northwest: Religion and Irreligion in Everyday Postwar Life*. Vancouver, BC: University of British Columbia Press.

Bramadat, Paul. 2022. "Reverential Naturalism in Cascadia: From the Fancy to the Sublime." In *Religion at the Edge: Nature, Spirituality, and Secularity in the Pacific Northwest*, edited by Paul Bramadat, Patricia Killen, and Sarah Wilkins-Laflamme, 21–39. Vancouver, BC: University of British Columbia Press.

Bramadat, Paul, Patricia Killen, and Sarah Wilkins-Laflamme, eds. 2022. *Religion at the Edge: Nature, Spirituality, and Secularity in the Pacific Northwest*. Vancouver, BC: University of British Columbia Press.

Bruce, Steve. 2017. *Secular Beats Spiritual: The Westernization of the Easternization of the West*. New York, NY: Oxford University Press.

Bunting, Robert. 1997. *The Pacific Raincoast: Environment and Culture in an American Eden, 1778–1900*. Lawrence, KA: University Press of Kansas.

Cragun, Ryan, and Kevin McCaffree. 2021. "Nothing Is Not Something: On Replacing Nonreligion with Identities." *Secular Studies* 3 (1): 7–26. doi:10.1163/25892525-bja10017

Cragun, Ryan, and Christina Pasca. 2021. *What We Find in Nature: Comparing the Religious and Nonreligious*. Presentation given at the virtual biennial meeting of the Nonreligion and Secularity Research Network. June 16, 2021.

Crawford O'Brien, Suzanne. 2022. "Border Crossings: Indigenous Spirituality and Culture in Cascadia." In *Religion at the Edge: Nature, Spirituality, and Secularity in the Pacific Northwest*, edited by Paul Bramadat, Patricia Killen, and Sarah Wilkins-Laflamme, 61–81. Vancouver, BC: University of British Columbia Press.

Davie, Grace. 1994. *Religion in Britain Since 1945: Believing Without Belonging*. Oxford, UK: Blackwell Publishing.

Drescher, Elizabeth. 2016. *Choosing Our Religion: The Spiritual Lives of America's Nones*. New York, NY: Oxford University Press.

Findlay, John. 1997. "A Fishy Proposition." In *Many Wests: Place, Culture, and Regional Identity*, edited by David M. Wrobel and Michael Steiner, 37–70. Lawrence, KA: University Press of Kansas.

Fiola, Chantal. 2015. *Rekindling the Sacred Fire: Métis Ancestry and Anishinaabe Spirituality*. Winnipeg, MB: University of Manitoba Press.

Fuller, Robert. 2001. *Spiritual But Not Religious: Understanding Unchurched America*. New York, NY: Oxford University Press.

Heelas, Paul, and Linda Woodhead. 2005. *The Spiritual Revolution: Why Religion Is Giving Way to Spirituality*. Oxford, UK: Blackwell.

Hervieu-Léger, Danielle. 1999. *Le pèlerin et le converti: La religion en mouvement*. Paris: Flammarion.

Houtman, Dick, and Stef Aupers. 2007. "The Spiritual Turn and the Decline of Tradition: The Spread of Post-Christian Spirituality in 14 Western Countries, 1981–2000." *Journal for the Scientific Study of Religion* 46 (3): 305–320. doi:10.1111/j.1468-5906.2007.00360.x

Lee, Lois. 2015. *Recognizing the Non-Religious: Reimagining the Secular*. New York, NY: Oxford University Press.

Luckmann, Thomas. 1967. *The Invisible Religion: The Problem of Religion in Modern Society*. London, UK: MacMillan.

Marks, Lynne. 2007. "'Leaving God Behind When They Crossed the Rocky Mountains': Exploring Unbelief in Turn of the Century British Columbia." In *Household Counts: Canadian Households and Families in 1901*, edited by Peter A. Baskerville and Eric William Sager, 371–404. Toronto, ON: University of Toronto Press.

Marks, Lynne. 2017. *Infidels and the Damn Churches: Irreligion and Religion in Settler British Columbia*. Vancouver, BC: University of British Columbia Press.

Morrill, Susanna. 2022. "Reverential Naturalism in Cascadia: Everything Old is New Again." In *Religion at the Edge: Nature, Spirituality, and Secularity in the Pacific Northwest*, edited by Paul Bramadat, Patricia Killen, and Sarah Wilkins-Laflamme, 228–247. Vancouver, BC: University of British Columbia Press.

Mossière, Géraldine, ed. 2021. *Dits et non-dits: Mémoires catholiques au Québec*. Montréal, QC: Les Presses de l'Université de Montréal.

O'Connell, Nicholas. 2003. *On Sacred Ground: The Spirit of Place in Pacific Northwest Literature*. Seattle, WA: University of Washington Press.

Pew Research Center. 2014. *Religious Landscape Study* [dataset]. https://www.pewforum.org/about-the-religious-landscape-study/

Putnam, Robert D. 2000. *Bowling Alone: The Collapse and Revival of American Community*. New York, NY: Simon and Schuster.

Robbins, William G., ed. 2001. *The Great Northwest: The Search for Regional Identity*. Corvallis, OR: Oregon State University Press.

Roof, Wade Clark. 1999. *Spiritual Marketplace*. Princeton, NJ: Princeton University Press.

Shaw, Phillip. 2006. *The Sublime*. New York, NY: Routledge.

Shibley, Mark A. 2011. "Sacred Nature: Earth-Based Spirituality as Popular Religion in the Pacific Northwest." *Journal for the Study of Religion, Nature and Culture* 5 (2): 164–185.

Stonechild, Blair. 2016. *The Knowledge Seeker: Embracing Indigenous Spirituality*. Regina, SK: University of Regina Press.

Taylor, Bron. 2010. *Dark Green Religion: Nature, Spirituality and the Planetary Future*. Berkeley and Los Angeles, CA: University of California Press.

Taylor, Charles. 1991. *The Ethics of Authenticity*. Cambridge, MA: Harvard University Press.

Taylor, Charles. 2007. *A Secular Age*. Cambridge, MA: The Belknap Press of Harvard University Press.

Thiessen, Joel, and Sarah Wilkins-Laflamme. 2020. *None of the Above: Nonreligious Identity in the U.S. and Canada*. New York, NY: New York University Press.

Todd, Douglas. 2008. *Cascadia: The Elusive Utopia; Exploring the Spirit of the Pacific Northwest*. Vancouver, BC: Ronsdale Press.

Watts, Galen. 2016. *The Personal Politics of Spirituality: On the Lived Relationship between Contemporary Spirituality and Social Justice among Canadian Millennials*. MA Thesis, Queen's University.

Watts, Galen. 2022. *The Spiritual Turn: The Religion of the Heart and the Making of Romantic Liberal Modernity*. New York, NY: Oxford University Press.

Wilkins-Laflamme, Sarah. 2017. "Religious-Secular Polarization Compared: The Cases of Québec and British Columbia." *Studies in Religion* 48 (2): 166–185. doi:10.1177/0008429817695662

Wuthnow, Robert. 1998. *After Heaven: Spirituality in America Since the 1950s*. Los Angeles, CA: University of California Press.

Young, Pamela Dickey, and Heather Shipley. 2020. *Identities under Construction: Religion, Gender, and Sexuality among Youth in Canada*. Kingston, ON: McGill-Queen's University Press.

5

THE CULTURAL BELIEVER MILLENNIAL

Similar in size to spiritual seeker Millennials in Canada, representing an estimated one fifth of young adults there, and the smallest of the four Millennial categories at 12% in the United States (see Figure 2.12 in Chapter 2), the cultural believer Millennial often gets overlooked or quickly passed over in many existing studies. Because of their low levels of religious and spiritual behavior, cultural believers are frequently lumped in with nonreligious Millennials. However, this masks the reality of a distinct group who are usually less religiously and spiritually active, but who mostly still assign importance to religious identity and hold a number of more religious beliefs. There may only be an estimated 13% of cultural believers who attend religious services at least once a month, and only 29% who pray at least once a week, but almost 90% are religiously affiliated and just over 70% believe in God or a higher power (Table 5.1), although it is a God or a higher power often according to their own views rather than the teachings of their religion.

Catholics are by far the largest religious tradition represented in this cultural believer category. Sixty-one percent of young adult cultural believers in Canada and 53% in the United States are Catholic. In turn, 8% of Millennial cultural believers in Canada and 16% in the United States are Protestant. Another 8% in Canada say they are spiritual with no religion. In the United States, another 8% are Christian Orthodox, and 8% indicate they have no religion with no particular preference for a nonreligious identity marker.

As the results in Table 5.1 indicate, the cultural believer Millennial is a little bit older than average among young adults (mean age of 26.6 years), especially when compared with the spiritual seeker Millennial (mean age of 25.9 years). Cultural believers are also slightly more likely to be female, especially when compared with religious Millennials. Compared with both religious and spiritual seeker Millennials, cultural believers are more likely to be White in both Canada and the

DOI: 10.4324/9781003217695-5

TABLE 5.1 Characteristics of cultural believer Millennials

	Cultural believer Millennials	*Rest of Millennials*
% weekly or more frequent childhood religious or spiritual education	52%	54%
% monthly or more frequent religious service attendance as adults	13%	37%
% weekly or more frequent prayer as adults	29%	38%
% belief in God or a higher power	71%	59%
% religiously affiliated	87%	49%
Mean age	26.6 years	26.0 years
% female	52%	48%
% non-White ethnic background/race	28%	33%
% university educated	21%	26%
% with less than $20,000 household income	18%	17%
% rural residents (pop. < 50,000)	35%	26%

Source: MTS 2019.

United States, as well as to have lower levels of university education and to live in more rural areas in the United States.

The religious identity of the cultural believer Millennial is often tied more to family, community, tradition and nostalgia rather than to religious or spiritual activity. It does provide a number of young adults with a positive sense of situated belonging at a time when identity formation is especially important during their emerging adulthood years (Arnett 2015; Whitney and King 2014; Young and Shipley 2020), even if in practice these individuals are physically removed from an actual religious group most of the time. Belonging and belief remain somewhat important to most cultural believers, but contact with a place of worship usually only happens for special holidays or occasions, if at all: 34% of cultural believers in Canada and 25% in the United States attend religious services a few times or once a year; and 55% of cultural believers in Canada and 50% in the United States say they always or sometimes celebrate or plan to celebrate rites of passage with a faith group (marriage, birth/initiation/baptismal rites for a child or a funeral, for example).

Yet, strong cultural identity can also lead to stronger in-group and out-group boundaries being created among some cultural believers, boundaries that are not mitigated by regular exposure to interfaith teachings, sermons and activities of friendship and love within many religious groups in North America. At times this can and does lead to more xenophobic attitudes toward individuals perceived as outside a cultural believers' frame of heritage and cultural reference.

This chapter explores in more depth these paradoxes that result from a strong cultural identity tied to a religious tradition without regular religious and spiritual behavior to match. We will also explore how, despite these paradoxes, the cultural believer acts in many ways as a bridge category between the larger more religious and spiritual populations on the one hand and the larger more nonreligious groups on the other among the Millennial generation today.

The Importance of Cultural Ties

Andrew, who we met in Chapter 2 when I introduced the category of cultural believer, spoke of ritual spaces, shared cultural experience, nostalgia, continued tradition, and community as key to his Jewish identity and occasional practice. Rachel, a Reformed Jew who we met in Chapter 1, similarly states:

> We, the Reform community, we say a lot, 'community.' A token word. So people are neither seeking to be religious nor are they seeking to be spiritual, they are seeking tradition. That tradition might mean Shabbat dinner. They might not know the prayers, but they still wanna come together for dinner at someone's house on Friday night and have a glass of wine. Or they grew up going to Yom Kippur services and they didn't want to fast when they were a kid, but now that they're an adult, they feel that it's important. They might not go to services but when they're at work they'll fast for the day and that's meaningful to them. … I don't think any of the conversations I have on a daily basis would ever say anything about spirituality within the Jewish communities that I'm a part of. It would be, "My traditions are …," or "My community is …" Rather than "My religion is …" or "I spiritually do …"

Cultural believers are found throughout North America. This said, certain regions do contain higher proportions of them. The province of Québec in Canada is the area *par excellence* where larger swaths of the population, including larger swaths of Millennials, can be defined as cultural believers. Twenty-three percent of Millennials residing in Québec fall into the cultural believer category according to the MTS 2019 data, compared with 17% in the rest of Canada and 12% in the United States. This cultural believer relationship with religion in the province, especially among the French-speaking majority with a form of cultural Catholicism, has been referred to as a love-hate relationship by Meunier and Nault (2014). Anti-(Catholic) Church sentiment has been a prevalent part of the social imaginary since the Quiet Revolution of the 1960s in the province. Adam, a practicing Catholic born in 1983, interviewed in Montréal in 2018, and who we first met in Chapter 3, refers to this as the general nausea of *La Grande noirceur* passed on to all Québécois. The mid-19th to mid-20th centuries are often remembered as a "black" period of Church and clerical domination during which regular citizens, especially women and LGBTQ2S+ individuals, were kept under the yoke of the Catholic way of life. Strict sexual morals and gender roles were taught and enforced by means of the Catholic Church's hold on social institutions and its general prevalence throughout social life. It was only with the "enlightenment" of the Quiet Revolution in the 1960s that Québec society was seen to be able to free itself not only from the economically dominant English-speaking minority in the province but also from the *Grande noirceur* of the Catholic Church's domineering influence (Zubrzycki 2016).

This view of the past has achieved a quasi-mythical status for most Québécois, being passed on to younger generations through family stories and history lessons at school, even if Gen X and Millennials were not alive during the period in question themselves. Many of the nuances and other complexities of the period and the role of the Catholic Church in French-speaking Canada are also often lost in the tale (Christiano 2007; Gauvreau 2005; Koussens and Foisy 2018; Meunier and Warren 2002). This view of the history of the Catholic Church in the province as well as a continued disagreement by many with its sexual morals and other institutional stances translates into extremely low levels of regular religious service attendance in current-day Québec (Bibby 2011; Meunier and Wilkins-Laflamme 2011; Wilkins-Laflamme 2014). It also translates into negative sentiments held by many not only toward the Catholic Church but also by proxy toward religion in general. These negative views, along with more general fears and discomfort toward non-Christian religions (especially Islam), have in turn manifested themselves most notably in social and political tensions arising since the 2000s. Issues of accommodating growing numbers of religious minorities in the province have surfaced with events such as the Bouchard-Taylor Commission in 2007–2008, the proposed Québec Charter of Values in 2013, the debate during the 2015 federal election campaign surrounding the wearing of the niqab in citizenship swearing-in ceremonies, Bill 62 brought into law in 2017, and most recently Bill 21 brought into law in 2019 and banning the wearing of most religious symbols and clothing among many provincial government employees.

Nevertheless, despite this particular history, the negative views it often generates toward the Catholic Church as an institution and toward religion in general, and the recent push to legislate State secularism policies in the province, there is also a hesitancy among a majority of Québécois to relinquish all cultural and identity ties to Catholicism. Fifty-four percent of residents in the province still declared themselves as Catholic in Statistics Canada's 2018 GSS (Cycle 33), although only 7% among them attend mass once a week. Public school boards remained denominational (Protestant or Catholic) until 2000, and Catholic and Protestant religion classes continued to be offered in public elementary and secondary schools until 2008. This ambivalent love-hate relationship with Catholicism is also evident in the practice of rites of passage. In 2001, the rate of newborns in the province that were baptized Catholic was still relatively high at an estimated 75%, compared with the province also housing the highest rate of couples living in common law partnerships in the Western world (as opposed to being married or religiously married) (Laplante 2006; Meunier and Nault 2014; Meunier and Wilkins-Laflamme 2011).

Cultural Catholic identity, not to be mistaken for actual ties with the Catholic Church, is still seen as the "default" option among many Québécois: an important aspect of group identity that maintains a link with culture and family tradition and is often seen as a way to distinguish the Québécois from a perceived Anglo-Protestant majority in the rest of North America (Lemieux and Montminy 2000; Meunier and Nault 2014; Meunier and Wilkins-Laflamme 2011; Milot 1991). This is an almost implicit dimension of francophone Québécois identity, referred to often quickly and without much fore- or afterthought in many of the Québec life history interviews. Research participants would often say they were baptized or did their first communion "like most Quebecers … because it was the normal thing to do." Guy, born in 1998, from Trois-Rivières, Québec and who does not attend Mass nor take part in other church activities regularly embodies this cultural Catholicism when he states:

> I'm Catholic because I was born Catholic. That's what it looks like. But, you know, I defend the fact that I'm Catholic. I'm Catholic and I'm proud to be Catholic. And I wouldn't want to be anything else but Catholic. And my kids will be Catholic. But nothing more than that.

Few residents of the province ever enter a place of worship anymore, but many will still cry out in shock and dismay when a village or city church must close due to financial difficulties and a lack of parishioners; or when a hospital or city building attempts to remove the crosses, crucifixes and statues of Mary, Jesus and Catholic saints that have long adorned their spaces.[1]

It is only with the arrival of Millennials that this cultural Catholicism, previously so prevalent in the province since the 1960s, has begun to show signs of fraying at its edges. Millennials are the first generation who went to non-denominational public schools (public school boards in Québec changed from being either Protestant or Catholic to either English- or French-speaking in 2000). Millennial parents in Québec were only baptizing their newborns into the Catholic community at a rate of 36% in 2016, compared with rates above 75% prior to 2001 (Meunier and Legault-Leclair 2021). Forty percent of Millennials in the province said they had no religion in the 2018 Statistics Canada GSS (Cycle 33), compared with only 28% among Gen X, and 10% among Boomers. Still, although cultural believers may not be as numerous now among Millennials in the province, compared with reaching their peak among Boomers and Gen X, they nevertheless do represent a large proportion of the younger Québécois generation. The ambivalent love-hate relationship with Catholicism and with religion in general may have softened among Millennial Québécois, but it has not disappeared entirely and will most likely be around for some time to come.

In some ways then, the distinct historical and socio-cultural dynamics of Québec make the experiences of its cultural believers unique to the region. Yet, in other ways, the Québécois cultural believer resembles those outside of the province and outside of Catholicism as well. Thiessen (2015, 65–93) for example explores the large category of marginal affiliates in Alberta, Canada, who keep their affiliation with a Christian denomination and occasional practice with a religious group for special holidays and occasions such as rites of passage. When interviewed, these individuals see this as an important dimension of their morality and of being a good person, as important family customs, and an important aspect of how it has always been during their lifetime and their parents' lifetimes. Voas (2009) in turn highlights the residual religious involvement and casual loyalty to Christian tradition among large segments of European populations, which he coins as "fuzzy fidelity." Not all marginal affiliates and fuzzies are cultural believers according to my categorization in this book: some marginal affiliates and fuzzies may instead fall into the spiritual seeker camp especially. But many are cultural believers who belong to a religious tradition, and have some beliefs tied to this identity, but little to no frequent behavior to match.

Stronger In-Group Identity Can Sometimes Also Mean Stronger Out-Group Sentiments

Some religious Millennials may see the cultural believers' relationship with religion as somewhat false, inauthentic, free-riding or hypocritical: the cultural believer identifying with a religious tradition, cherry-picking some of this tradition's beliefs, parachuting into one of its places of worship to get married or to welcome their newborn into the community, but not really walking the walk by regularly taking part in this tradition's religious or spiritual activities and rituals. For example, William, a practicing Catholic from Laval who we first met in Chapter 1 and then again in Chapter 3, makes a clear distinction between cultural and religious Catholics in his interview:

> ... the distinction that I make between on the one hand the more social practice of religion, being born in a religion, being baptised, physically being in Church; and on the other hand the practice from the heart, the real conversion of the heart, trying to practice this profoundly. The latter is what I myself humbly try to do.

This said, religious belonging and some religious beliefs are usually meaningful for the cultural believer, just not always in the same ways as for the religious Millennial. For the cultural believer, it is especially a question of family tradition and cultural heritage, rather than reinforcing and developing one's faith through ritual and community; family tradition and cultural heritage which should nevertheless not be downplayed or brushed aside.

Whereas this sense of belonging can have a positive impact on a cultural believer's life, family ties and sense of identity, it can also lead to what can be considered more negative social outcomes. Being part of a distinct "Us" can also in turn negatively affect attitudes toward others considered as outsiders or members of out-groups, such as religious minorities and immigrants when viewed from the position of the religious and cultural majority. American sociologist Herbert Blumer (1958) famously put forward in his work on social identity and inter-group relations that individuals often feel the need to differentiate themselves and members of their own social, cultural and national group from those perceived as part of out-groups, drawing the line between "Us" and "Them," as a fundamental process in constructing conceptions of the self (Bello 2016; Kehrberg 2007).

Cultural Catholics and Bill 21 in Québec

Let us return to Québec for a few moments. Its recent State secularism Bill 21, passed and brought into law in 2019, is framed by the provincial government as a way to protect and enforce *laïcité*, or in other words State/religion separation and State neutrality toward religion in the province. The law's measures of banning the wearing of religious symbols and clothing among many provincial government employees as well as requiring persons to uncover their faces to receive some governmental services are considered to fall under a more "strict" form of State secularism (Milot 2009). These measures would bring Québec closer to the French model of *laïcité* where a "neutral" State is envisioned as a public sphere devoid of all signs of religion, rather than a softer model of *laïcité* more common elsewhere in North America and earlier in Québec's contemporary history where all religions are meant to be given equal opportunity in the public sphere, without the State supporting one over another; although in practice this usually still means a greater prevalence of Christianity and Christian symbolism in the public sphere, given the regions' histories and current population compositions.

Despite provincial government rhetoric of equality within *laïcité* for all citizens, the stricter *laïcité* measures in Bill 21 do disproportionately target and affect religious minorities in the province, notably the larger Muslim communities of the province, members of which are the ones who tend to wear "religious" symbols and clothing in their daily lives and to work. These more strict measures do not really impact cultural Catholics in the province who still make up the majority of its residents, and who for the most part do not wear any symbols or garb considered as "religious" or problematic by the government.

In fact, efforts have been made by the Québec government to redefine Christian symbols so that its recent State secularism policies do not apply to them. Beaman (2020) highlights the legal and societal push by the shrinking Christian majority in many Western liberal democracies, including in Québec, to redefine Christian symbols such as crosses, crucifixes, prayer and sacred heart statues as "culture" and "heritage," rather than "religion," in order to circumnavigate religious freedom as well as State secularism policies and to keep these symbols within the public sphere in contexts of growing religious diversity and nonreligion. "The move to culture is a protective strategy, an attempt to reframe majoritarian religion as a heritage to be protected against both religious "others" and the nonreligious" (Beaman 2020, 6). Protecting cultural heritage was originally the argument made for keeping the crucifix in the Québec

National Assembly legislature's *Salon bleu* room: provincial premier Legault referred to the crucifix in October 2018 as a historical symbol, and said that "In our past we had Protestants and Catholics. They built the values we have in Québec. We have to recognize that and not mix that with religious signs."[2] Bill 21 also allows for the premier's argument by stating that "The bill may not be interpreted as affecting the emblematic or toponymic elements of Québec's cultural heritage that testify to its history" (p. 2 of Bill 21).

Nevertheless, in June 2019, the government finally bowed to public pushback and moved the crucifix to another corridor space, all the while still keeping it in the parliamentary building. So these attempts at keeping Christian symbolism in the public sphere while excluding minority religions by redefining the symbols of the majority as culture rather than religion have achieved mixed results so far.

Meunier and Legault-Leclair (2021) find that it is not the nonreligious in the province who show the largest amount of public support for the strict State secularism measures in Bill 21 that tend to target religious minorities. Rather, this largest public support comes from the cultural Catholics in the province. Catholics, who for the most part are not practicing in the province, oppose the wearing of religious symbols in schools and government services at a rate of 74%, compared with 64% among the religiously unaffiliated. Looked at from a generational perspective, whereas more than 80% of Boomers and between 70% and 75% of Gen Xers support this measure in Bill 21 (older age groups among whom Catholic cultural believers are more numerous), only 45–55% of respondents among Millennial age groups show the same support for the law's key measure (younger age groups among whom cultural believing is less common as well as nonreligion and non-Christian religions are more common).

The remaining cultural ties to Catholicism and the fear of losing them among the French-speaking population can be a contributing factor to more negative feelings toward non-Christian groups in the province, most notably toward Muslim communities (Bouchard and Taylor 2008; Wilkins-Laflamme 2018) who have in recent years born the brunt of Québec's new *laïcité* laws. Whereas there are many dynamics at play with these *laïcité* laws, it would be naïve to think that anti-Muslim sentiment is not one of them. In the 2015 Canadian Election Study (CES) survey, Québec respondents' answers to two questions about on the one hand negative feeling scores for Muslims "living here" and on the other hand being in favor of laws banning women from covering their faces (wearing the niqab) in public, showed positive moderate correlation with each other (a significant Spearman correlation coefficient of 0.343). In other words, for a number of Québec respondents, the two sets of attitudes do not appear to be all that distinct. Additionally, when asked to rank different minority groups on feeling thermometer scales in the 2019 CES survey, cultural Catholic respondents who affiliate with the religious tradition but who attend religious services less than once a month were the ones in the province who scored Muslims living in Canada the lowest (Table 5.2).

TABLE 5.2 Feeling thermometer scores toward Muslims living in Canada (0 = really dislike; 100 = really like), among different groups of Québec respondents, CES 2019

Groups of Québec respondents	*Average feeling thermometer scores toward Muslims living in Canada*
Catholics who attend religious services less than once a month	**46**
Catholics who attend religious services at least once a month	49
Religiously unaffiliated	57
Other Christian religious affiliates	61
Non-Christian religious affiliates, excluding Muslims	61

Anti-Group Sentiment in the 2019 MTS

This greater dislike of certain minority groups among some cultural believers is not just found in Québec either, nor just among older populations. In the 2019 MTS data, cultural believer Millennials in the United States with a Christian religious affiliation or no religious affiliation are those of their generation who associate more negative scores with the words "immigrants," "Judaism" and "Islam," compared with religious, spiritual seeker and nonreligious American Millennials with a Christian religious affiliation or no religious affiliation (Table 5.3). For the whole of Canada, it is only "immigrants" who receive the lowest (most negative) word association scores from cultural believer Millennials, and not the listed minority religions (Table 5.4). So it is not all religious minorities who feel the dislike from cultural believers. It is also not all cultural believers who have these more negative attitudes toward some religious minorities. And it is not only among cultural believers that we see negative attitudes toward religious minorities:

TABLE 5.3 Average feelings scores, "Select all words that generally have positive or negative associations or meanings for you," among the four categories of Millennials, U.S. respondents 18–35 years old who affiliate with a Christian tradition or no religion, MTS 2019

	United States			
	Religious	*Spiritual seeker*	*Cultural believer*	*Nonreligious*
Immigrants	3.9	22	**−13**	14
Judaism	−2	11	**−6**	−2
Hinduism	−7	6	**−2**	−1
Islam	−17	−5	**−24**	−18
Sikhism	−8	9	**−7**	−2
Buddhism	−8	20	**3**	6
Atheism	−28	−20	**−12**	16
Christianity	55	23	**46**	−20

TABLE 5.4 Average feelings scores, "Select all words that generally have positive or negative associations or meanings for you," among the four categories of Millennials, Canadian respondents 18–35 years old who affiliate with a Christian tradition or no religion, MTS 2019

	Canada			
	Religious	*Spiritual seeker*	*Cultural believer*	*Nonreligious*
Immigrants	25	21	**17.5**	26
Judaism	−2	6	**10**	−3
Hinduism	−2	11	**11**	4
Islam	−13	−15	**−10**	−18
Sikhism	−2	3	**6**	1
Buddhism	6	28	**23**	20
Atheism	−22	−3	**3**	19
Christianity	63	27	**21**	−17

we also find them among other categories of Millennials. Yet, as a trend, cultural believers do assign more negative scores on average for some minority groups.

Why Cultural Believers?

Why are negative attitudes toward some minority groups more prevalent among cultural believers affiliated with a religious tradition, but not practicing that religion regularly with a religious group, rather than say among actively religious and spiritual individuals? A number of researchers have specifically applied Blumer's social identity theory to the study of the effects of religion and religiosity on attitudes toward immigrants (Bloom, Arikan, and Courtemanche 2015; Daniels and Von Der Ruhr 2005; Doebler 2014; Leon McDaniel, Nooruddin, and Shortle 2011), and on prejudicial attitudes in general (Banyasz, Tokar, and Kaut 2016; Blogowska and Saroglou 2013; Goplen and Plant 2015). For these scholars, religious nationalism, or in other words an individual's belief that their own specific religious identity, set of practices and beliefs are tied to their country's or region's national identity (and specifically Christian nationalism in the Western context), is a key reason why many who are religiously affiliated also tend to hold more negative attitudes toward immigrants, especially toward non-Christian immigrants (Leon McDaniel, Nooruddin, and Shortle 2011; Pew Research Center 2018; Scheepers, Gijsberts, and Hello 2002; Whitehead and Perry 2020).

> … certain groups, particularly religious minorities and the nonreligious, are excluded from the narrative of "we" in the public sphere, and as contributors to nation in the present tense, the past, and potentially the future. What is worth preserving and protecting does not belong to them and does not originate with them. To be clear, not all Christianities are

> welcome in this "we." It is often a specific formulation of Christianity that provides a language, symbols and framework for a particular social order. Moreover, narratives of values and community circulate to reinforce boundaries of belonging. A "we" can situate itself in alignment with culture and heritage, excluding those who do not share this tradition. (Beaman 2020, 19)

This seems to be especially prevalent in countries where there are high levels of state support for a specific religion, officially tying religious identity with state and national identity, and often making it more difficult in practice to accommodate religious minorities (Helbling and Traunmüller 2016). These sentiments of religious group threat also seem to be especially prevalent toward Muslim immigrants arriving in Europe and North America, to the extent that many in these host societies tend to directly associate immigration with Islam (Anderson and Antalíková 2014; Ribberink, Achterberg, and Houtman 2017).

Whitehead and Perry (2020) examine more specifically Christian nationalism in the United States, defined as "a cultural framework—a collection of myths, traditions, symbols, narratives, and value systems—that idealizes and advocates a fusion of Christianity with American civic life" (Whitehead and Perry 2020, 10); a cultural framework through which many Americans navigate their social world. This Christian nationalism ideology is not simply religious, it is also ethnic and political in nature; about power and maintaining a specific social order:

> … the "Christianity" of Christian nationalism represents something more than religion. … it includes assumptions of nativism, white supremacy, patriarchy, and heteronormativity, along with a divine sanction for authoritarian control and militarism. … Understood in this light, Christian nationalism contends that America has been and should always be distinctively "Christian" (reflecting this fuller, more nuanced sense of the term) from top to bottom—in its self-identity, interpretations of its own history, sacred symbols, cherished values, and public policies—and it aims to keep it that way. (Whitehead and Perry 2020, 10)

Symbolic, and at times physical, boundaries and hierarchies are drawn among natives and foreigners, whites and nonwhites, men and women, as well as heterosexuals and others, which encourages "… antipathy and mistrust toward those who do not meet the membership requirements of *native-born, Christian, and white*—namely, racial minorities, nonwhite immigrants, and Muslims" (Whitehead and Perry 2020, 16).

Although strong supporters of such Christian nationalism are getting older on average in the United States, declining in numbers and proportionally with younger cohort replacement (Whitehead and Perry 2020, 23–53), these types of Christian nationalist beliefs nevertheless remain present among some Millennials today. It is likely that at least some Millennial Christian cultural believers, who tend to hold onto religious identity more for family, heritage and cultural reasons, would hold these nationalist beliefs as well. This may be one of the main reasons why we see more negative word association scores toward many minorities among U.S. Millennial cultural believers, compared with only toward "immigrants" among the same group in Canada in Tables 5.3 and 5.4. Although Canadian versions of Christian nationalism do exist, they are not usually as widespread among the population on average and do not have nearly the same public presence and influence as in the United States.

Religious nationalism, especially Christian nationalism in Western contexts, is a key mechanism then driving more negative sentiments toward at least some minority groups in society. Yet, there is also a countervailing factor identified in the existing literature that could mitigate these more xenophobic attitudes among more active religious affiliates who are in regular contact with their religious group and hold stronger beliefs: the role of compassion beliefs taught by most major religious traditions toward one's fellow human beings (Knoll 2009; Schwartz and Huismans 1995). These compassion beliefs include an emphasis on values of brotherly and sisterly love for all, as well as of understanding, appreciation, benevolence, tolerance and protection for the welfare of all people, including for those coming from outside one's cultural and religious group. Whitehead and Perry (2020) find for example that, although stronger Christian nationalism beliefs and higher individual religiosity are positively correlated in the United States, the two variables nevertheless impact Americans' political views in the opposite direction when it comes to attitudes toward out-groups. Christian nationalism beliefs worsen attitudes toward out-groups such as Muslims, immigrants and racial minorities, whereas personal religiosity improves such attitudes on average.

This compassion and openness could also extend to spiritual seekers who still usually have some contact with organized religion, but who are also usually quite open to spiritual exploration outside their traditional religious group and for whom religious nationalism may not be as strong. Spiritual seekers may be more open and curious toward many other faith traditions, including minority faith traditions in the Western context, notably Eastern religions in their more Westernized forms (yoga, meditation, mindfulness activities, etc.). This in turn may make spiritual seekers more amenable to those who practice these minority religious traditions in society, as indicated in the more positive scores found among Millennial spiritual seekers in both the United States and Canada in Tables 5.3 and 5.4 toward most minority groups.

Bloom, Arikan, and Courtemanche (2015) argue that these opposing *religious nationalism* and *religious compassion* mechanisms are the reason that some researchers have found the effect of religiosity on attitudes toward immigrants and minorities to be curvilinear (Eisinga, Felling, and Peters 1990). As theorized by Bloom, Arikan, and Courtemanche (2015), those without any ties to religion (non-religious) would hold on average the most positive attitudes toward minorities, due to a lack of religious nationalism and religious group markers; marginal religious affiliates or cultural believers who have cultural identity ties to a religious tradition, but who do not have regular contact with a religious group nor very strong religious beliefs, would have on average the most negative attitudes toward minorities; and active affiliates who identify as part of a religious tradition and partake regularly in religious group activities, who are consequently regularly exposed to religious group teachings of compassion, and who often hold stronger religious beliefs would fall somewhere in between the nonreligious and cultural believers in their attitudes toward minorities (Figure 5.1).

There could also be other mechanisms contributing to this curvilinear effect of religiosity on attitudes toward immigrants. The nonreligious, those with no ties to organized religion, have historically been minorities in Western societies, and have only more recently begun to form majorities among younger demographics in some nations. It is possible then that in many countries and regions, the nonreligious still share a marginalized experience with other minority groups, including immigrants and religious minorities, and see members of these other minority groups more as allies to defend their minority rights in the face of a Christian majority, and thus share stronger inter-group bonds with them (Fetzer 1998; Knoll 2009). The nonreligious have also been shown to hold on average more progressive or left-wing value orientations in general compared with the more religious (Bruce 2003; Putnam and Campbell 2010; Wilkins-Laflamme 2016), as we previously saw in Chapter 3, which in turn may extend to more positive attitudes toward minorities among their ranks.

Additionally, it is especially active religious and spiritual affiliates in many current-day Western societies, including in Canada and the United States, who are coming into regular contact with non-Western immigrants and minorities, since many new arrivals and minorities originally from outside the West have higher levels of religiosity and spirituality than most members of the host society. The composition of active affiliates has diversified in recent decades in

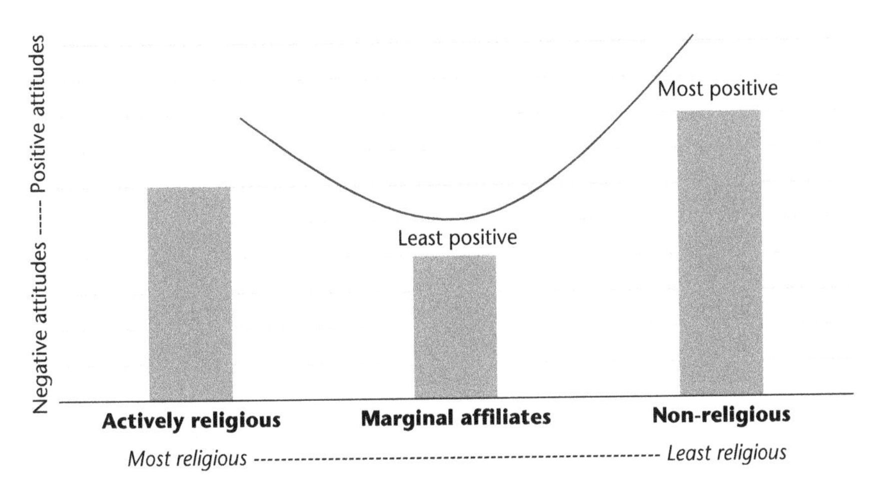

FIGURE 5.1 Theoretical curvilinear distribution of attitudes toward immigrants and minorities, among the actively religious, marginal affiliates and the nonreligious.

North America, Europe and Oceania, even among Christian groups (Beaman and Beyer 2008; Bramadat and Seljak 2008; Sherkat 2014), and so native-born religious and spiritual affiliates who regularly partake in religious and spiritual group activities have a higher likelihood of entering into constructive day-to-day contact with these more actively religious and spiritual minorities. This greater level of positive contact may thus help develop more positive attitudes toward minorities (Allport, Clark, and Pettigrew 1954; McLaren 2003; Schneider 2008), especially compared with cultural believers who are potentially much less likely to have this regular contact.

The Transitional Category

In some ways then, the presence of religious nationalism combined with an absence of regular exposure to religious compassion teachings and constructive contact with actively religious and spiritual minorities can lead larger numbers of cultural believers to hold stronger in- and out-group boundaries as well as more negative attitudes toward some minorities. Yet, in other ways, cultural believers can act as an intergenerational bridge category among the four types of individuals studied in this book; between the more religious and spiritual on the one hand, and the nonreligious on the other.

Some observers see the cultural believer, with their remaining religious identity, some beliefs and infrequent contact with religious groups, as a potential pool for religious revival. Since the cultural believer has not yet cut all ties to religion, many religious leaders who see their numbers in places of worship tantalizingly swell on holidays and special occasions ponder and plot how to engage these individuals during the rest of the year. For Canadian sociologist of religion Reginald Bibby, the cultural believer along with marginal affiliates in general still show signs of spiritual needs and interest in religion, and so Bibby posits that these individuals will return to active religiosity if and when religious groups can better meet these needs and interest (Bibby 2004; Bibby, Thiessen, and Bailey 2019).

And there are some instances of cultural believers becoming more involved with their religious group, especially during key moments in life, including when they have children and are thinking about how to raise them, or when they face particularly difficult hardships, or more generally once they have gone through the transitional years of emerging adulthood. Daniel, Solange, Emilie and William from the Québec life history interviews all mentioned how they were less religious during their CÉGEP years (Québec's equivalent of early college years), but returned to church more often afterward. Adam, who we met earlier in this chapter, was raised as a cultural Catholic during his childhood, but became more religious during his university years in part from his studies with the Dominicans in Ottawa, but also tied to life hardships including traversing a serious illness and witnessing a murder in his early twenties. Catholicism became a sanctuary, a safe space, for him through these hardships.

Yet, there are many more instances of persistent indifference and even dislike toward active religiosity among cultural believers. Thiessen (2015) for example found very little interest for more religious engagement among the marginal affiliates he interviewed, and virtually no active searching among these same marginal affiliates for a faith community that would meet their so-called spiritual needs among the many available religious groups in interviewees' local areas.

On the whole, the available empirical evidence in fact points to cultural believers being more often than not a transitional group away from active religiosity and spirituality, and instead toward nonreligion and toward post-Christian societies in North America; not a source of religious revival, but rather a delayed indicator of religious decline. This falls more in line with the secular transition framework introduced in Chapter 1. A reminder that, although secular transition theory sees modern Western contexts as unfavorable to the continued prevalence of identities, beliefs and behavior related to the supernatural and transcendent, religious decline can nevertheless be triggered at different moments in different regions due to specific socio-historical conditions. Once this decline is triggered in a given region at a given time though, a similar process begins to unfold where religiosity decreases across generations. For Voas (2008, 2009), British sociologist of religion and the main proponent of the secular transition framework, this process of religious decline often unfolds in a very similar way across regions and countries, even if its beginnings may be timed differently in different areas.

This process of secular transition involves an initial swell of marginal affiliates, or fuzzy fidelity as Voas coins individuals with irregular or mid-levels of religiosity, as many individuals transition from more active religiosity and spirituality to a more cultural believing relationship with religion. It is rare for an individual to go from being actively religious to being completely removed from all forms of religious and spiritual identity, belief and behavior over the course of one lifetime. Much more common is this slower, intergenerational transition from religious to fuzzy to secular. The popularity of more fuzzy forms of fidelity would be a transitional phase then in the larger process of decline: populations having been religiously socialized as children but no longer religiously active in the conventional sense as adults would be those especially likely to practice more individualized forms of personal spirituality and retain cultural ties to their religious tradition (Bruce 2017). As younger birth cohorts receiving less or no religious socialization as children begin to replace these older cohorts though, even these forms of less conventional religion and spirituality also begin declining cross-generationally.

Figure 5.2 is a visualization of these expected trends, based on secular transition theory. There would be an initial moment when religious decline is triggered, variable in timing depending on the national or regional context. This would then start the clock on a similar process unfolding as the years advance and as younger cohorts replace older ones: (1) a decline in the proportion of the population who is actively religious; (2) an initial swell in fuzzy fidelity as large segments of the population transition from active to more cultural forms of believing; (3) then a decline of fuzzy fidelity and a rise in nonreligiosity as larger segments of younger

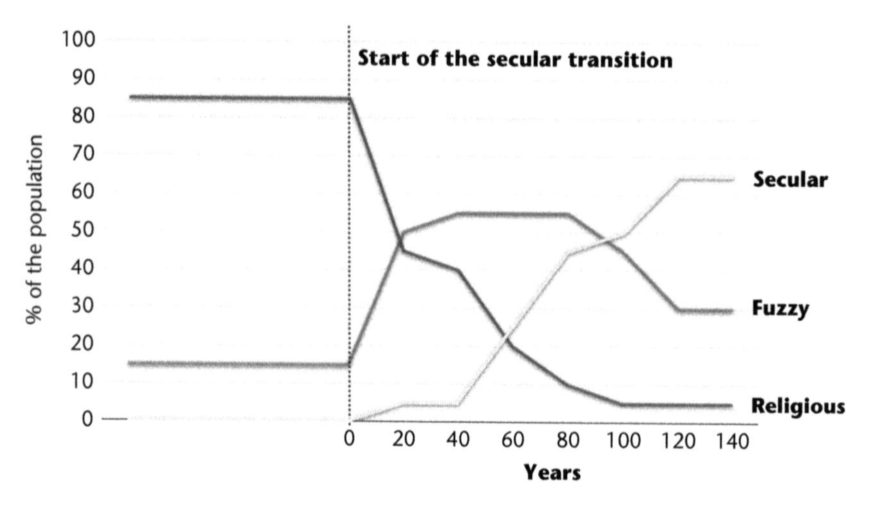

FIGURE 5.2 Theoretical distribution of religious, fuzzy and secular individuals, secular transition theory.

birth cohorts are raised without explicit religious socialization in markedly more secular social surroundings.

Figure 5.2 is a conceptual visualization: theoretically, not empirically, driven. Figures 5.3 and 5.4 in turn map the empirical trends of the population distribution of religious individuals (attend religious services at least once a month), marginal affiliates (religiously affiliated, but attend religious services less than once a month) and nonreligious individuals (no religious affiliation and attend religious services less than once a month) across Silent, Boomer, Gen X and Millennial birth cohorts in both the United States (Figure 5.3) and Canada (Figure 5.4) in 2018. From the results in Figure 5.3, we can see that the United States does not quite match the secular transition model in its empirical trends across birth cohorts, although it does come very close. There is a decline of the more religious population across 5-year birth cohorts; there is also a parallel rise in no religion; but the marginally affiliated population, roughly representing fuzzy fidelity here and at least partly made up of cultural believers, remains stable in proportional size across cohorts, rather than starting smaller, swelling in size among Boomer cohorts, and then declining in size among Gen X and Millennials. Most likely is that the transition from religious to marginal affiliation to no religion began later in the United States (especially in the 1990s; Sherkat 2014; Voas and Chaves 2016), but has developed more quickly since, foregoing the swell of fuzzy fidelity as such in more recent years among Boomers and Gen X.

This said, the American Millennial cohorts in Figure 5.3 still appear to be in a more advanced stage of secular transition. Millennials born between 1985 and 1989 are the first cohort in which the three categories of religious, marginal affiliate and no religion are roughly the same proportional size in 2018 in the United States, due to increases in the size of the no religion group. Then, for those

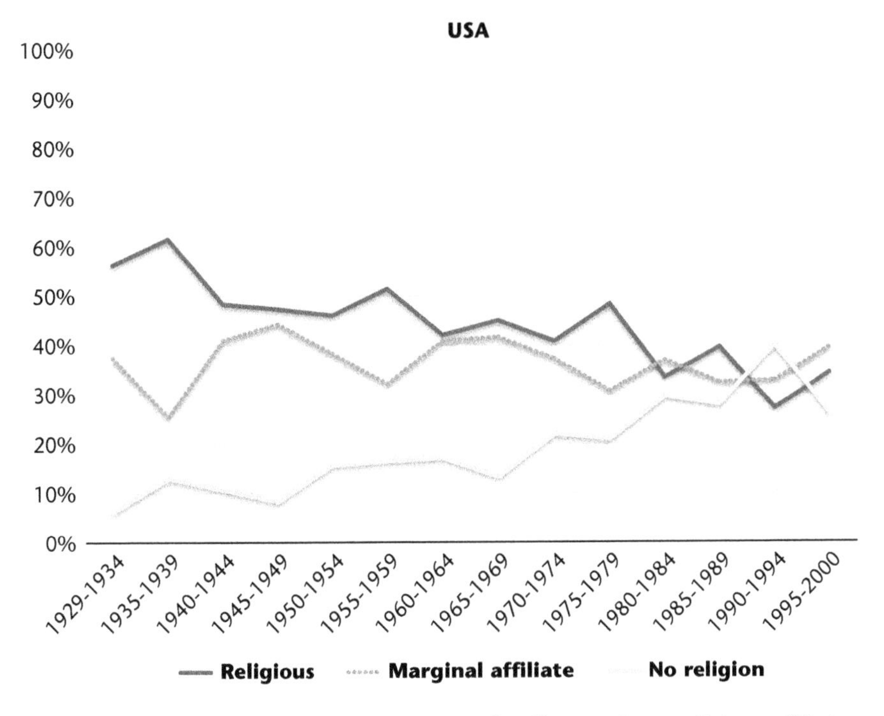

FIGURE 5.3 Distribution of religious, marginal affiliate and no religious affiliation individuals, by 5-year birth cohort, United States 2018.

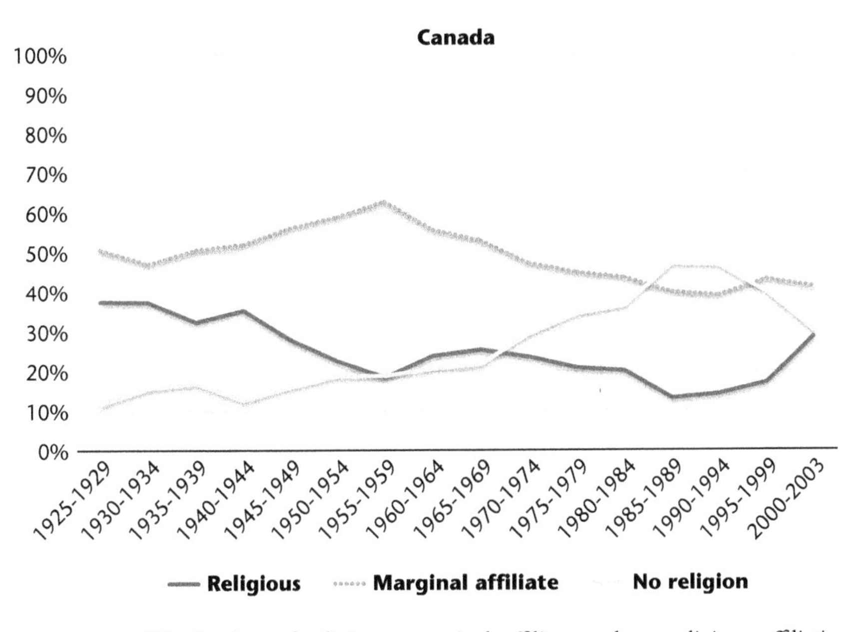

FIGURE 5.4 Distribution of religious, marginal affiliate and no religious affiliation individuals, by 5-year birth cohort, Canada 2018.

Millennials born between 1990 and 1994, no religion becomes the proportionally largest group, followed by marginal affiliates and then religious individuals. There is then a dip in no religion among the youngest Millennials, born between 1995 and 2000 (even referred to by some as the beginnings of Gen Z). Since many among this youngest cohort are still living with their parents at the time of the 2018 GSS, and that the transition from the parental household to one's own household in emerging adulthood is a crucial time for religious disaffiliation (Manning 2013; Thiessen and Wilkins-Laflamme 2017), we will have to wait and see if this younger group manages to catch up and even surpass older Millennial cohorts when it comes to no religion.

From the results in Figure 5.4, we can see that Canada more closely resembles the secular transition model. There is a decline of religious individuals across 1925–1994 birth cohorts. There is a swell in marginal affiliates among Boomer cohorts born between 1945 and 1964. There is a slight rise in no religion beginning with cohorts born in 1940–1944, and then a more rapid increase in no religion rates among cohorts born in the 1970s and 1980s.

We also see the same dip in rates of no religion and rise in rates of religious individuals for Canada among younger cohorts born from 1995 to 2003 as we do in the United States, bringing their rates closer to those of Gen X cohorts born in the 1970s. Again, this could be due to many of them not having left their original parental household yet and going through a life transition that is often conducive to religious disaffiliation. We may also be seeing the impact of the cultural generation gap here too when it comes to religiosity trends: with younger cohorts born from 1995 onward having higher rates of non-Judeao-Christian religions that also have higher rates of religious practice. We'll have to wait for future data and studies on late Millennials and early Gen Z for more certainty.

The transitional category of cultural believer, often part of the larger marginally affiliated group, seems then to have been more prevalent in generations prior to Millennials, especially in Canada. This speaks to the difficulty of passing on a nominal religious identity and some beliefs without a more structured institutional-, community- and family-based religious socialization during childhood.

Millennials now seem to represent a tipping point where nonreligion has become larger and more of the norm among their birth cohorts. Cultural believers are still present among Millennials, but now in smaller numbers. The cultural believer is a bridge between categories in a sense, but a bridge where most of the traffic so far has been moving in one direction across generations: from religious and spiritual toward nonreligion. Let us now explore this last category of the nonreligious Millennial in more detail in Chapter 6, the end point on the other side of the bridge for many young adults.

Notes

1 See Wilkins-Laflamme (2017) where I compare this love-hate relationship with religion in Québec with socio-historical dynamics in another Canadian region: British Columbia.

2 See CBC Montreal article "Crucifix Represents Christian Values but isn't a Religious Symbol, Québec's Incoming Premier Says," October 11, 2018. https://www.cbc.ca/news/canada/montreal/quebec-francois-legault-crucifix-religious-symbols-1.4858757

References

Allport, Gordon Willard, Kenneth Clark, and Thomas Pettigrew. 1954. *The Nature of Prejudice*. Cambridge, MA: Addison-Wesley.

Anderson, Joel, and Radka Antalíková. 2014. "Framing (Implicitly) Matters: The Role of Religion in Attitudes toward Immigrants and Muslims in Denmark." *Scandinavian Journal of Psychology* 55 (6): 593–600. doi:10.1111/sjop.12161

Arnett, Jeffrey Jensen. 2015. *Emerging Adulthood: The Winding Road from the Late Teens through the Twenties*. New York, NY: Oxford University Press.

Banyasz, Alissa M., David M. Tokar, and Kevin P. Kaut. 2016. "Predicting Religious Ethnocentrism: Evidence for a Partial Mediation Model." *Psychology of Religion and Spirituality* 8 (1): 25–34. doi:10.1037/rel0000020

Beaman, Lori G. 2020. *The Transition of Religion to Culture in Law and Public Discourse*. New York, NY: Routledge.

Beaman, Lori G., and Peter Beyer, eds. 2008. *Religion and Diversity in Canada*. Leiden: Brill.

Bello, Valeria. 2016. "Inclusiveness as Construction of Open Identity: How Social Relationships Affect Attitudes towards Immigrants in European Societies." *Social Indicators Research* 126: 199–223. doi:10.1007/s11205-015-0881-1

Bibby, Reginald W. 2004. *Restless Gods: The Renaissance of Religion in Canada*. Toronto, ON: Novalis.

Bibby, Reginald W. 2011. *Beyond The Gods & Back: Religion's Demise and Rise and Why It Matters*. Lethbridge, AB: Project Canada Books.

Bibby, Reginald W., Joel Thiessen, and Monetta Bailey. 2019. *The Millennial Mosaic: How Pluralism and Choice Are Shaping Canadian Youth and the Future of Canada*. Toronto, ON: Dundurn.

Blogowska, Joanna, and Vassilis Saroglou. 2013. "For Better or Worse: Fundamentalists' Attitudes toward Outgroups as a Function of Exposure to Authoritative Religious Texts." *International Journal for the Psychology of Religion* 23 (2): 103–125. doi:10.1080/87567555.2012.687991

Bloom, Pazit Ben-Nun, Gizem Arikan, and Marie Courtemanche. 2015. "Religious Social Identity, Religious Belief, and Anti-Immigration Sentiment." *American Political Science Review* 109 (2): 203–221. doi:10.1017/S0003055415000143

Blumer, Herbert. 1958. "Recent Research on Race Relations: United States of America." *International Social Science Bulletin* 10: 403–477.

Bouchard, Gérald, and Charles Taylor. 2008. "Fonder l'avenir. Le temps de la conciliation." *Rapport final intégral, Commission de consultation sur les pratiques d'accommodement reliées aux différences culturelles*. https://numerique.banq.qc.ca/patrimoine/details/52327/66284 (accessed 3 May 2022).

Bramadat, Paul, and David Seljak, eds. 2008. *Christianity and Ethnicity in Canada*. Toronto, ON: University of Toronto Press.

Bruce, Steve. 2003. *Politics and Religion*. Cambridge, UK: Polity.

Bruce, Steve. 2017. *Secular Beats Spiritual: The Westernization of the Easternization of the West*. New York, NY: Oxford University Press.

Christiano, Kevin J. 2007. "The Trajectory of Catholicism in Twentieth-Century Québec." In *The Church Confronts Modernity: Catholicism Since 1950 in the United*

States, Ireland and Québec, edited by Leslie Woodcock Tentler, 21–61. Washington, DC: Catholic University of America Press.

Daniels, Joseph P., and Marc Von Der Ruhr. 2005. "God and the Global Economy: Religion and Attitudes Towards Trade and Immigration in the United States." *Socio-Economic Review* 3 (3): 467–489. doi:10.1093/SER/mwi020

Doebler, Stefanie. 2014. "Relationships between Religion and Intolerance towards Muslims and Immigrants in Europe: A Multilevel Analysis." *Review of Religious Research* 56 (1): 61–86. doi:10.1007/s13644-013-0126-1

Eisinga, Rob, Albert Felling, and Jan Peters. 1990. "Religious Belief, Church Involvement, and Ethnocentrism in the Netherlands." *Journal for the Scientific Study of Religion* 29 (1): 54–75. doi:10.2307/1387030

Fetzer, Joel S. 1998. "Religious Minorities and Support for Immigrant Rights in the United States, France, and Germany." *Journal for the Scientific Study of Religion* 37 (1): 41–49. doi:10.2307/1388028

Gauvreau, Michael. 2005. *The Catholic Origins of Québec's Quiet Revolution, 1931–1970.* Montréal, QC: McGill-Queen's University Press.

Goplen, Joanna, and E. Ashby Plant. 2015. "A Religious Worldview: Protecting One's Meaning System through Religious Prejudice." *Personality and Social Psychology Bulletin* 41 (11): 1474–1487. doi:10.1177/0146167215599761

Helbling, Marc, and Richard Traunmüller. 2016. "How State Support of Religion Shapes Attitudes toward Muslim Immigrants: New Evidence from a Sub-National Comparison." *Comparative Political Studies* 49 (3): 391–424. doi:10.1177/0010414015612388

Kehrberg, Jason E. 2007. "Public Opinion on Immigration in Western Europe: Economics, Tolerance, and Exposure." *Comparative European Politics* 5: 264–281. doi:10.1057/palgrave.cep.6110099

Knoll, Benjamin R. 2009. ""And Who Is My Neighbor?" Religion and Immigration Policy Attitudes." *Journal for the Scientific Study of Religion* 48 (2): 313–331. doi:10.1111/j.1468-5906.2009.01449.x

Koussens, David, and Catherine Foisy, eds. 2018. *Les catholiques québécois et la laïcité.* Québec, QC: Presses de l'Université Laval.

Laplante, Benoît. 2006. "The Rise of Cohabitation in Québec: Power of Religion and Power over Religion." *Canadian Journal of Sociology* 31 (1): 1–24. doi:10.2307/20058678

Lemieux, Raymond, and Jean-Paul Montminy. 2000. *Le catholicisme québécois.* Québec, QC: Les Éditions de l'IQRC, Collection Diagnostic.

Leon McDaniel, Eric, Irfan Nooruddin, and Allyson Faith Shortle. 2011. "Divine Boundaries: How Religion Shapes Citizens' Attitudes toward Immigrants." *American Politics Research* 39 (1): 205–233. doi:10.1177/1532673X10371300

Manning, Christel. 2013. "Unaffiliated Parents and the Religious Training of their Children." *Sociology of Religion* 74 (2): 149–175. doi:10.1093/socrel/srs072

McLaren, Lauren M. 2003. "Anti-Immigrant Prejudice in Europe: Contact, Threat Perception, and Preferences for the Exclusion of Migrants." *Social forces* 81 (3): 909–936. doi:10.1353/sof.2003.0038

Meunier, E.-Martin, and Jacob Legault-Leclair. 2021. "Nones and Catholics in Québec: The Social Reconfiguration of Bill 21." *Secular Studies* 3: 93–117. doi:10.1163/25892525-bja10013

Meunier, E.-Martin, and Jean-François Nault. 2014. "Vers une sortie de la religion culturelle: les transformations du catholicisme au Québec et au Canada (1968-2008)."

In *La longue transition du catholicisme. Gouvernementalité et influence*, edited by François Mabille, 27–63. Paris: Éditions du Cygne.

Meunier, E.-Martin, and Jean-Philippe Warren. 2002. *Sortir de la « Grande noirceur ». L'horizon personnaliste de la Révolution Tranquille*. Sillery: Éditions de Septentrion.

Meunier, E.-Martin, and Sarah Wilkins-Laflamme. 2011. "Sécularisation, catholicisme et transformation du régime de religiosité au Québec. Étude comparative avec le catholicisme au Canada (1968-2007)." *Recherches Sociographiques* 52 (3): 683–729. doi:10.7202/1007655ar

Milot. Micheline. 1991. "Le catholicisme au creuset de la culture." *Studies in Religion* 20 (1): 51–64.

Milot, Micheline. 2009. "Laïcité au Canada. Liberté de conscience et exigence d'égalité." *Archives de Sciences Sociales des Religions* 146: 61–79. doi:10.4000/assr.21233

Pew Research Center. 2018. *Being Christian in Western Europe*. Accessed December 28, 2018. http://www.pewforum.org/2018/05/29/being-christian-in-western-europe/

Putnam, Robert, and David Campbell. 2010. *American Grace: How Religion Divides and Unites Us*. New York, NY: Simon and Schuster.

Ribberink, Egbert, Peter Achterberg, and Dick Houtman. 2017. "Secular Tolerance? Anti-Muslim Sentiment in Western Europe." *Journal for the Scientific Study of Religion* 56 (2): 259–276. doi:10.1111/jssr.12335

Scheepers, Peer, Merove Gijsberts, and Evelyn Hello. 2002. "Religiosity and Prejudice Against Ethnic Minorities in Europe: Cross-National Tests on a Controversial Relationship." *Review of Religious Research* 43 (3): 242–265. doi:10.2307/3512331

Schneider, Silke L. 2008. "Anti-Immigrant Attitudes in Europe: Outgroup Size and Perceived Ethnic Threat." *European Sociological Review* 24 (1): 53–67. doi:10.1093/esr/jcm034

Schwartz, Shalom H., and Sipke Huismans. 1995. "Value Priorities and Religiosity in Four Western Religions." *Social Psychology Quarterly* 58 (2): 88–107. doi:10.2307/2787148

Sherkat, Darren E. 2014. *Changing Faith: The Dynamics and Consequences of Americans' Shifting Identities*. New York, NY: New York University Press.

Thiessen, Joel. 2015. *The Meaning of Sunday: The Practice of Belief in a Secular Age*. Montréal, QC: McGill-Queen's University Press.

Thiessen, Joel, and Sarah Wilkins-Laflamme. 2017. "Becoming a Religious None: Irreligious Socialization and Disaffiliation." *Journal for the Scientific Study of Religion* 56 (1): 64–82. doi:10.1111/jssr.12319

Voas, David. 2008. "The Continuing Secular Transition." In *The Role of Religion in Modern Societies*, edited by Detlef Pollack and Daniel V. A. Olsen, 25–48. New York, NY: Routledge.

Voas, David. 2009. "The Rise and Fall of Fuzzy Fidelity in Europe." *European Sociological Review* 25 (2): 155–168. doi:10.1093/esr/jcn044

Voas, David, and Mark Chaves. 2016. "Is the United States a Counterexample to the Secularization Thesis?" *American Journal of Sociology* 121 (5): 1517–1556. doi:10.1086/684202

Whitehead, Andrew L., and Samuel Perry. 2020. *Taking America Back for God: Christian Nationalism in the United States*. New York, NY: Oxford University Press.

Whitney, William B., and Pamela Ebstyne King. 2014. "Religious Congregations and Communities." In *Emerging Adults' Religiousness and Spirituality*, edited by Carolyn McNamara Barry and Mona M. Abo-Zena, 133–151. New York, NY: Oxford University Press.

Wilkins-Laflamme, Sarah. 2014. "Towards Religious Polarization? Time Effects on Religious Commitment in US, UK and Canadian Regions." *Sociology of Religion* 75 (2): 284–308. doi:10.1093/socrel/sru001

Wilkins-Laflamme, Sarah. 2016. "Secularization and the Wider Gap in Values and Personal Religiosity between the Religious and Non-Religious." *Journal for the Scientific Study of Religion* 55 (4): 717–736. doi:10.1111/jssr.12307

Wilkins-Laflamme, Sarah. 2017. "Religious-Secular Polarization Compared: The Cases of Québec and British Columbia." *Studies in Religion* 48 (2): 166–185. doi:10.1177/0008429817695662

Wilkins-Laflamme, Sarah. 2018. "Islamophobia in Canada: Measuring the Realities of Negative Attitudes towards Muslims and Religious Discrimination." *Canadian Review of Sociology* 55 (1): 86–110. doi:10.1111/cars.12180

Young, Pamela Dickey, and Heather Shipley. 2020. *Identities under Construction: Religion, Gender, and Sexuality among Youth in Canada*. Kingston, ON: McGill-Queen's University Press.

Zubrzycki, Geneviève. 2016. *Beheading the Saint: Nationalism, Religion, and Secularism in Québec*. Chicago, IL: University of Chicago Press.

6

THE NONRELIGIOUS MILLENNIAL

According to the latent class typology first discussed in Chapter 2 and derived from the 2019 MTS data, over a third of Canadian Millennials and over a quarter of American Millennials are nonreligious. This group of individuals has lower than average levels of religious childhood socialization, and score low as young adults on all religiosity and spirituality indicators, including those in Table 6.1. Frequent religious service attendance and prayer as well as religious affiliation: virtually absent among this category. Belief in God or a higher power and frequent unchurched spiritual activities: rare phenomena among the nonreligious, with only about one fifth holding this belief and fewer still taking part in such activities.

As well as scoring much lower on all religiosity and spirituality measures than religious, spiritual seeker and cultural believer Millennials, the nonreligious also show signs of some socio-demographic distinctions from the other three categories. The results in Table 6.1 indicate a higher rate of women among nonreligious Millennials, especially compared with religious young adults. There are fewer ethnic and racial minorities among the nonreligious than among the religious, spiritual seekers and cultural believers. In both Canada and the United States, there are slightly lower rates of university education among nonreligious Millennials than among the religious, a reversal of trends from earlier generations when the nonreligious tended to have higher levels of education (Mayrl and Oeur 2009). In the United States specifically, the nonreligious Millennial does have higher rates of university education than the cultural believer though, as well as proportionally fewer young adults in the lowest household income bracket. In Canada, the nonreligious are found proportionally less in rural areas than cultural believers, but proportionally more in rural areas than religious or spiritual seeker Millennials. In the United States, a larger proportion of nonreligious Millennials reside in rural areas, more so than among the religious, spiritual seekers and cultural believers.

DOI: 10.4324/9781003217695-6

TABLE 6.1 Characteristics of nonreligious Millennials

	Nonreligious Millennials	Rest of Millennials
% weekly or more frequent childhood religious or spiritual education	33%	64%
% monthly or more frequent religious service attendance as adults	4%	49%
% weekly or more frequent prayer as adults	2%	53%
% belief in God or a higher power	20%	82%
% religiously affiliated	0%	84%
% monthly or more frequent unchurched spiritual activities as adults	15%	32%
Mean age	26.2 years	26.1 years
% female	51%	48%
% non-White ethnic background/race	17%	40%
% university educated	23%	27%
% with less than $20,000 household income	15%	18%
% rural residents (pop. < 50,000)	28%	27%

Source: MTS 2019.

Defining and Measuring Something That Is Not

As discussed in the previous chapter, this category of the nonreligious has been growing in size over the past few generations in both the United States and Canada. It now represents the largest category of Millennials in Canada (36%; see Figure 2.12 in Chapter 2), and although not yet the largest in the United States it still makes up a sizable proportion there as well (26%). What does it mean to be "nonreligious" exactly? How do we define the concept of nonreligion? Like when defining key concepts in any discipline, there is much discussion and debate surrounding the nature of nonreligion in the fields of sociology of religion, religious studies, and the burgeoning subfield of nonreligion and secularity studies.

To first understand "nonreligion," we have to outline a definition of its direct opposite: religion. So far in this book, the definitions of religion and spirituality I have been using have mostly been pragmatic, hinging on the survey questions in the 2019 MTS as well as the other surveys analyzed, and on how interviewees define religion and spirituality themselves. I have ended up here mainly with a more substantive definition of religion and spirituality, focused more on its content rather than functionality, referring especially to identities, beliefs and behaviors related to the superempirical and transcendent. In Chapter 4, I made the distinction between more traditional-looking institutional and organized forms of such identities, beliefs and behaviors (religion) vs. their less conventional forms (spirituality). Given the nature of the data examined, the focus has also mainly been on the individual, studied through the lens of surveys and interview data, rather than on larger social institutions and cultural frameworks, although all are interrelated.

Classically, some of the key 19th-century founding fathers of sociology established a conceptual binary between the opposite categories of religion and nonreligion. Whether it be Max Weber's enchanted world vs. disenchanted world dichotomy, or Emile Durkheim's sacred and profane binary, these were crucial in the establishment and development of the fields of sociology of religion and religious studies. Such binary conceptions of religion and nonreligion, or of the religious and the secular, were the product of a social context that was coming to understand religion more and more as a social domain separate from others; more and more distinct from health, education, politics, work and the economy in the late stages of 19th-century Western societies. The religious/secular binary was also used for years afterward in the social scientific disciplines, and can still be found today in some studies.

However, as our understanding of individual-level belonging, believing and behavior developed, so too did the sophistication of our measures. Now, we often utilize a multidimensional continuum of levels of religiosity if we can, rather than bluntly dividing individuals into two camps only. Elements of such a continuum can be seen in the categories I work with in this book. Religious, spiritual seeker, cultural believer and nonreligious Millennials can be seen in many ways as falling at different points on the same religious/nonreligious spectrum, with perhaps a few distinct elements separate from this spectrum thrown into the mix once in a while.

Yet, as Cragun and McCaffree (2021) point out, having a religious or spiritual identity, set of beliefs and practices is something; not having them, so being nonreligious at the other end of the continuum as the term is used in the present book, is not something. Defining some Millennials by what they are not, so not religious nor spiritual, thus nonreligious, is a negative or subtractive definition. It is an absence category in a sense. By contrast, Lee (2012) as well as Cragun and McCaffree (2021) advocate for a shift in focus to the more positive and substantive elements of nonreligion; "… a new research program that examines the positive substance of nonreligious worldviews and identities along with their effects on behavior" (Cragun and McCaffree 2021, 8–9). Nonreligious individuals have other worldviews and identities, and Cragun and McCaffree (2021) feel that should be the focus of studies on the nonreligious moving forward.

I hear and agree with this call to research action made by Lee (2012), Cragun and McCaffree (2021), as well as by many others in the subfield of nonreligion and secularity studies. At times in the coming pages of this chapter, I will be exploring some of the substantive elements that make up the internal diversity of worldviews, identities and behaviors within the category of the nonreligious Millennial. This said, I also think that "nonreligion" as a concept and phenomenon only makes sense and is only present in relation to religion, in relation to that religiosity continuum, in line with what Lee (2015) and Quack (2014) argue. Away from religion, an individual is not thinking of it, and is not in relation to it. This individual would be identifying in different ways and taking part in different activities that we already have other names for, such as outdoor person, traveler, student, pet lover, career driven, mother or father, social media influencer and so forth. These other substantive elements of their lives are very important and often fascinating to study, but they are not the focus of my research here. As my PhD student Zachary Munro (2021) argues, it is only at the border regions, where an individual is confronted with others who are more religious and a social milieu where religion is more present that this individual would define themselves as not being part of this life world that is "religion": "Nonreligious interaction with religion forces a discursive positioning of being in-relation to religion but distinct from it" (Munro 2021, 28).

I use the category of nonreligious here, in a book focused on religion and spirituality among Millennials, to highlight that many emerging adults today just do not do religion and spirituality as I substantively define these terms as well as according to what research participants themselves say about their lives. We can speak of nonreligion among the Millennial generation, because many members of these younger birth cohorts, even if nonreligious themselves, still encounter religion and spirituality in the media and pop culture, among older living generations, and among many minority cultural groups and races who form large subsections of the Millennial generation in both the United States and Canada and among whom religion and spirituality are much more present. Consequently, nonreligious Millennials do end up thinking about themselves as nonreligious at least on some occasions when they still encounter religion and find themselves in that border region of having contact with religion without being part of it.

If the nonreligious category continues to grow among even younger Gen Z cohorts and beyond, it is conceivable that at some point the category will no longer make sense to use. With less and less likelihood of encountering religion and spirituality in their everyday lives as these become rarer and rarer phenomena, individuals would not find themselves in border regions anymore where they would have to engage with religion, but rather would be completely removed from thinking about religion and spirituality as well as thinking of themselves as nonreligious. Nonreligion is a concept that is used in contexts where religion and spirituality are more normalized. When religion is no longer the norm, but rather the exception, using a term like nonreligion makes less sense, a categorization that will become less and less relevant if trends continue (Cragun and McCaffree 2021).

Yet, Millennials still seem to be a transition generation when it comes to nonreligion. Religion and spirituality are still present enough among subsections of the generation as well as in the social world around them from prior generations that the border regions between religion and nonreligion still exist in many social milieus. Religion, spirituality and nonreligion currently coexist in U.S. and Canadian societies among Millennials, and so this coexistence is the main name of the game for this generation at this point in time. This said, the scales seem to be tipping in nonreligion's favor more and more among the Millennial generation, which I will demonstrate in the next section with intergenerational religious and nonreligious switching and retention trends between Millennials and their parents.

(Non)Religious Switching and Retention from Parent to Millennial[1]

As trends of mainline Protestant decline, conservative Protestant growth, as well as the rise in rates of nonreligion developed across time and cross-generationally over the past 60 years in the United States, so too did research in the sociology of religion documenting, exploring and explaining these changes through rates of religious switching and retention. Although many Americans and Canadians stick with the inherited religion of their parents (Newport 2006; Pew Research Center 2015; Putnam and Campbell 2010; Sherkat 2014), others instead switch their religion for a variety of reasons. These reasons can include childhood socialization into a different (non)religion, a change in socioeconomic, community or theological preferences as adults within a (non)religious marketplace (Barro, Hwang, and McCleary 2010; Loveland 2003; Putnam and Campbell 2010; Sherkat and Wilson 1995), the pull of other family and friendship ties (Roof 1989; Sherkat 2014), geographic mobility (Sherkat 2014, 76–79; Smith and Sikkink 2003) or to match a spouse's (non)religion in initially exogamic marriages and partnerships (Hadaway and Marler 1993; Hoge, Johnson, and Luidens 1995; Musick and Wilson 1995; Newport 1979; Sherkat 1991). Along with the demographic realities of fertility, migration and mortality, switching and retention are key factors in a (non)religious group's numeric and proportional growth, stability or decline—and so are crucial to tracking and understanding evolving religious landscapes, including among the Millennial generation.

Almost all the religious switching and retention literature to date lumps together the phenomena of conversion (switching from one religion to another, or from nonreligion to a religion) and disaffiliation (leaving a religion for nonreligion).[2] For example, Putnam and Campbell (2010, 160) find an increase in rates of religious switching among younger Gen X and Millennial birth cohorts, and make the argument that these younger cohorts find themselves in a more open religious marketplace than their parents and grandparents: "One result of all these changes is that individual choice has become virtually as important as inheritance in explaining Americans' religious affiliations, raising the stakes for religious marketing and innovation." Yet, these authors include disaffiliation as a type of switching, and then seem to neglect this fact when making their general argument of greater religious mobility. I put forward the argument here, supported by my MTS 2019 data, that when intergenerational change does happen for Millennials, it is first and foremost a change of disaffiliation (leaving organized religion) within a social location much more post-Christian than that of their parents and grandparents. Unlike most of the existing religious switching and retention literature, I understand the phenomena of conversion and disaffiliation as distinct, with often distinct causes and implications for society, and so measure them separately here.

Due to the nature of the MTS 2019 data, I focus on inherited (non)religion from respondents' parents. Key variables for this analysis include respondent's religious (non)affiliation as a young adult: "What, if any, is your religion?" Respondents were given 18 categories to select from for this question, including aboriginal/Indigenous spirituality, Buddhism, Chinese religion, Christianity—Catholic, Christianity—Orthodox, Christianity—Protestant (prompted to specify denomination or church), Christianity—other (prompted to specify tradition, group or church), Hinduism, Islam, Judaism, Sikhism, other religion (prompted to specify), multiple religions (prompted to specify), no religion—agnostic, no religion—atheist, no religion—secular humanist, no religion—spiritual with no religion, and no religion—no particular preference. These categories were then grouped into the RELTRAD categorization for most of the analyses in this section (evangelical Protestant, mainline Protestant, Black Protestant, Jewish, Catholic, other religion and no religion; Steensland et al. 2000), with Black Protestants, Jewish and other smaller affiliations grouped together at times into a larger "other religions" category due to small sample size.

Parents' (non)religion(s) are also crucial for this section's results, declared by the respondent in their answers to the two questions "When you were growing up as a child (between the ages of 5–12 years old), what was your mother's primary religion?" and "When you were growing up as a child (between the ages of 5–12 years old), what was your father's primary religion?" A homogenous (non)religion parental background is defined as a respondent either having two parents of the same (non)religion when growing up, or declaring the (non)religion of one parent while not knowing the (non)religion of the other (or not having another parent). A mixed (non)religious parental background is defined as a respondent having two parents of different (non)religions when growing up.[3] Inherited (non)religion, along with intergenerational conversion and disaffiliation, are measured by comparing the respondent's (non)religious group they are affiliated with as a young adult with their declared parents' (non)religion(s).

Intergenerational Disaffiliation

Overall in the MTS data, 31% of Canadian and 37% of U.S. young adults switched between the groups of Indigenous spiritualties, Buddhism, Chinese religion, Catholicism, Christian Orthodox, mainline Protestantism, evangelical Protestantism, Black Protestantism, Hinduism, Judaism, Islam, Sikhism, other religions (grouped together) and no religion. In other words, these respondents have no parent from the (non)religious group that they themselves identify with as young adults. When broken down between disaffiliation and conversion, 24% of the Canadian sample disaffiliated (parents had a religion, but the respondent did not as a young adult), compared with 23% of the U.S. sample; and only 7% of the Canadian sample converted (different religion from their parents as a young adult, or have a religion as a young adult when their parents did not), compared with 14% in the United States.[4]

Pew Research Center (2015, 33) estimates that 34% of all adult Americans have switched from their childhood religion, and Sherkat (2014, 60) puts this rate at 32%. For 18–29 years old Americans in 2010, Pew estimated switching rates to be at 42% overall, with the disaffiliation rate reaching 18% (Pew Research Center 2010, 88). However, since these studies focus on childhood (non)religion (rather than parents' (non)religion) to measure switching in adult years, these works are not directly comparable with the MTS 2019 data. Putnam and Campbell's (2010, 136) study is more comparable to mine, and these two researchers put the proportion of all adult Americans who have switched from the religion of their parents at just over one quarter. When compared with my results here, this indicates that Millennials' intergenerational switching rates, especially for disaffiliation, are higher than among older Americans; a finding also supported by Newport (2006), Pew Research Center (2010), Sherkat (2014) and Smith and Snell (2009).

Based on these results so far, it is first important to note that the main story here is still one of inherited (non)religion. A majority of Millennials (69% in Canada and 63% in the United States) affiliate with the (non)religion of at least one of their parents. As sociologist Frank Newport (1979, 549) stated: "We live … in a nation of church-like religious groupings in which membership is largely a between-generational hand-me-down, produced from within." Yet, when switching does occur among Millennials, disaffiliation is by far the most common change from their parents' religion. This is even more the case in Canada than in the United States: conversion rates are slightly higher south of the 49th parallel (in line with findings from Haskell, Burgoyne, and Flatt 2016 as well as Sherkat 2014), but still not high enough to offset the larger trends of Millennial inherited (non)religion and disaffiliation in the United States.

Table 6.2 contains more detailed results regarding the distribution of parental (non)religion and respondent's (non)religion as a young adult between the five broad categories of Catholicism, mainline Protestantism, evangelical Protestantism, other religions and no religion, to better parse out the overall winners and losers when it comes to conversion and disaffiliation among Millennials. Column (a) contains the percentage of young adult respondents coming from a homogenous (non)religion parental background of the group in question; column (b) contains the percentage of young adult respondents coming from a mixed (non)religion parental background with one of their parents from the group in question; column (c) in turn contains the percentage of respondents who identify with the group in question at the time of the survey (as young adults); and column (d) indicates the proportional intergenerational gains or losses for the group in question. If a (non)religious group has the same share of young adult affiliates as the share of respondents coming from the homogenous (non)religion parental background in question, in addition to half of those coming from a mixed (non)religion parental background of the group in question, then it is considered not to have experienced any proportional intergenerational loss or gain (0%).

TABLE 6.2 Parental and young adult (non)religious group, respondents 18–35 years old, Canada and the United States, 2019

Canada					*United States*			
	(a) % of respondents with two parents (or single-parent family) from group	*(b) % of respondents with one parent from group, in a mixed (non) religious family*	*(c) % of respondents who affiliate with group as young adults*	*(d) % gain or loss for group: ((c/(a + 0.5b)) * 100) – 100*	*(a) % of respondents with two parents (or single-parent family) from group*	*(b) % of respondents with one parent from group, in a mixed (non) religious family*	*(c) % of respondents who affiliate with group as young adults*	*(d) % gain or loss for group: ((c/(a + 0.5b)) * 100) – 100*
Catholic	38%	13%	30%	−33%	35%	11%	29%	−28%
Mainline Protestant	5%	6%	4%	−45%	5%	4%	5%	−27%
Evangelical Protestant	3%	1%	3%	−14%	7%	2%	9%	+2%
Other religion	20%	6%	20%	−13%	22%	8%	20%	−22%
No religion	16%	10%	43%	+102%	13%	11%	37%	+102%

Source: Millennial Trends Survey. *N* Canada = 1,452. *N* USA = 934. Percentages weighted to be representative of the 18–35 Canadian and U.S. populations. Any discrepancies in the table are due to rounding.

The results in Table 6.2 indicate that Catholicism is suffering large intergenerational losses between Millennials and their parents: a loss of 33% overall in its proportional share of respondents across a generation in Canada, compared with a 28% loss in the United States. Mainline Protestants are also characterized by these large intergenerational losses: a loss of 45% in Canada and 27% in the United States. This even after mainline Protestants have already experienced substantial declines among earlier generations in both countries (Bibby 2017; Pew Research Center 2015; Putnam and Campbell 2010; Sherkat 2014).

In Canada, evangelical Protestants as well as other religions are also experiencing intergenerational losses overall, but not as large as among Catholics and mainline Protestants. In the United States, the losses for "other religions" are higher at 22% (compared with 13% in Canada), potentially due to the different compositions of this broad category in the two countries. For example, the MTS Canadian subsample contains lower rates of Orthodox Christians and Black Protestants, and higher rates of Hindus, Muslims and Sikhs than the U.S. subsample. Evangelical Protestants are faring better in the United States though, by making enough gains from intergenerational conversions to at least offset any of their losses from out-conversion or disaffiliation (+2% overall).

Nevertheless, the group that is making by far the most intergenerational gains from switching among Millennials is the "no religion" category: a growth rate of 102% in both countries. Although their calculation methods vary from those in this chapter, our findings generally match those from other recent studies (Jones, Cox, and Banchoff 2012; Pew Research Center 2015; Putnam and Campbell 2010; Reimer and Hiemstra 2018; Sherkat 2014), while trends of disaffiliation are more pronounced here due to our focus on Millennial cohorts only.

In our previous work, Joel Thiessen and I identify four key biographic factors that drive disaffiliation, based on Joel's interview data from Alberta, Canada as well as other existing qualitative studies from the United States (Thiessen and Wilkins-Laflamme 2017, 2020). These factors do not always lead to disaffiliation among all individuals, but are identified by those who have disaffiliated as crucial to that process. Sometimes individuals would only identify one of these factors as being especially important for their disaffiliation; for others, a combination of them came into play.

The first key factor is parents giving choice to their Millennial children when it comes to religious matters. Many individuals describe how their parents had raised them within a religious tradition as children (would take them to church, would pray and read the Bible at home, etc.), with sometimes varying levels of intensity and frequency, but would then give them the choice during their tween and teen years if they wanted to continue with this faith lifestyle. Some chose to continue with it, but others, especially among whom faith had never been that salient for them personally, took the opportunity to break off their ties to religion. In prior generations and time periods, that choice would not likely have been given by parents and surrounding social ties, and the social pressure to remain actively religious even if not personally all that faithful would have been greater. Now, however, values of expressive individualism and internal authority are reflected in many parents' decisions, even among many religious parents, to give this choice and autonomy to their children during their development. Jayden, born in 1994, interviewed in Seattle, Washington in 2018 and who we first heard from in Chapter 3, identifies this as a key moment in the development of her nonreligious agnostic identity:

> … the thing in my family was like, you have to go to church until you're 15, so I think I was 16 when I told her [that I wasn't going to church anymore]. Until you were 15, and then when you were 15 you were allowed to choose. … then I stopped going [to church]. I was like, "I'm not going anymore." … I've struggled with, like, trying to believe in God for, like, a long time. Because my parents believe really strongly in God. And a lot of people possibly do. It just like, it just never, like, really, like resonated, or like made logical sense to me, so I just, like, logically have not been ever really able to bring that together, and like, when I try to, it just like, it drives me crazy. I'm just like, this does not make sense to me. … Being able to leave the church gave me a lot of freedom to be myself.

Georges, born in 1992, interviewed in St-Julie, Québec and another self-identified agnostic, recounts how he was raised more as a cultural Catholic: he was baptized, did his first communion and his parents brought him and his older sister to Mass for special holidays when they were kids, especially at Easter and Christmas. Yet, later in their childhood Georges and his sister said "no more!" and they stopped going to Mass for special holidays. They both felt visiting the church was no longer necessary to celebrate these holidays, and their parents went along with it. Georges and his sister still had to go to church with his dad's parents in Florida though during his youth when visiting. Georges and his sister did not have the same choice to stay away from church when with their paternal grandparents.

A second factor driving disaffiliation, not unrelated to the first, is having what Joel and I call intellectual disagreements with religion. Some would not share core beliefs or would disagree with moral and social teachings of their religious tradition, and so would often get disillusioned and choose to leave religion altogether, rather than finding another religious group to be part of. This can take many forms, including a dislike of exclusivist religious claims (one Truth; i.e. the Right beliefs) in a plural and diverse society, a lack of belief in God or a higher power, a disagreement with socially conservative religious teachings on sexuality and the body, etc. In the West Coast and Québec focus groups and interviews, this factor played an especially important role for LGBTQ+ research participants leaving religion. Caitlin, born in 1998, who self-identifies as nonreligious and who took part in one of the Portland, Oregon focus groups in 2018, explains:

> I remember I was 16 and there were speakers that would come [when in church] and tell us that being gay was a sin, just like, 'You know, you don't

> hit your Uncle Jack in the head with a pogo stick, just like you know that being gay is not okay.' So, sitting there, I was just astonished that the most liberal Catholic church in Eugene is still saying this?

Max, born in 1995, nonreligious and interviewed in Monteál, Québec in 2018 describes how he left the Catholic Church at around the age of 13–14 as he found out he was gay and religion was no longer for him. He mainly left because of the Church's stance toward the LGBTQ+ community, but also because he considers himself pro Science, holding a scientific and rationalist worldview, which he sees in opposition to religion.

Many others experience our third factor driving disaffiliation: meeting new people and forming new relationships with less or nonreligious friends and new family. These social influences would pull some individuals away from religion, either by normalizing nonreligion for the individual (and sometimes stigmatizing religion for them) or by simply occupying their time with other activities which eventually led the individual to leave religion behind. For example, Avril, nonreligious and who we first met in Chapter 4, recounts in her interview how her extended family used to all go to Midnight Mass together on Christmas Eve during the earlier years of her childhood. Then, her uncle began dating a woman who later would become Avril's new aunt. This aunt was nonreligious, and did not want to attend Midnight Mass with Avril's grandparents. The extended family as a whole consequently diminished this annual activity to still be able to celebrate the holiday together at home and not cause any discord.

Finally, a fourth factor for disaffiliation is life transitions. When individuals would move away from their original parental household, geographic area and religious group, or when they would experience the death of a family member or other loved one who had been the main driver of religious activity in their lives, for example, some individuals would leave religion to the wayside rather than renewing their religiosity once they had reached the other side of their life transition. Sarah, born in 1986, nonreligious and who we first heard from in Chapter 2, identifies a combination of this factor and others listed above as part of her pathway to leaving religion. Her quote in Chapter 2 highlighted her dislike of Christian teachings. Let us now look at more of that narrative to illustrate these multiple factors triggering her religious disaffiliation:

> Growing up, my parents, probably when I was about 5, started going to a Presbyterian church. Because neither of them had grown up going to church and they didn't feel deprived but they wanted to make sure that their children had some sort of spiritual grounding. I remember being the kid who would always ask really difficult questions and was never really satisfied with the answers. But we had a good library in the church so I read as much as I could read. I even went and I got confirmed when I was 14. I had to learn a lot, I memorized a lot of things for that. It wasn't common that people just get confirmed in the Presbyterian Church. But

> even so, as I was going through that, I knew that I didn't take any of the things I read as literal truth in the same way that people from my church did, because for me religion had always been about the symbolism, and then going to church had been about family. And about community. And so, when I stopped, when I went away and went to college, I lost that connection to that family, so there was no real reason for me to go to a church, because all the—the ritual is fine, and some of the songs are really comforting because they're part of my childhood. But, for me, the whole—in the teaching of Christianity, there's just not much there for me. It doesn't serve my needs, and there's too much I find really repulsive, and really antagonistic towards queer people like me, and towards women, and just unsuitable to living a life in this world, where we need to get along with each other, and where we need to really respect our relationships with other creatures and other beings, whether or not they're sentient. And so I've always erred more towards science and looking for ways to show that empathy is more important than religion. Or empathy is more important than winning. That if we want to survive, we should be looking out for the best for everybody. So even though I'm not religious, I have very strong convictions about morality and justice and the common humanity among people.

Although religious disaffiliation can happen at any point during an individual's lifetime, what Joel and I kept finding and what I see here with many of the nonreligious West Coast and Québec research participants is that the late teen and early emerging adulthood years are often crucial for this change. Hiemstra, Dueck, and Blackaby (2018) and Smith et al. (2014, 159) also find this in their respective studies. This is especially the case for Millennials who come from parental households that were somewhat but not all that religious to begin with, as illustrated in many of the interviewee quotes listed above. Many of the previously identified factors driving disaffiliation appear during young adulthood: greater independence from parents, greater focus on self-understanding and self-development, new and growing social networks, as well as many life transitions. As I discussed in Chapter 1, emerging adulthood is a period in an individual's life usually defined by mobility and transitions, and for some these life changes are the moments when disaffiliation crystalizes and becomes part of their lived reality.

Strong Intergenerational Transmission of Parental Nonreligion

To summarize so far, whereas intergenerational transmission of religion remains present among many Millennials, intergenerational disaffiliation is nonetheless also an important trend among this generation in North America; more important than it has ever been among living adult cohorts today. Only an estimated 48% of the religiously unaffiliated young adult respondents from Canada and 45% from the United States have at least one nonreligious parent. This means that, more

Millennials in my study have joined the ranks of "no religion" than inherited this identity from their parents.

Yet, despite a slim majority of Millennial religious nones being intergenerational disaffiliates, retention rates for those who do have nonreligious parents are also very high. I want to take a bit of time and space here to explore this other way of acquiring nonreligion: inheriting nonreligion from one or both parents.

Figure 6.1 illustrates the results of where respondents from two types of nonreligious parental backgrounds end up as young adults in terms of their own (non)religious belonging. Eighty-nine percent of Canadian Millennials and 91% of

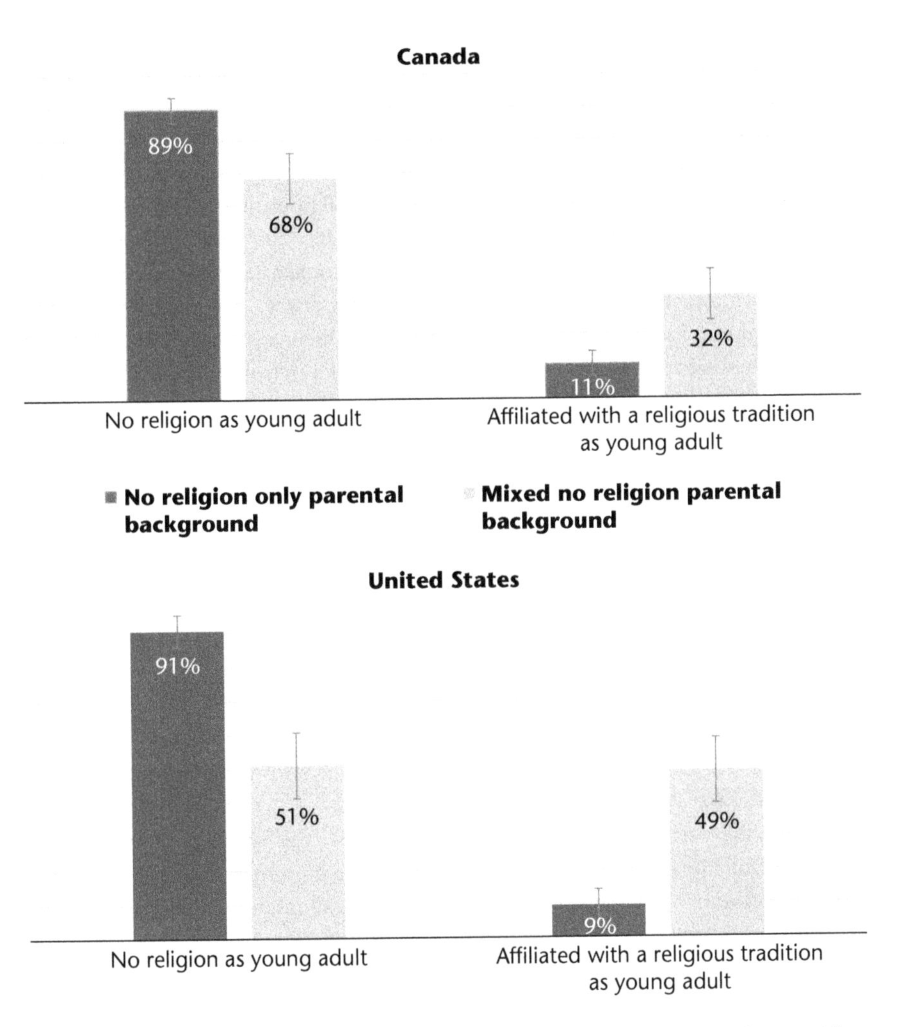

FIGURE 6.1 Religious (non)affiliation among 18–35 years old respondents with a nonreligious parental background (in %), 2019, with CI (95%)

Source: Millennial Trends Survey. Percentages weighted to be representative of 18–35 Canadian and U.S. populations

U.S. Millennials in the MTS sample who come from a nonreligious only family remain religiously unaffiliated as young adults. Among the Canadian and U.S. respondents who come from mixed nonreligion/religion parental backgrounds, 68% are religiously unaffiliated as young adults in Canada, compared with 51% in the United States.

Putnam and Campbell (2010, 139) have previously shown intergenerational retention rates among the religiously unaffiliated were only around 30% for cohorts reaching adulthood between the 1920s and 1950s in the United States, but have been climbing steadily ever since. With their 2006 data, they put retention rates of religious nonaffiliation among Millennial birth cohorts between 65% and 80%. With my 2019 MTS data, these rates reach an even higher threshold of 91% among American Millennials coming from homogenous nonreligious parental backgrounds. This is impressive when we consider that most nonreligious parents do not expressly aim to socialize their children strictly as nonreligious, but rather take a more "hands-off" choice-based approach when it comes to religion. Nonreligious parents especially will often leave religious matters open and up to their children. As Zuckerman, Galen, and Pasquale (2016, 127) note, "Secular people tend toward nonconformity, independence, and antiauthoritarianism … to base their maturational goals on personal independence, and their childrearing philosophy emphasizes autonomy rather than obedience to authority." Yet, our results show that the vast majority of Millennial children from nonreligious parents nevertheless go on to be religiously unaffiliated themselves as young adults in recent years. This further supports the finding in Thiessen and Wilkins-Laflamme (2020, 53) that:

> … modeling a 'hands-off' approach to religion in the home does, in fact, pass on a particular individualist and secular orientation to religion and the world more generally. Such an approach strengthens the likelihood that someone who identifies as a religious none will raise children who also say they do not identify with a religion.

Without any direct exposure to religion coming from parents during childhood, individuals will rarely pick religion up themselves, even if in theory they could if they wanted to.

These very strong intergenerational retention rates among religiously unaffiliated Millennials also indicate the extent to which nonreligion has become the default option of sorts among their generation's social milieu. In the past, the pull from surrounding social ties and their environment in general used to be strong enough to convert many adults to a religion who were initially socialized as nonreligious. Now, the opposite seems to be playing out among Millennials in both Canada and the United States. Now, nonreligion persists among most who were raised without religion from their parents, and also pulls in many who had a more religious upbringing. The "no religion" group not only saw the most proportional intergenerational gains by means of disaffiliation but is also bolstered by very strong intergenerational retention rates among those from a nonreligious parental background—a first among living adult generations.

Different Ways of Being Nonreligious

I realize I have mainly been discussing religious nonaffiliation in the previous section when it comes to switching and retention, rather than the broader non-religiosity category touching a wide variety of religiosity and spirituality beliefs, behaviors and identities that I first introduced in Chapter 2 and began the present chapter with here. Nonetheless, the majority of Millennial respondents who have no religious affiliation also find themselves within the category of nonreligious Millennial: an estimated 81% of the religiously unaffiliated are also nonreligious Millennials in Canada; and 67% in the United States. These nonreligious young adults share in common extremely low levels of religiosity and spirituality, despite experiencing various biographic pathways into nonreligion. Yet, they also have different ways of being nonreligious and considering religion from their non-religious viewpoint. As the category of nonreligious individual has grown in proportional size cross-generationally, its internal diversity has also grown as more and more different types of people move away from religion and spirituality (Cragun and McCaffree 2021; Strawn 2019).

Some seek out communities of like-minded nonreligious individuals for social support and to build, reinforce and share their views and nonreligious identities (Cimino and Smith 2014; LeDrew 2015; Smith 2013, 2017). Researchers such as Brewster (2014), LeDrew (2015) and Smith (2013) add that atheist and secular humanist organizations can be helpful spaces for atheists to "come out." When facing stigmatization and discrimination for their non-religious identities, individuals may seek out community to cope with psy-chological stress, to mitigate an otherwise marginalized and stigmatized status, and to build a new positive social support system. The primary goals of atheist and secular humanist organizations are to gather with others who think similarly about the world, to reinforce their shared nonbelieving worldview and, in some cases, to actively oppose the influence and spread of religion in society by creating a secular social movement and strengthening the secular voice and impact in society (Niose 2012). This is especially the case in contexts where normative pressures surrounding religion remain, where religious ideas and leaders hold more political sway, and where it may be difficult to find non-religious individuals among one's existing family and social networks (Garcia and Blankholm 2016; Wilkins-Laflamme and Thiessen 2020).

Five percent of nonreligious Millennials in the United States and 2% in Canada take part in meetings or activities with an atheist, humanist or secularist organi-zation at least once a year according to the 2019 MTS data; 16% in the United States and 14% in Canada post on social media about atheist, humanist, secularist or nonbelief values, views or practices; and 19% in the United States and 41% in Canada read or watch online content on atheism, humanism or secularism.

Yet, many more nonreligious Millennials do not take part in such atheist, humanist or secularist activities. Joel Thiessen and I have previously found that on the one hand it is especially religious disaffiliates who had a religious upbringing during childhood who are the most likely to take part in atheist and secular humanist organized activities. These individuals are more likely to face social pressures and discrimination for leaving religion as young adults from their family, friends and social environments. They also often continue to appreciate a certain kind of in-person community support they grew up with among their prior religious group, just minus God (Wilkins-Laflamme and Thiessen 2020). On the other hand, the cradle nonreligious who had little or no religious upbringing as children and who do not find themselves in contexts where religion is still very normative are the ones who are often completely disinterested in religious, atheist and secular humanist activities alike. Consequently, the distinction between religious disaffiliate, where someone has more religious parents and was raised within a religious tradition only to leave it later in life, and cradle nonreligious, where someone was raised with little or no religion and has always been nonreligious, is an important one here.

As indicated by the results in Tables 6.3 and 6.4, it is among nonreligious Millennials who were regularly religiously socialized as children, who broke away from a religious group or tradition in their teen or young adult years, that we find the more negative associations with the word "religion" and the more positive associations with the word "atheism" (as well as the word "spirituality" in the United States). By contrast, for those nonreligious Millennials who had little regular religious socialization as children, their mean word association scores for "religion" and "atheism" alike are closer to 0, indicating fewer negative or positive associations with either of these concepts.[5] Rather than most cradle nonreligious Millennials showing signs of anti-religion sentiment, indifference seems to be more prevalent among this subgroup. More of this subgroup also selected the "no religion—no particular preference" option when asked about their religious

TABLE 6.3 Mean word association scores by frequency of childhood religious socialization, among nonreligious U.S. Millennials, MTS 2019

	Nonreligious U.S. Millennials		
	Received religious or spiritual education at school, at home or at a place of worship at least once a month on average between the ages of 5 and 12 years old	*Received religious or spiritual education at school, at home or at a place of worship less than once a month on average between the ages of 5 and 12 years old*	*All nonreligious U.S. respondents*
Religion	−39	−17	−25
Spirituality	20	8	12
Atheism	22	13	16

TABLE 6.4 Mean word association scores by frequency of childhood religious socialization, among nonreligious Canadian Millennials, MTS 2019

	Nonreligious Canadian Millennials		
	Received religious or spiritual education at school, at home or at a place of worship at least once a month on average between the ages of 5 and 12 years old	*Received religious or spiritual education at school, at home or at a place of worship less than once a month on average between the ages of 5 and 12 years old*	*All nonreligious Canadian respondents*
Religion	−39	−20	−28
Spirituality	34	36	35
Atheism	26	14	19

affiliation in the 2019 MTS, compared with religiously socialized disaffiliates, over the specific identities of agnostic and spiritual with no religion in the United States, and agnostic and atheist/secular humanist in Canada (see results in Tables 6.5 and 6.6).

It is a kind of indifferent openness that is found among many nonreligious Millennials, especially among the cradle nonreligious: a "you do you" sentiment indicative of this generation, while the "I do me" is done without any reference to religion or spirituality for many. Kelly, a cradle nonreligious Millennial from the

TABLE 6.5 Nonreligious identity distribution by frequency of childhood religious socialization, among nonreligious U.S. Millennials, MTS 2019

	Nonreligious U.S. Millennials		
	Received religious or spiritual education at school, at home or at a place of worship at least once a month on average between the ages of 5 and 12 years old	*Received religious or spiritual education at school, at home or at a place of worship less than once a month on average between the ages of 5 and 12 years old*	*All nonreligious U.S. respondents*
Agnostic	38%	18%	25%
Atheist or secular humanist	33%	36%	34%
Spiritual with no religion	17%	7%	11%
No particular preference	13%	39%	30%

TABLE 6.6 Nonreligious identity distribution by frequency of childhood religious socialization, among nonreligious Canadian Millennials, MTS 2019

	Nonreligious Canadian Millennials		
	Received religious or spiritual education at school, at home or at a place of worship at least once a month on average between the ages of 5 and 12 years old	*Received religious or spiritual education at school, at home or at a place of worship less than once a month on average between the ages of 5 and 12 years old*	*All nonreligious Canadian respondents*
Agnostic	21%	19%	20%
Atheist or secular humanist	34%	25%	29%
Spiritual with no religion	9%	13%	11%
No particular preference	35%	43%	40%

Pacific Northwest, illustrated this in her quote that we saw in Chapter 2. Claire, born in 1985, raised with no religion and now living in Montréal, Québec, provides another example:

> … here [in Montréal] you quickly realise that there are lots of other things [referring to religious groups, when compared with her childhood city of Rimouski, Québec], even if you knew, here you see it and it's in the open, there's openness and not closure. So I think in this sense, it [her life transition to Montréal] led to more openness, more possibilities, more choices, but not necessarily a desire to go further, to explore further nor to participate more [in religion]. I never felt that need.

Georges, who we heard from earlier in this chapter, makes a point of mentioning in his interview that everyone has their own spirituality, that it is a personal thing that he respects although he does not know much about religion.

A number of nonreligious Millennial interviewees, including Claire, also make a point of mentioning that this openness only extends to those religious individuals not trying to convert them. Religious individuals trying to convert is not cool in their eyes, breaking the "you-do-you" principle, although none of these cradle nonreligious interviewees mentioned ever actually experiencing a conversion attempt from a religious person.

Many nonreligious interviewees, including both Claire and Georges, also mentioned they had some (not a lot of) friends more into religion than themselves, but usually also admitted they did not talk much if at all about religion with these or other friends. Along a similar line, Kelly, who we first met in Chapter 2, says:

> … I can really only think of one friend who identifies as religious, and she doesn't, I wouldn't even consider it being a huge identifier for her. I think she goes to church very rarely, I think she went for Easter this year. So no, not, it's never something we've really talked about. I think it's something that's been approached but nothing that we've ever, like, dug deep into and had full conversation about. Because she's really the only one that I can, that I know of that actively goes to church. And by actively I mean maybe six times a year. … It's [religion] never been something that's deterred me from being somebody's friend. … it's never made me uncomfortable. I would say, if I'm being 100% honest, if they are overly religious or, like, pushing it upon me or, you know, saying things that are, "oh like, God this, God that." Maybe that would make me less likely to become a solid grounded friendship with them. But other wise no, I don't mind that my friend goes to church. She's invited me once and I politely declined. Saying I didn't want to spend my time doing that. But no, it would never prevent me from being somebody's friend or something.

Among the nonreligious Millennials in the 2019 MTS who had little to no religious socialization as children, only 8% in the United States and 6% in Canada said they discussed religion or spirituality at least once a month with their close friends.

This widespread indifference toward religion among many nonreligious Millennials was also identified by Smith and Snell (2009) in their study, these researchers giving this group of indifferent nonreligious individuals their own category. This indifference goes beyond just toward religion though, and also seems to extend to nonreligion. In the 2019 MTS, 70% of 18–35 years old respondents who said they had no religious or spiritual beliefs and who had little to no religious socialization as children also said that not having these beliefs was not very or not at all important for their lives.

For the cradle nonreligious, especially those finding themselves in contexts where nonreligion is considered "normal," religion does not even enter into their frame of mind for the most part. Religion for them is this bizarre thing, removed from most of their family and social networks, that they probably only see in the media once in a while in its more sensationalized forms. Many of the cradle nonreligious have not even developed the language to conceptualize religious experiences and to discuss them with others, let alone to even think of religious activities as a possibility to occupy some of their time. This is almost akin to someone who has never been exposed to skydiving, for example, and so does not even think of it as a possible activity for a Friday evening or a Sunday morning nor is able to or cares to discuss its various realities and experiences. This is possible when it comes to religion for the Millennial generation because social change among previous generations has led to many social environments where this nonreligion is common and socially acceptable in both the United States and Canada. The more widespread it becomes, the more individuals in turn will grow up with this as the "new normal" away from any religion as well as away from any border regions where nonreligion exists in relation to religion.

This does not mean that the nonreligious are empty in mind and spirit, nor lead empty lives. They instead have alternative worldviews, identities, attitudes, behaviors and sources of meaning. Many nonreligious worldviews are subjectively constructed, but also share in common more naturalistic explanations of phenomena (Cragun and McCafree 2021, 9). Work, online subcultures, travel, nature and the environment, everyday experiences, sexual orientation (especially for sexual minorities), racial identity (especially for racial minorities) and nationality often take on greater importance for the nonreligious. Their more left-leaning socio-political values and issue stances often play a key boundary-marking role to delineate their self-identities. Life meaning for the nonreligious is often self-made, rather than dictated by a higher being or universe, and often comes from what Drescher (2016) calls the four Fs: friends, family, food and fido (pets). I could also add a fifth F here, for "function" or one's occupation or work in life.

The need for specifically atheist or secular humanist activities and organizations may be much less prevalent with the growing number of social environments where nonreligious individuals do not experience discrimination and social penalties for being nonreligious, where they are not confronted with a religious majority with different values and issue positions to themselves, and where they already have access to friends and family who are also nonreligious and share their worldview.

Many atheist and secular humanist organizations are now seeing their membership age and are struggling to attract younger individuals, similar to many religious groups for that matter. On top of a general decline in popularity among the Millennial generation of many organizations with more in-person and traditional membership structures, organized atheist and secular humanist groups may find it difficult to flourish in contexts and generations where nonreligion becomes less stigmatized, and growing numbers of individuals are raised without religion and do not care as much about religious/nonreligious issues. If the shared goal of atheist and secular humanist organizations is to normalize nonreligion in society (Cragun and Manning 2017), what happens when that goal is achieved? They may have sowed the seeds of their own destruction in this sense.

***

Overall, we found less evidence in this chapter for Millennials circulating within a religious marketplace with fewer constraints and enabling greater rates of conversion, and much more evidence for a majority of intergenerational switcher Millennials just leaving organized religion altogether. This finding, coupled with the very high rates of intergenerational retention of nonreligion found here, are indicators that nonreligion has become a default option of sorts among the

Millennial generation; that their social environments have become much more secular and post-Christian, compared with that of their parents and grandparents. The vast majority of individuals raised with no religion remain unaffiliated as young adults now, and many more coming from more religious backgrounds switch into nonreligion. This is not just happening in Canada where religiosity indicators have long been weaker and declining since the 1960s (Bibby 2017; Clarke and Macdonald 2017), but also in the United States. I will not go so far as to call the Millennial generation post-Christian full stop here, since a majority in both countries still affiliate with a religion and the most popular of these religions remains Christianity, but I will say that we see a trend moving in this post-Christian direction with this younger generation: growing religious pluralism, as well as growing nonreligion.

Those who were raised in a religious tradition but disaffiliated sometime during their teens or young adult years show signs of remaining closer in relation to religion than the cradle nonreligious. On the one hand, disaffiliates seem to care more about their nonreligion, and have more negative associations with religion within this border region. The cradle nonreligious, on the other hand, seem much more indifferent to all of it, focused on their other worldviews, identities and behaviors completely outside of what can be substantively defined as religious or spiritual. This distinction between religious disaffiliation and cradle nonreligion is a relatively new dynamic among the Millennial generation, being the first adult birth cohorts that have substantial groups of both among them.

The impact of these nonreligious life pathways and identities are likely to last a lifetime, with the cradle nonreligious especially much less likely to engage with religion and nonreligion as they grow older. As the number of nonreligious Millennials has grown from prior generations, so too will the number of their children raised without religious socialization. This means that the proportion of cradle nonreligious is likely to grow in both the United States and Canada among Gen Z and beyond, and more individuals will grow up not only completely removed from religion itself but also from the border region where nonreligion remains in relation with religion.

Notes

1 Findings from this section were initially published in Wilkins-Laflamme (2020).
2 With the notable exceptions of Jones, Cox, and Banchoff (2012), Newport (2006), Sherkat (2014, 50–89) and Suh and Russell (2015).
3 Respondents who indicated they did not know both their mother's and father's (non)religion(s), or did not answer both questions, were excluded from the analyses (128 respondents, or 5% of the full sample). Due to space limitations, outcomes between mother's and father's (non)religion are not compared here. Similar to findings in the existing literature (Arweck and Nesbitt 2010; Nelsen 1990), in the MTS data intergenerational retention rates are lower among mixed (non)religion parental backgrounds. This said, retention rates are a bit higher among mixed (non)religious families where the mother identifies with the group in question, compared with only the father identifying with this group.

4 In some ways, these are lowballed conversion and disaffiliation estimates. In these estimates, I do not include conversions between mainline Protestant denominations (notably between Anglicans, Episcopalians, Presbyterians, members of the United Church of Canada, Lutherans, more liberal Baptists, and Methodists), nor between the many evangelical Protestant denominations and groups, nor between the many smaller religious groups in the "other religions" category; only conversions between the 14 major groups listed in the previous paragraph. I also do not account for switches between the different nonreligious identities (agnostic, atheist, secular humanist, spiritual with no religion, and no particular preference); only to and from "no religion" in general. I also count having one parent in a mixed (non)religious family from the group the respondent is affiliated with as a young adult as inherited religion (not converted, nor disaffiliated), along with coming from a homogenous (non)religion background of the same group. Additionally, I am only measuring religious (non)affiliation of the respondent when they are young adults. For those who have not yet switched, they have the rest of their lifetime to potentially do so, although late teen and young adult years have been shown to be the most common time when switching does occur (Sherkat 2014; Thiessen and Wilkins-Laflamme 2017).

In other ways, these are highballed estimates of conversion and disaffiliation. I am purposefully comparing a respondent's religious (non)affiliation as a young adult with their parents' (non)religion(s) here, not with the (non)religion the respondent was raised in as a child (which for some may be different than their parents and the one they have kept into adulthood, especially when it comes to nonreligion). And once again, religious (non)affiliation of the respondent is only measured at one time point during their young adult years. Those who have converted or disaffiliated at this time point have the rest of their lives to potentially go back to the (non)religion of their parents.

5 This is also reflected in the larger proportion of cradle nonreligious Millennials not selecting "religion" as having positive or negative associations for them: 63% of the cradle nonreligious Millennials in the 2019 MTS did not select this word either way, compared with only 45% of nonreligious disaffiliates.

References

Arweck, Elisabeth, and Eleanor Nesbitt. 2010. "Growing Up in a Mixed-Faith Family: Intact or Fractured Chain of Memory?" In *Religion and Youth*, edited by Sylvia Collins-Mayo and Pink Dandelion, 167–174. Aldershot, UK: Ashgate.

Barro, Robert, Jason Hwang, and Rachel McCleary. 2010. "Religious Conversion in 40 Countries." *Journal for the Scientific Study of Religion* 49 (1): 15–36. doi:10.1111/j.1468-5906.2009.01490.x

Bibby, Reginald W. 2017. *Resilient Gods: Being Pro-Religious, Low Religious, or No Religious in Canada*. Vancouver, BC: University of British Columbia Press.

Brewster, Melanie E., ed. 2014. *Atheists in America*. New York, NY: Columbia University Press.

Cimino, Richard, and Christopher Smith. 2014. *Atheist Awakening: Secular Activism and Community in America*. New York, NY: Oxford University Press.

Clarke, Brian, and Stuart Macdonald. 2017. *Leaving Christianity: Changing Allegiances in Canada since 1945*. Montréal, QC: McGill-Queen's University Press.

Cragun, Ryan, and Christel Manning. 2017. "Introduction." In *Organized Secularism in the United States*, edited by Ryan Cragun, Lori Fazzino, and Christel Manning, 1–12. Berlin: De Gruyter.

Cragun, Ryan, and Kevin McCaffree. 2021. "Nothing Is Not Something: On Replacing Nonreligion with Identities." *Secular Studies* 3 (1): 7–26. doi:10.1163/25892525-bja10017

Drescher, Elizabeth. 2016. *Choosing Our Religion: The Spiritual Lives of America's Nones*. New York, NY: Oxford University Press.
Garcia, Alfredo, and Joseph Blankholm. 2016. "The Social Context of Organized Nonbelief: County-Level Predictors of Nonbeliever Organizations in the United States." *Journal for the Scientific Study of Religion* 55 (1): 70–90. doi:10.1111/jssr.12250
Hadaway, C. Kirk, and Penny Long Marler. 1993. "All in the Family: Religious Mobility in America." *Review of Religious Research* 35 (2): 97–116. doi:10.2307/3511778
Haskell, David Millard, Stephanie Burgoyne, and Kevin N. Flatt. 2016. "Mainline Denominational Switching in Canada: Comparing the Religious Trajectories of Growing and Declining Church Attendees." *Canadian Journal of Sociology* 41 (4): 493–524.
Hiemstra, Rick, Lorianne Dueck, and Matthew Blackaby. 2018. *Renegotiating Faith: The Delay in Young Adult Identity Formation and What It Means for the Church in Canada*. Toronto, ON: Faith Today Publications. Accessed December 15, 2021. www.RenegotiatingFaith.ca
Hoge, R., Benton Johnson, and Donald A. Luidens. 1995. "Types of Denominational Switching among Protestant Young Adults." *Journal for the Scientific Study of Religion* 34 (2): 253–258. doi:10.2307/1386770
Jones, Robert P., Daniel Cox, and Thomas Banchoff. 2012. *A Generation in Transition: Religion, Values, and Politics among College-Age Millennials. Findings from the 2012 Millennial Values Survey*. Public Religion Research Institute and Georgetown University's Berkley Center for Religion, Peace, and World Affairs. Accessed December 15, 2021. https://repository.library.georgetown.edu/bitstream/handle/10822/1052347/120419BC-PRRIMillennialValuesSurveyReport[1].pdf?sequence=1
LeDrew, Stephen. 2015. *The Evolution of Atheism: The Politics of a Modern Movement*. New York, NY: Oxford University Press.
Lee, Lois. 2012. "Research Note: Talking about a Revolution: Terminology for the New Field of Non-Religion Studies." *Journal of Contemporary Religion* 27 (1): 129–139. doi:10.1080/13537903.2012.642742
Lee, Lois. 2015. *Recognizing the Non-Religious: Reimagining the Secular*. New York, NY: Oxford University Press.
Loveland, Matthew T. 2003. "Religious Switching: Preference Development, Maintenance, and Change." *Journal for the Scientific Study of Religion* 42 (1): 147–157. doi:10.1111/1468-5906.00168
Mayrl, Damon, and Freeden Oeur. 2009. "Religion and Higher Education: Current Knowledge and Directions for Future Research." *Journal for the Scientific Study of Religion* 48 (2): 260–275. doi:10.1111/j.1468-5906.2009.01446.x
Munro, Zachary. 2021. "Proximity of Borders: Locating Nonreligion and Secularity." *Secular Studies* 3 (1): 27–48. doi:10.1163/25892525-bja10014
Musick, Marc, and John Wilson. 1995. "Religious Switching for Marriage Reasons." *Sociology of Religion* 56 (3): 257–270. 10.2307/3711822
Nelsen, Hart M. 1990. "The Religious Identification of Children of Interfaith Marriages." *Review of Religious Research* 32 (2): 122–134. doi:10.2307/3511760
Newport, Frank. 1979. "The Religious Switcher in the United States." *American Sociological Review* 44 (4): 528–552. doi:10.2307/2094586
Newport, Frank. 2006. "A Look at Religious Switching in America Today." *Gallup News Service*. Accessed September 11, 2019. https://news.gallup.com/poll/23467/look-religious-switching-america-today.aspx
Niose, David. 2012. *Nonbeliever Nation: The Rise of Secular Americans*. New York, NY: Palgrave Macmillan.

Pew Research Center. 2010. *Millennials: A Portrait of Generation Next. Confident. Connected. Open to Change*. Accessed December 2, 2020. https://www.pewsocialtrends.org/2010/02/24/millennials-confident-connected-open-to-change/

Pew Research Center. 2015. *America's Changing Religious Landscape*. Accessed September 11, 2019. https://www.pewforum.org/2015/05/12/americas-changing-religious-landscape/

Putnam, Robert, and David Campbell. 2010. *American Grace: How Religion Divides and Unites Us*. New York, NY: Simon and Schuster.

Quack, Johannes. 2014. "Outline of a Relational Approach to 'Nonreligion.'" *Method &Theory in the Study of Religion* 26 (4–5): 439–469. doi:10.1163/15700682-12341327

Reimer, Sam, and Rick Hiemstra. 2018. "The Gains/Losses of Canadian Religious Groups from Immigration: Immigration Flows, Attendance and Switching." *Studies in Religion* 47 (3): 327–344. doi:10.1177/0008429818754786

Roof, Wade Clark. 1989. "Multiple Religious Switching: A Research Note." *Journal for the Scientific Study of Religion* 28 (4): 530–535. doi:10.2307/1386582

Sherkat, Darren E. 1991. "Leaving the Faith: Testing Theories of Religious Switching Using Survival Models." *Social Science Research* 20 (2): 171–187. doi:10.1016/0049-089X(91)90015-U

Sherkat, Darren E. 2014. *Changing Faith: The Dynamics and Consequences of Americans' Shifting Identities*. New York, NY: New York University Press.

Sherkat, Darren E., and John Wilson. 1995. "Preferences, Constraints, and Choices in Religious Markets: An Examination of Religious Switching and Apostasy." *Social Forces* 73 (3): 993–1026. doi:10.1093/sf/73.3.993

Smith, Christian, Kyle Longest, Jonathan Hill, and Karl Christoffersen. 2014. *Young Catholic America: Emerging Adults In, Out of, and Gone from the Church*. New York, NY: Oxford University Press.

Smith, Christian, and David Sikkink. 2003. "Social Predictors of Retention In and Switching From the Religious Faith of Family of Origin: Another Look Using Religious Tradition Self-Identification." *Review of Religious Research* 45 (2): 188–206. doi:10.2307/3512582

Smith, Christian, and Patricia Snell. 2009. *Souls in Transition: The Religious and Spiritual Lives of Emerging Adults*. New York, NY: Oxford University Press.

Smith, Jesse M. 2013. "Creating a Godless Community: The Collective Identity Work of Contemporary American Atheists." *Journal for the Scientific Study of Religion* 52 (1): 80–99. doi:10.1111/jssr.12009

Smith, Jesse M. 2017. "The Secular as Object of Belief and Belonging? The Case of the Sunday Assembly." *Qualitative Sociology* 40 (1): 83–109. doi:10.1007/s11133-016-9350-7

Steensland, Brian, Lynn D. Robinson, W. Bradford Wilcox, Jerry Z. Park, Mark D. Regnerus, and Robert D. Woodberry. 2000. "The Measure of American Religion: Toward Improving the State of the Art." *Social Forces* 79 (1): 291–318. doi:10.1093/sf/79.1.291

Strawn, Kelley D. 2019. "What's Behind the 'Nones-sense'? Change Over Time in Factors Predicting Likelihood of Religious Nonaffiliation in the United States." *Journal for the Scientific Study of Religion* 58 (3): 707–724. doi:10.1111/jssr.12609

Suh, Daniel, and Raymond Russell. 2015. "Non-Affiliation, Non-Denominationalism, Religious Switching, and Denominational Switching: Longitudinal Analysis of the Effects on Religiosity." *Review of Religious Research* 57 (1): 25–41. doi:10.1007/s13644-014-0197-7

Thiessen, Joel, and Sarah Wilkins-Laflamme. 2017. "Becoming a Religious None: Irreligious Socialization and Disaffiliation." *Journal for the Scientific Study of Religion* 56 (1): 64–82. doi:10.1111/jssr.12319

Thiessen, Joel, and Sarah Wilkins-Laflamme. 2020. *None of the Above: Nonreligious Identity in the U.S. and Canada.* New York, NY: New York University Press.

Wilkins-Laflamme, Sarah. 2020. "Like Parent, Like Millennial: Inherited and Switched (Non)Religion Among Young Adults in the USA and Canada." *Journal of Religion and Demography* 7 (1): 123–149. doi:10.1163/2589742X-12347103

Wilkins-Laflamme, Sarah, and Joel Thiessen. 2020. "Religious Socialization and Millennial Involvement in Organized and Digital Nonbelief Activities." *Secularism & Nonreligion* 9 (2): 1–15. doi:10.5334/snr.126

Zuckerman, Phil, Luke W. Galen, and Frank L. Pasquale. 2016. *The Nonreligious: Understanding Secular People and Societies.* New York, NY: Oxford University Press.

7

CONCLUSION

Ah, it [my worldview] must be pretty similar, more or less [to that of my parents]. Yeah, we're pretty close, we're in pretty close harmony, my parents, my brother, my sister in-law … we're not completely opposed, so we're pretty close.

Claire, born in 1985 and living in Montréal, Québec; nonreligious all her life

But I think that the way people practice their religion is different. And I feel like I practice it very differently than my parents do for instance. I think my brother who is several years younger than me, and some of my close friends who are also from the faith, are now very much questioning the faith and the ideas behind it and are slowly starting to phase out of it. … For example, my parents' social life revolves around … the prayer space, and including all of their activities and their friends. That's just basically home for them, in a way. Whereas I think people in my generation are now expanding to other circles and we want to know more of what's going on in the world, how people practice different things. So I think there is a lot of questioning. That being said, there are also lots of people that I know, including my brother-in-law or my sister, who are very much practicing without questioning. So I think there are different versions of practicing the faith and I think even in my network I see an entire range of different ways in which people are responding to or participating in religious life.

Shirin, born in 1985 and living in Victoria, British Columbia; identifies as Ismaili

… I think my generation was kind of the Millennial generation, none of us really seem to spend our time on Sundays or, you know, going to Wednesday night mass or anything like that. I don't think that's something that people are finding a good way to spend their time. Which sounds bad if that's their

DOI: 10.4324/9781003217695-7

religion and how they were raised, but I think that people are just choosing not to for whatever reason.

Kelly, born in 1992 and living in Seattle, Washington; nonreligious all her life

... I have the impression that what differentiates my generation a lot, at least speaking for myself, I don't want to generalise to my generation, but myself from my parents it's that we don't all have the same sort of negative prior attitudes [towards religion, and towards minority religions like Islam] that maybe my mother and my father have, or at least their brothers and sisters have ... myself I'm interested in religious diversity and they [my parents] know that I work with Muslims, and it [my parents' attitudes] come out from time to time.

Martine, born in 1992 and living in Saint-Augustin, Québec; nonreligious

One of the main goals of this book was to compare Millennials with prior generations when it comes to their religion, spirituality and secularity, as this younger generation now begins to transition from emerging to middle adulthood. Research participants Claire, Shirin, Kelly and Martine all illustrate different aspects of these generational dynamics that we have discussed throughout this book: most notably some continuity with prior generations, greater diversity and greater openness toward diversity among Millennials, and growing nonreligion—albeit without a total disappearance of religion and spirituality among Millennials today.

Cross-Generational Continuity

As Claire points out in the context of her own family, there is still much generational continuity when it comes to religion, spirituality and secularity. In many ways, Millennials have not made some cataclysmic break when it comes to these phenomena compared with older adults. Few generations ever really do. Even for Boomers, who broke away from their Greatest and Silent Generation parents in perhaps a more dramatic fashion with the counter-cultural movement of the 1960s, most still inherited their religious identity, core beliefs and key ways of practicing their faith from these same parents. Many just took part in rituals less frequently when they reached adulthood, and did not bestow upon religious leaders the same kinds of recognized authority that many in prior generations had. As we saw in Chapter 6, a majority of Millennials have also inherited and kept the religious identity of one or both their parents, and with it some key beliefs and practices. This means a large proportion of Millennials in both Canada and the United States still identify as affiliated to a Christian tradition, and still believe in God or a higher power, in life after death and in religious miracles. Most Millennials also continue the Boomer and Gen X trends of not attending religious services regularly in both the United States and Canada, and not praying frequently in Canada.

Further reflecting on the main results of this book, the four categories we explored in depth of the religious, spiritual seeker, cultural believer and nonreligious Millennial can also be found among older generations. These categories are by no means unique to cohorts born in the late 1980s, 1990s and early 2000s, but instead are found among all living adults to a certain degree. It is more the prevalence of these categories that seems to vary between living generations today, rather than their core nature and definitional boundaries as such. Actively religious individuals were and still are found in much larger proportions among Silent and older generations, although from a more limited number of religious traditions given these older generations' less widespread cultural, ethnic and religious diversity. As discussed in Chapters 4 and 5, spiritual seekers and cultural believers seem to have reached their peak among Boomers and Gen X who had higher rates of religious socialization during their childhoods, but also came to maturity in a post-1960s culture that de-emphasized and de-traditionalized in many ways frequent communal religious activities and external religious authority.

Cross-Generational Difference

Social change can be slow coming, often developing gradually across a number of generations. But it does happen. Building on earlier changes that occurred among their parents and grandparents, now it is the nonreligious category that seems to have grown and gained more popularity especially among Millennials in both the United States and Canada, as interviewees Shirin and Kelly point out in their own contexts. When cross-generational change has happened between Millennials and their parents, it has often been a change toward nonreligion within a much more secular Millennial social location, social environment and social imaginary. This change has in turn reverberated across the entire Millennial generation, impacting dynamics among all four categories explored in this book. The religious Millennial, who now finds themself a minority, is the one especially experiencing cross-pressures from a generally less religious generation overall, often having to justify and defend their religious worldview and practices to others and to themselves. Spiritual seekers and cultural believers are faced in turn with a social context on the one hand more accepting of their less conventional ways of doing religion and spirituality, and with new technologies expanding the availability of a wider variety of spiritual materials and digital communities. Yet, on the other hand, these individuals are also confronted with widespread indifference from many nonreligious members of their own generation toward these spiritual practices and cultural religious identities. Finally, as the nonreligious Millennial population grows, it is less defined by one specific type of individual, notably the White, male, university-educated Atheist or Freethinker of the past, and becomes more diverse in terms of individuals' backgrounds and ways of living their nonreligion. One important distinction made in Chapter 6, less prevalent in prior generations due to higher past rates of religious socialization, is the distinction between Millennial disaffiliates and cradle nonreligious Millennials. The latter of these two subtypes, born of nonreligious parents, reaches new heights among Millennials in terms of size of the nonreligious population as well as in terms of their levels of indifference and lack of knowledge toward the religious.

Earlier observers thought, and hoped in some cases, higher rates of non-religion among Millennials would only be a life cycle effect: a phenomenon present during youth that would gradually disappear with a return to religion as individuals age into middle adulthood, "settle down" and start families of their own. In some cases, this does happen. Take Fiona for example, born in 1990, from one of the Seattle, Washington focus groups, and who just had a baby at the time of the focus group:

> I got my Master's in Food Science also in California. In that time I wasn't really as involved with church because I was trying to finish a thesis, but you know, I was still in transition from campus ministry to real life and so trying to figure out what religion looked like for my life when I moved to Washington. I have been here for four years. It took a while, but I eventually got plugged into the church I am at right now, and sort of self-driven to be very involved. So I'm on the leadership council right now for my church and I consider myself very religious.

Yet, Fiona seems to be the exception, rather than the rule. With the current data we have on Millennial cohorts in the United States and Canada, this return to religion among large segments of the Millennial generation as they begin to enter middle adulthood is looking less and less likely. Despite some variations present across some life cycles, continued higher proportions of nonreligion are looking more and more like a permanent generational shift tied to Millennials' distinct social location that will last many a Millennial's lifetime. We saw in Tables 2.7 and 2.8 in Chapter 2 that religiosity indicators have declined among individuals in their twenties across Boomer, Gen X and Millennial generations. In Table 7.1, we can see with 2019 MTS data that older Millennial cohorts now in their early thirties and many beginning to enter into middle adulthood are not scoring substantially higher on a number of religiosity and spirituality indicators compared with those 18–24 years old and 25–29 years old. For some indicators, including religious affiliation, frequency of prayer and salience of belief, rates among 30–35 year olds are similar to those 18–24 years old. For other indicators, including frequency of religious service attendance, unchurched spiritual activity, digital content consumption, reading religious or spiritual materials and discussing religion or spirituality with friends, rates among 30–35 year olds are instead similar to those 25–29 years old.

Higher rates of nonreligiosity are the big generational difference between Millennials and prior generations then, a difference that looks like it is here to stay

TABLE 7.1 Religiosity and spirituality indicators among different Millennial age cohorts, United States and Canada, MTS 2019

	18–24 years old	*25–29 years old*	*30–35 years old*
Religiously affiliated	57%	50%	58%
Attend religious services at least once a month	37%	30%	30%
Pray at least once a week	37%	33%	38%
Unchurched spiritual activity at least once a month	25%	27%	28%
Consume digital content on religion or spirituality at least once a month	37%	31%	32%
Read religious or spiritual materials at least once a month	35%	31%	31%
Belief in God or a higher power	60%	60%	63%
Religious and spiritual beliefs are somewhat or very important in life	57%	53%	56%
Discuss religion or spirituality with friends at least once a month	36%	29%	30%

as this generation ages. Still, there exist other key differences between Millennials and older adults that affect the ever-changing religious, spiritual and secular landscapes. One of these, as we explored in Chapter 3, is the broad progressive movement left along the political spectrum that characterizes large swaths of Millennials compared with older adults, including among groups which have been traditionally more conservative such as among more actively religious individuals. Not only is this causing large political upheavals across society in general as these Millennials vote more and some are entering positions of influence and power as they age, but it is also having a big impact within religious organizations themselves. Especially in the United States, but also in some instances in Canada, religious Millennials hold on average more progressive attitudes on abortion, immigration, the environment and LGBTQ2S+ communities than their older religious counterparts. This is causing many a religious group and leader to rethink their stances on a number of socio-political issues, or risk losing their precious 18–35 year olds that many religious groups already experience difficulty in attracting in the first place and who are crucial to their groups' survival and flourishment.

As we also saw in Chapter 3, digital religion along with the cultural values it is a vehicle for, including interactivity, audience-generated content and expressive individualism, play a much larger role for a substantial amount of religious and spiritual Millennials than among older birth cohorts. In-person religious and spiritual activities are only part of the larger experience now, often paired with digital content consumption, interactive sharing with online communities and social media posting. For a smaller minority of Millennials, in-person activities are even completely absent, and religion and spirituality only happen online.

The cultural generation gap is also another cross-generational difference that extends to religion and spirituality. Not only is the Millennial generation more ethnically and racially diverse than older generations but also more (non)religiously diverse with slimmer Christian majorities, more ethnic and racial diversity within Christianity, and larger proportions of both nonreligion and non-Judeo-Christian religions.

This cultural generation gap also extends to attitudes toward religious and spiritual outgroups, as Martine points out in her quote from the start of this chapter. Millennials are the most accepting and open adult generation today when it comes to religious minorities and generally to groups different from their own (Young and Shipley 2020). However, as we saw in Chapters 2, 3 and 5, this openness and acceptance at times has its limits, with certain minority groups still the target of more negative Millennial public opinion and discrimination. At other times, Millennial attitudes can be better described as ignorance and indifference toward religion, rather than engagement with and interest in (non)religious difference as such.

Nevertheless, more favorable—or at least indifferent—public opinion generally toward religious and spiritual difference as well as a decline in conventional forms of religion have on the one hand opened up both cognitive and social spaces for alternatives such as nature spiritualities and nature spiritual experiences as explored in Chapter 4. On the other hand, the prevalence of these spiritual alternatives may be more limited among Millennials than among Boomers and Gen X due to a lack of religious and spiritual socialization during childhood. If not exposed to more structured and consistent forms of spiritual activities and teachings as children in the home, at school or by close family members, the more secondary forms of spiritual socialization found in pop culture for example (think of movies such as Avatar or Marvel's Doctor Strange, or Hollywood star influencers such as Gwyneth Paltrow and her Goop brand) or within holistic milieus and available spiritual materials today may not be as effective in transmitting interest for spiritual matters from one generation to the next. Smith et al. (2014, 198) argue that socialization is only effective when reinforced by direct social relationships in an individual's life, which such secondary sources of spiritual socialization do not necessarily have. Much more future research is needed regarding the intergenerational transmission of less conventional spiritualities, but for now it looks like this transmission is not as prevalent from parents to Millennials as more conventional religious transmission was in the past among prior generations. Spiritual seeker Millennials are an important part of their generation, but also do not encompass a majority of younger birth cohorts as far as my data can measure. More generally, as societies grow in size, population, complexity and diversity, perhaps we should no longer expect one specific form of religion, spirituality or secularity to become prevalent among a vast majority of people in younger generations. In other words, we should not expect just one thing to replace conventional forms of Christianity which are on the decline, but rather to see a plurality of religious, spiritual and nonreligious ways of thinking and doing expand and coexist moving forward.

Comparing the United States and Canada

Another comparison that traversed this book has been between the U.S. and Canadian Millennial religious, spiritual and secular contexts. Canadian and U.S. societies share many commonalities overall: both being European settler majority English-speaking liberal democratic nations on the same continent; both having a rich dominant Christian heritage along with the influence of many diverse Indigenous, linguistic, religious, racial and ethnic minorities; both sharing much pop culture in common; both defined by the advances and excesses of neo-liberal capitalism; and so forth. In this light, it is no great surprise that there are many similarities between Millennials in both countries when it comes to their religion, spirituality and secularity. The main similarities found in this book are shared trends of growing religious pluralism paired with growing nonreligion among Millennials in both nations, along with similar religious, spiritual seeker, cultural believer and nonreligious categories existing among both Canadian and American Millennials. Other similarities include important overlap in digital and in-person religious and spiritual activities among individuals in both countries, nature activities as spiritual activities for many Millennials in both the United States and Canada, cultural believers having more negative attitudes toward immigration in both countries, as well as rates of disaffiliation and the cradle nonreligious being quite similar within both countries' nonreligious subpopulations.

Still, there are also some key distinctions to be made between American and Canadian Millennials when it comes to their religion, spirituality and secularity, tied to distinct national and regional social environments. It is sometimes hard to believe, but Canada was once a more religious and conservative place on average than the United States prior to the 1960s. Tied to a prevalent British-Canadian White Anglo-Saxon Protestant majority national identity in English-speaking Canada as well as a strong French-Canadian Catholic identity in French-speaking Canada, rates of frequent religious service attendance and socio-political attitudes were generally higher and more conservative north of the 49th parallel during the first half of the 20th century (Grant 1966; Lacombe 2002; Lipset 1991; Noll 1992). Yet, like with most Western nations, Canadian society underwent some important changes throughout the 1960s and early 1970s. The Boomer counter-cultural movement discredited many traditional sources and figures of authority, including the church minister or priest. It also pushed for and normalized much more progressive sexual, family and gender values. Civil rights movements began to carve out more social and political spaces for their members and more equal treatment and opportunities for racial minorities, members of LGBTQ2S+ communities, those with disabilities and women—although much more work remains to be done to achieve true equity goals for these and other vulnerable groups.

Something more happened in Canada though during this period of the long 1960s, something that did not happen to the same extent in the United States: the de-coupling of Christian and national identities in both English-speaking and

French-speaking Canada. In English-speaking Canada, with the final collapse of the British Empire unfolding during the independence movement of India in the 1930s and 1940s, the end of the Second World War, the Suez Canal crisis of 1956 and the UK joining the European Economic Community in 1967, the British-Canadian national identity of the past began to crumble; a national identity that was once so reliant on the British Empire's ideals, worldview and colonial membership (Buckner 2005; Igartua 2006). This crumbling of British-Canadian national identity was evident in events such as the flag debate of 1964 when political leaders decided to remove the union jack from the new Canadian national flag.

In response, a socio-political move was made first toward a bilingual and bicultural national identity combining French and English heritage, as articulated and promoted during the Laurendeau-Dunton Commission of 1963–1970. Then a further move was made toward a multicultural national identity in the 1970s and 1980s focused on celebrating politically accepted (and often watered-down and Westernized) forms of cultural and ethnic diversity; a national identity which is still prevalent today in much of English-speaking Canada. Christianity in the form of Protestantism, which was closely tied to the old British-Canadian national identity and its (problematic) ideals of civilization, did not really go with and was not really transferred onto this new multicultural vision of the nation (Grant 1998; Rawlyk 1990). In fact, although religious diversity more broadly is an important part of the Canadian mosaic, it is often not the form of diversity touted and celebrated explicitly within Canadian multiculturalism discourse. More often than not, it is treated as an afterthought, or as a potential source of unwanted controversy, that does not receive much attention nor discussion by key leaders and influencers (Biles and Ibrahim 2005). From the 1960s onward, with there being less or no social pressure to be "a good Christian" to be a "Good Canadian" and with many even associating a number of historical and present social ills with Christianity (such as clergy child sexual abuse scandals as well as the running of Indigenous residential schools in the 19th and 20th centuries), large segments of the Canadian Boomer majority and subsequent generations began and continue today their move away from conventional forms of Christian belonging, belief and ritual.

As discussed in Chapter 5, in French-speaking Canada, the Quiet Revolution of the 1960s brought about an end to the direct links between on the one hand the Catholic Church and way of life and on the other hand the new emerging Québécois national identity (Zubrzycki 2016). Although Catholic and Christian heritage remains an important part of national identity today for many Québécois, it is a much-weakened form of cultural Catholicism that does not imply regular practice of specific Catholic rituals nor adherence to specific Catholic beliefs by the individual, and is often not explicitly expressed in public (Lemieux and Montminy 2000; Meunier and Wilkins-Laflamme 2011). Rates of frequent religious service attendance plummeted in the 1960s and subsequent decades in Québec, more quickly than in most other Western nations during the period, and have never recovered since. Most other religiosity measures have also followed in decline among French-speaking populations both within Québec and to a lesser extent in the rest of Canada.

Many of these changes Canada underwent in the 1960s had their roots in developments over the course of prior decades (Gauvreau 2005; Meunier and Warren 2002), which paved the way for the more dramatic and visible changes that erupted in the 1960s. Still, the long 1960s were crucial in setting the core conditions for the next 50 years of religious, spiritual and secular transformation (Clarke and Macdonald 2017). The United States, however, did not experience the same de-coupling of Christian and American national identity in the 1960s, and ties between Christianity and American patriotism arguably remain strong to this day. As we also saw in Chapter 5, Whitehead and Perry (2020) show that a certain form of heteronormative, patriarchal and White-supremacist Christian nationalism is still present today among important segments of the U.S. population. Even for those groups who do not espouse this specific form of Christian nationalism, other types of ties between individuals' Christian faith and their identities as Americans and their American citizenship also remain prevalent in much public and private discourse in the country.

More conservative forms of evangelicalism also experienced a revival of sorts in the United States in the 1980s and the 1990s, notably by means of the Christian Right that emerged politically during this period, a revival that did not even come close to developing in Canada to the same degree. Putnam and Campbell (2010) understand this later return of conservative evangelicalism to the American political sphere as a counter-shock to the civil rights movement and progressive sexual, family and gender norms of the 1960s and 1970s, many in America fearing the socio-political disappearance of their more conservative values and so reacting politically to defend them. This also had the effect of reinvigorating certain ties between Christian and American identity and ensuring that this link would persist for most Americans into the 1990s. It has only been since the start of the 21st century that we have begun to see signs of Christianity fraying at the edges among certain demographics in the United States, notably among many Millennials, and not to the same extent that we have seen in Canada.

Whenever I compare the U.S. and Canadian contexts in my own work, I keep coming back to these key developments explored in the past few paragraphs, to the point that for those readers familiar with my past work I may start to sound like a broken record on the topic. Nevertheless, I do think these changes in Christianity's ties to political, regional and national identity, changes that seem to have been more significant in Canada than in the United States since the 1960s, are crucial to understanding the different social environment religion and Millennials now find themselves in within Canada compared with the United States. As mentioned in Chapter 1, religion is not isolated from transformations in other parts of society, but is very much a part of them and affected by them.

These distinct elements of the Canadian and American socio-historical contexts are reflected in this book's data by the fact that Canadian Millennials systematically score even lower on religiosity measures than their American counterparts.

Religious affiliation, digital religious or spiritual content consumption, social media posting about religion or spirituality, frequency of religious service attendance, frequency of prayer, reading religious or spiritual materials, making offerings to ancestors at temple, belief in God and salience of belief in life; all are lower among Canadian Millennials. As given in Chapter 3, religious Millennials are not all that more left-leaning politically than their religious counterparts from older generations in Canada, because most in the country are already more left-leaning anyways. There is a lingering reality for many Millennials in the United States that religion and Christianity more specifically have a positive individual and social desirability within American society, and this in turn does impact many an individual's relationship with and perception of religion.

As discussed in Chapter 6, it is not so much that many Canadian Millennials take a squarely anti-religious stance. In fact, tied to the greater national celebration of diversity in English-speaking Canada, more among this generation have favorable attitudes toward religious minorities than in the United States. Additionally, dislike for Christianity is muted in the word association and feelings scores measured among 18–35 year old Canadians in the 2019 MTS: the word "Christianity" for example still receives a feeling score of +3 overall among those who are not actively religious in Canada. Some have instead inherited or taken on more cultural forms of believing, notably in Québec, as more active and conventional forms of Christianity have declined. In other cases, there appear to be slightly higher levels of interest and participation in less conventional spiritualities among Canadian Millennials, as we saw in Chapters 2 and 4. A less conventionally religious context allows more space for greater openness toward less conventional spiritualities, and many of these spiritualities have received mostly positive public exposure through the counter-cultural New Age movement, Westernized elements of Eastern religions, an emphasis on spiritual journeys seeking personal authenticity, and especially in Canada the more recent greater public presence of Indigenous spiritualities.

In other cases still, a number of Canadian Millennials just seem to be removed from religion and spirituality in most or all of the ways I measured these phenomena in my study, and indifference seems to be the main (non)approach to these phenomena among this demographic. As we saw in Figure 2.10 in Chapter 2, Canadian Millennials score words such as "religion," "Christianity" and "Catholicism" closer to zero (closer to no positive nor negative associations with these words) than their U.S. counterparts who tend to score them more positively overall. As we saw in Tables 6.5 and 6.6 in Chapter 6, a larger proportion of nonreligious Millennials in Canada also have no preference for atheist, secular humanist, agnostic or spiritual labels (40%), compared with nonreligious Millennials in the United States (30%).

With rates of religious nonaffiliation rising and many religiosity indicators declining in the United States especially since the 1990s and especially among Millennials, could this be where America is headed in the next few decades when it comes to religion, spirituality and secularity? Will the United States begin to look more and more like what Canada is now? In some ways, probably. Rates of religious nonaffiliation in the United States have already matched those in Canada in recent General Social Surveys (Thiessen and Wilkins-Laflamme 2020, 7–8). Rates of the multi-dimensional nonreligious category as measured in this book will likely continue to rise in the United States, potentially also matching those in Canada in the near future and among Gen Z.

In other ways though, the United States will probably remain distinct from Canada when it comes to its religious, spiritual and secular landscapes over the coming years and decades. American Millennials are already showing signs of being slightly more polarized between the religious on the one hand, and the nonreligious on the other hand, with fewer U.S. Millennials falling into the more middle categories of spiritual seekers and cultural believers combined. This is most likely both a product and a factor of the more politically polarized landscape now found in the United States, and that Millennials have dealt with for most, if not all, of their lives. Party affiliation and issue stance are tightly linked with (non)religious identity in the American political context, and republican and democrat political divisions are found more and more between on the one hand White evangelicals and practicing Catholics (strong support for Republicans and their conservative value orientation) and on the other hand Black Protestants, more liberal Protestants and the nonreligious (strong support for Democrats and their progressive value orientation; Smidt et al. 2010). Under these circumstances, holding a less conventional middle ground when it comes to (non)religion may be more difficult for U.S. Millennials. If you are not at one end of the polarized political and religious spectrum, then you may feel the need and be socially pressured into occupying the other end rather than a middle ground. We will have to wait and see if this religious polarization trend becomes more prominent among Millennials as they age, as well as with the next cohorts of Gen Z.

As the Republican Party has claimed they are "God's Party" more and more over the years (Smidt et al. 2010), Millennials who do not share this party's conservative value orientation may have moved away from God altogether along with moving away from the Republicans, potentially as another counter-shock to the conservative evangelical revival of the 1980s and 1990s. When religion and politics become so closely intertwined, religion may also get left behind if an individual does not agree with such politics (Hout and Fischer, 2002). The American context may thus have the potential for more political, social and religious shocks and counter-shocks between the two polarized sides moving forward, much more so than in Canada. North of the national border, Canadian Millennials are for the most part very aware of the more polarized political situation in the United States, and may use it as a cautionary tale to avoid some of its outcomes. Many Canadian Millennials may become wary of religion due to its ties to politics in the United States, and evangelical Christianity more specifically even though some may or may not be able to distinguish it from other forms of Christianity with their little knowledge of religious content and differences. This in turn may further entrench many Canadian Millennials in nonreligion, which they may feel better reflects their progressive views, as they are impacted by developments among their neighbors to the south.

Looking Forward to Middle Adulthood

As U.S. and Canadian Millennials alike begin the move into middle age, I do not expect a return to religion for many. As discussed earlier in this chapter, none of the religiosity measures show signs of this, and fundamental social conditions among the generation do not look set to change the situation either. What can we expect then during Millennials' next life phase? This is probably a good time to add an important caveat about predicting the future based on present social scientific research. In short, sociologists are not great at making such predictions, along with pretty much anyone else from all other scientific disciplines for that matter. Track records on making accurate predictions are definitely mixed, to say the least. Our main job and expertise are instead to explain things as they are, and why they are, at the time we observe them. This said, it is always important to have a longer view and to look to the future for how things could potentially play out, given what we know today. What we can expect from Millennials during their middle adulthood years is also a question I am asking myself as I begin this life transition in my thirties. I am sure I am not the only one wondering about what is to come. Just take my forecasts in this concluding chapter with a grain of salt: this is a discussion of what we might expect, not what we know for sure will happen (because obviously we do not).

I want to return here in this section to each of the eight aspects of the Millennial social location initially discussed in Chapter 1, and then referred back to from time to time throughout this book, to examine how they might play out on religion and spirituality during middle adulthood in the years and decades to come. First, the digital age, an age the COVID-19 pandemic and its multiple lockdowns have sped up. Many religious groups in North America were repeatedly forced to move entirely online during 2020 and 2021, to offer their services and gatherings in a remote virtual format to ensure their members' health and safety. Many groups had already begun offering online resources to varying degrees before the pandemic, and many more were planning to prior to 2020. Nonetheless, the pandemic lockdowns sped up and expanded in many cases this process by many years, like with the digital expansion in most other social sectors during the same period. Now, as I finish writing this book and as we slowly begin to emerge (hopefully) from the worst of the pandemic at the end of 2021, most religious groups still have the online tools, resources and know how they developed during the pandemic lockdowns available for continued use. As discussed in Chapter 3, it is likely that many will develop a much more hybrid in-person and virtual experience for their members moving forward, in order to integrate the best of both worlds as it were. This means that Millennials who are so inclined will probably have access to a lot more options, in-person and virtually, to connect with their religious group. This may come in handy when getting to your religious groups' in-person activities may be too much to handle with infants or small children, a house to maintain, a full-time job to juggle, as well as all middle-aged life's other activities. When making it in person is not possible, more connections can now be maintained online for the individual to stay in touch with their group.

In other ways though, online religious and spiritual activity may slow down for individuals entering middle adulthood. They may just have less time to spend browsing and exploring content online as they develop serious romantic relationships, buy and maintain a home, work on their career and begin raising a family. They may not feel the need for such browsing and exploring online anyways, since their self-identity and values usually become more settled during this later life phase and they become sure of who they are as a person, their habits become steadier, and their self-exploration may wane. I expect to see a shoring up of two distinct groups among Millennials in the years to come regarding digital religion, more so than we see now: those interested by religious and spiritual activities both in-person and online, and those who are not. I expect to see fewer Millennials just infrequently accessing digital content on religion and spirituality in a more exploratory manner without more solid in-person ties. This said, like with all my prognostications in this chapter, much more research will be needed in the years to come to see if this is how things play out.

Second, the years of economic precarity and the subsequent prolonged emerging adulthood that many have experienced as a consequence will leave deep financial, psychological and social scars and effects for many Millennials over the whole of their lifetimes. Many are pushing home ownership and family formation further and further back into their late thirties, either by choice or as a result of the economic insecurity and job market volatility of the Great Recession, the COVID-19 pandemic, unaffordable housing markets as well as more general neoliberal policies and realities. As discussed in Chapter 1, this in turn can have a negative impact on individual religiosity, with religious service attendance usually going hand in hand with weekly family life and a stable home location near one's local religious group. I would argue that the longer this phase of emerging adulthood lasts for someone, the more likely it is to have a lasting impact for the rest of their lives on their relationship with religion and on their worldview: a relationship and worldview which may be less and less likely to subsequently change in middle adulthood as (nonreligious) identities and habits become ingrained.

Third, pluralism in all its forms is likely to continue to factually grow due especially to immigration within both Millennial and younger birth cohorts, higher than average birth rates among many racial, ethnic and religious minorities in both the United States and Canada, as well as growing LGBTQ2S+ social acceptance which creates a safer environment for more individuals of these communities to be comfortable "coming out." This said, the ideals of youth of widespread "deep equality" (Beaman 2017) and of utopic multiculturalism may give way among aging Millennials to a more pragmatic thinking of what can be achieved on the ground regarding equality goals as Millennials enter middle adulthood and take over more positions of influence in society. As many Millennials are given more responsibility to address systemic inequality in all its forms, many are also beginning to realize it is not a problem that is solved overnight. Bringing in more racial and gender diversity into positions of influence, such as in politics and in business in order for directly-affected individuals to make the important decisions, is a push that has started now in many sectors but where there is still much work to be done. This push will be a big part in addressing issues of systemic inequality moving forward. Nevertheless, it can be a long process with many setbacks. Ask members of the second- and third-wave feminist movements who have only seen the slow trickle of more women in positions of power in many fields to this day, along with persistent gender inequities in pay, occupational status and beyond.

Religion has the potential to be forgotten in the current pushes to address systemic inequities in race, ethnicity, sexual orientation and gender. Religion is often another target of systemic as well as overt violent discrimination. Negative stereotyping of Muslims by State actors and in the enforcement of state policies, as well as overt Islamophobic attacks which have plagued both Canada and the United States over notably the past 20 years are clear examples of this. Yet, rarely do discussions on systemic inequalities in both societies focus on religious diversity and inequity, rather than or in addition to those of race, ethnicity, sexual orientation and gender. Religious diversity and discrimination should be part of the conversation here, especially with this diversity growing among younger generations, but may not end up being as much as it should be. The growing indifference toward and lack of exposure to religion among large segments of Millennials, as well as a growing lack of knowledge about religions due to a lack of religious education and literacy, will likely have long-term consequences for public discussions and debates on both religion itself as well as on diversity and systemic inequities more broadly. Some nonreligious Millennials in positions of influence may not consider religion all that important to take into consideration, or may only see religion as part of the problem, influenced by a narrow media focus only on religious extremism and conservatism, rather than as part of potential solutions. This would be a mistake that we should aim to avoid. Because religion remains important in our societies, even if its forms and roles have changed with younger generations. Religious discrimination remains present today, and religion needs to be part of the wider conversation to address systemic inequities.

Fourth, even as Millennials enter middle adulthood, values of expressive individualism so prevalent in our current-day Western societies will continue to put individual choice and the search for "authentic" personal experiences and ways of being first. As Watts (2022) convincingly shows, although individuals will usually perceive these searches and experiences of personal authenticity as getting at a presocial version of the self devoid of the pressures of social structures, in reality this expressive individualism comes from a long social tradition of romantic liberalism especially prevalent in our societies since the 1960s and ingrained in many of our social institutions and socialization today. This expressive individualism will continue to shape the internal workings of many religious and spiritual groups for the foreseeable future, with many emphasizing first and foremost the individual experiential aspects of faith. Nevertheless, as extreme individualism can lead for some to excess individualism and negative outcomes such as addiction or loneliness, some groups may be able to position themselves as milieus of resistance and alternative havens for those who are most impacted by these extremes and excesses. Somewhat ironically, as religion was once very much part of mainstream culture among older generations, it could instead become a type of countercultural institution in this sense for some Millennials within a larger generation where religion is no longer the mainstream. Active religion and spirituality may only appeal to a minority of Millennials moving into middle adulthood, but among whom some may be looking for something different or more than the majority values of expressive individualism.

Fifth, as we saw in Chapter 6, the growing nonreligious Millennial subpopulation now encompasses a wider diversity of peoples than among prior generations. The same is also happening with the expansion of access to higher education. As the college- and university-educated population has expanded among Millennials, it is no longer just the White, male, secular elite who achieves higher education. Although disparities in this regard do still exist and need to be addressed, they have lessened over the past few generations. The expansion of who is on campuses over the past few generations has also driven a greater diversity of religious and spiritual practices on many of these campuses in both the United States and Canada through student associations and activities, along with a growing diversity of secular student associations as well (such as the Secular Student Alliance), better reflecting the pluralism present in the wider Millennial population. Under these less homogenous conditions, a more specific secularizing influence of the university years later in an individual's life that some studies have found in the past among certain segments of older generations (Mayrl and Oeur 2009) may be waning. Higher education has become more widespread, and more diverse peoples bring with them their more diverse worldviews and ways of doing to these campus environments.

Additionally, as nonreligion has become more prevalent among Millennials compared with prior generations, it is not just at college or university that Millennials are exposed to nonreligious worldviews, but rather in many social milieus of their generation. This in turn may also reduce the specific secularizing influence of university life observed in prior generations, as these secularizing influences are more widespread now beyond higher education.

Finally, we arrive at the potential impact environmental degradation and climate change may have on the religion, spirituality and secularity of Millennials later in their adult lives. Throughout this book, I have either implied or explicitly stated that, for a reversal of the current Millennial trends of growing nonreligion paired with growing religious and spiritual pluralism to happen, change would have to occur among the more fundamental structures of how our societies currently function in both the United States and Canada. Our current values of choice and expressive individualism as well as the wide availability of secular alternatives in ways of thinking and doing would probably have to change for us to also see a change in (non)religiosity trends. Although tomorrow always has a better chance of being like today than not, if there is one area that is most likely to drive such fundamental structural social change in our societies over the next few decades, I see it coming from the environmental crisis. As I write this book, things are starting to get noticeably bad not just to scientists but also now to many everyday people. We just lived through record-breaking heat, hurricanes, droughts, floods and forest fires over the past couple of years, and look set to continue to live through them in the years to come. Even residents of urban areas are feeling the effects more and more, urban residents especially prevalent among the Millennial generation and who have usually been more removed in the past from the direct impact of extreme weather phenomena. Many climate scientists argue we are on track for some of their worst-case scenario models of at least a 3°C increase in world average temperatures by the end of the 21st century from preindustrial levels.[1]

Of all the elements of the Millennial social location, I think these major changes in the natural environment and climate have the greatest potential to drive major social change. As environmental degradation and the effects of climate change get worse, it may not spell the end of humanity and the human species as such, but it very well may spell the end of how we currently function in our societies. It may be more difficult for example to live outside of urban centers in the future, given climate effects such as droughts and forest fires often hitting rural areas hardest and with fewer societal resources to dedicate to the countryside to stave off the worst of these effects. Yet, more fundamental still, some of the key ways of doing in our societies, notably our rampant consumerism and fossil fuel burning, will have to end. Along with them, some of the core values attached to this current way of life, such as an emphasis on personal happiness, choice and expressive individualism, may also have to shift in favor of a different, more environmentally friendly, social order and cultural framework (hopefully not going in the direction of Margaret Atwood's *A Handmaid's Tale* or George Miller's *Mad Max*). This could happen abruptly if things get really bad really fast, or more gradually as the environmental crisis evolves over the next few decades and centuries.

These are potential future period effects that may impact the current generational trends of growing nonreligion paired with growing religious and spiritual pluralism. Some readers may have the reflex of thinking that such future changes could lead to a return of religion among large segments of populations, including among Millennials in later life phases, as material conditions worsen and existence becomes less certain for them. Maybe. But not necessarily. Future change to social structures could just as well drive a greater decline of worldviews and practices related to the supernatural and superempirical than we are currently seeing now cross-generationally with Millennials. Such worldviews and practices, along with religious discourses of dominion over nature, for example, could receive more of the blame than they currently do for environmental degradation, and so could be discarded to a greater extent among populations—depending on the circumstances. Only time will really tell.

What became apparent when I was reading the transcripts from the Millennial West Coast focus groups and from the Québec life history interviews is that most of the research participants had yet to face real hardships in their own lives and severe illness and deaths near to them. Many, not all, had a mostly comfortable upbringing and young adult life, and most had not lost anyone close to them yet: for the most part, their parents, siblings, close friends and even many grandparents were still alive and well. Consequently, it is yet to be seen how facing such hardships later in life will affect their Millennial worldviews and ways of living. For most, these hardships and loss are not yet on their radar; they are not something Millennials are necessarily spontaneously thinking about a lot yet, at least not in the focus groups and interviews my research teams conducted.

There were a few exceptions to this though among the research participants. Jason, for example, born in 1994 and living in Montréal, went through a lot of anxiety and an existential crisis during the period of his mother's two severe illnesses in his early adulthood. These were impactful years for him, and he discusses them at length in his interview. In the end though, this period of hardship generated some spiritual seeking on Jason's part, but not a complete change of worldview: he still identified as nonreligious at the time of his interview. My prediction here is that many Millennials will have a similar experience to Jason when they do have to face severe hardship, illness and death close to them: they will have moments when they become more aware of their worldview in the face of big life and death questions, they may think on it more than they have before, but most probably will not change their worldview fundamentally. We have not seen big changes in worldviews among prior generations as they have aged; I do not expect to see them among Millennials either. Still, more future research is needed on this as Millennials age and enter later life stages.

Looking to Raising Their Children

Something many Millennials were definitely thinking about in our research focus groups and life interviews is the prospect of having and raising kids. Some had already entered this new family reality, with their newborns, infants and young children already arrived. Others were planning for childrearing in their near future. Many Millennial research participants, often those who were more religious and spiritual themselves, told us of how they were looking to explicitly pass on their own religious and spiritual beliefs and practices to their children, despite what may come. In the 2019 MTS, respondents were asked if they agreed or disagreed with the following statement: "I want to pass on my religious, spiritual or nonreligious beliefs to my children." Seventy-nine percent of religious Millennials in the sample agreed or strongly agreed with the statement, compared with 52% of cultural believers, 32% of spiritual seekers and only 12% of nonreligious

Millennials. William, a practicing Catholic who we first met in Chapter 1, gives us an example of this desire for religious transmission in his interview:

> … for sure for me it's essential to pass on the faith to them [future children], to pass on, not just to get them baptised and to let them go, but to pass on the importance of having a relationship with God and to have a life of prayer. … Obviously to pass this on in freedom, because I also think that all of this, that spirituality means nothing if it's imposed. So for sure as a parent there's this fine line which I'll try and walk, but for sure I'll try and pass this on effectively. That faith is, that spirituality and faith are the most important things in life.

Interviewees also often discussed their struggles of figuring out how best to pass on their religion within their Millennial social location. Fiona, who we first met in Chapter 4, who we heard from again earlier in this chapter, and who recently had her first child, discusses this struggle:

> … we are getting him [baby son] baptised in July and then also being a convert I am very unfamiliar with cradle Catholic and with what that means, the classes he took as a kid, what that even looks like, summer camps, all of that. I think I'll do it, but I am still trying to figure out what I do as a mother for him and I also know many cradle Catholics who say, "my mom taught me my faith," and so I'm thinking, "what I am I supposed to do? How does this kid learn what does it mean to be Catholic?" I have no idea. … you don't you know, the church shouldn't just have classes, have kids, and put them there and then take them out and say, "you're done, you're Catholic," but that the parents should be Catholic and drive the teaching of the kid to be Catholic and what that means. And so for me that means I can't just throw my kid there, I actually have to develop my relationship with God and try to figure out how to teach that to my kid. I still don't know, so still on the journey, but he can't talk yet, I have some time. … Before I got pregnant I did have this idea I do want to do be more structured in saying a prayer before meals or saying a prayer before bed and teach that to my kid, but I haven't done that yet. … He is pretty young, but I could theoretically start now, but you know when his, when my husband's parents were visiting they would do that, and for my husband I think that's natural for him to have his dad pray over a meal, but I haven't really figured out how to get my husband to do that role for himself now that he's a father. And I don't necessarily, don't want to force him to as well, but still trying to figure out what my role is if you know, if for me, religion and spirituality is more vocal, what does that, is my kid going to see a different faith from his dad versus his mom or is it going to be more of a family faith thing. And then again what role does the church play in terms of classes or structures. I do want to, we have a maybe three other people that I know around my age

> who also had kids this year and we try to meet up and in my head I had this idea my kid is going to be surrounded by Catholic kids and maybe that would help teach them the faith, but I don't really know if that's going to happen that way.

Andrew who we first met in Chapter 2 also discusses this struggle from his point of view. Andrew loves his Jewish faith, but part of that love for him is bringing a healthy amount of critique to the tradition. Yet, he worries that his future children may only take away the critique, not the love:

> ... I don't have children and don't have any immediate plans to have them, but at some point and I think I share some of those same questions of how I would raise them within my [Jewish] tradition ... I think that for me, I mean there was this quote in Lady Bird that sometimes paying attention is love and I think that critique for me, within my tradition, is an act of love, but I always have this concern that if I am leading with a critique then that will be all these kids walk away with, I want them to be critical and I don't want them to just buy into my criticism, but I want them to approach that with a buy in that isn't just, "screw this, like ..."

Another distinct planned approach to parenting identified by our research participants both in the Pacific Northwest and in Québec is a choice-based approach: giving their children choice on religious and spirituality matters, and leaving religious and spiritual exploration, knowledge acquisition and experience up to their children. This is an approach especially found among our less or nonreligious research participants. For example, Guy, a cultural Catholic we first met in Chapter 5, states in his life history interview that:

> My kids will be, will have, will be baptized. But after that, they'll decide what they want to do. ... they [his future kids] will know we are Catholic, but at a certain age, I imagine that if they want to continue being Catholic, they'll be Catholic. But, I don't think my kids will waste their time going to another church to look for another identity in another religion. I don't think so. In today's generation, I don't think that. There are some who do, but I don't think so. Anyways, maybe my kids will. They'll do what they want at that point. [sigh] I don't care. They'll be the religion they want.

Claire, a nonreligious Montréal resident who we met for the first time in Chapter 6 and heard from again at the start of this chapter, says the following while discussing values she received from her parents and that she would also like to pass on to her children someday: "... free choice, and respecting the free choice of others, that's something that I also put forward a lot, I try." Georges, who we also met in Chapter 6, states in his life history interview that he and his partner will leave the decision to get baptized up to their child when they can make that decision for themselves. He repeatedly says that it will be his child's choice, that he and his partner will not baptize their future children at birth. Georges feels that having his future kids baptized would force them down a certain path that is hard to reverse later in life. He does not want to impose anything, but instead aims to provide all the information possible, open all the doors possible for them to make an informed choice, whether that choice is to do nothing, to adhere to a religion or to believe in a certain spirituality.

As we discussed in Chapter 6, this choice-based approach favored by nonreligious parents often ends up leading to a more secular upbringing, often despite the best intentions of parents and even though not explicitly sought after by them as such. Without parents or other key socializing agents signaling the value of religious and spiritual matters in daily life, it is rare for children to spontaneously pick up an interest for such matters on their own.

***

Most people, especially most Millennials, do not usually like the idea of being boxed into generalized categories. Talk about doing away with binaries and instead being more fluid, malleable, and identities being under constant construction and negotiation is common among Millennials (Young and Shipley 2020). I am aware of the irony then that my book about Millennial religion, spirituality and secularity is structured around four categories derived from my survey data. Nevertheless, these four categories of the religious, the spiritual seeker, the cultural believer and the nonreligious Millennial have been useful in crunching a lot of empirical information and being able to pull from it some of the key similarities and distinctions among Millennials on these topics. Whereas many often think they are doing their own personal and unique thing, in some ways they may be, but in other ways they share important similarities with other individuals that impact wider society. One key take-away from the four categories explored in this book: the nonreligious category has gotten very large among Millennials. I reiterate here my main argument first discussed in Chapter 1: whereas Charles Taylor's secular age is mainly defined by the philosopher as the coexistence of belief and unbelief, and a decline of certainty in worldviews all around, I posit that this uncertainty seems to be favoring unbelief among Millennials and younger generations more and more. This period of coexistence that we currently find ourselves in seems to be one of long transition, with a steady movement toward nonreligion becoming the new default or majority reality. We are not quite there yet, and trends can always change in the future, but Millennials are the first generation where we have seen nonreligion really emerge as the new default that other groups now have to contend with. This does not mean that all beliefs are declining: I am mainly referring here to a decline of beliefs and related practices tied to the superempirical, and to Christianity specifically. And beliefs in the superempirical do still remain among Millennials, just now among significant minorities of more traditionally religious as well as less conventionally spiritual individuals.

To what extent will all of this get passed on to the next generation, Gen Z and beyond? The Millennial trend of growing nonreligion seems to be continuing, and even becoming more pronounced in some cases, among the first data we are now getting for Gen Z (Barna Group 2018; Manning 2019). Most new Gen Z data are coming from teenagers and very young adults who are still living with their parents though. Most members of Gen Z have yet to traverse that transitional life period of setting out on their own in the world that has been key to religious disaffiliation and decline among many Millennials. When this time does arrive, I expect to see Gen Z nonreligion growth become even more pronounced. Still, we will have to wait for future research to see. Gen Z could push back and define themselves differently from their Millennial counterparts, which we have seen prior generations do from time to time, and which might affect their religious, spiritual and secular dynamics. Only time, not this book, will tell. The journey continues: as one generation ages, another arrives.

Note

1 See, for example, the World Economic Forum's 2020 report "The World Is on Track to Warm by 3 Degrees Celsius," available at https://www.weforum.org/agenda/2020/12/global-emissions-record-covid19-green-stimulus/; and the UN's 2019 emissions report, available at https://news.un.org/en/story/2019/11/1052171

References

Barna Group. 2018. *Atheism Doubles Among Generation Z*. Accessed November 25, 2021. https://www.barna.com/research/atheism-doubles-among-generation-z/

Beaman, Lori G. 2017. *Deep Equality in an Era of Religious Diversity*. New York, NY: Oxford University Press.

Biles, John, and Humera Ibrahim. 2005. "Religion and Public Policy: Immigration, Citizenship, and Multiculturalism—Guess Who's Coming to Dinner?" In *Religion and Ethnicity in Canada*, edited by Paul Bramadat, David Seljak, 154–177. Toronto, ON: Pearson Longman.

Buckner, Phillip, ed. 2005. *Canada and the End of Empire*. Vancouver, BC: University of British Columbia Press.

Clarke, Brian, and Stuart Macdonald. 2017. *Leaving Christianity: Changing Allegiances in Canada since 1945*. Montréal, QC: McGill-Queen's University Press.

Gauvreau, Michael. 2005. *The Catholic Origins of Québec's Quiet Revolution, 1931–1970*. Montréal, QC: McGill-Queen's University Press.

Grant, George. 1966. *Lament for a Nation. The Defeat of Canadian Nationalism*. Toronto, ON: McClelland and Stewart Limited.

Grant, John W. 1998. *The Church in the Canadian Era*. Second revised edition (first edition published in 1988). Vancouver, BC: Regent College Publishing.

Hout, Michael, and Claude S. Fischer. 2002. "Why More Americans Have No Religious Preference: Politics and Generations." *American Sociological Review* 67 (2): 165–190. doi:10.2307/3088891

Igartua, José E. 2006. *The Other Quiet Revolution: National Identities in English Canada, 1945-71*. Vancouver, BC: University of British Columbia Press.

Lacombe, Sylvie. 2002. *La rencontre de deux peuples élus. Comparaison des ambitions nationale et impériale au Canada entre 1896 et 1920.* Québec, QC: Les Presses de l'Université Laval.

Lemieux, Raymond, and Jean-Paul Montminy. 2000. *Le catholicisme québécois.* Québec, QC: Les Éditions de l'IQRC, Collection Diagnostic.

Lipset, Seymour M. 1991. *Continental Divide: The Values and Institutions of the United States and Canada.* New York, NY: Routledge, Chapman and Hall.

Manning, Christel. 2019. "Gen Z is the Least Religious Generation. Here's Why That Could Be a Good Thing." *Pacific Standard*, May 6, 2019. Accessed November 25, 2021. https://psmag.com/ideas/gen-z-is-the-least-religious-generation-heres-why-that-could-be-a-good-thing

Mayrl, Damon, and Freeden Oeur. 2009. "Religion and Higher Education: Current Knowledge and Directions for Future Research." *Journal for the Scientific Study of Religion* 48 (2): 260–275. doi:10.1111/j.1468-5906.2009.01446.x

Meunier, E.-Martin, and Jean-Philippe Warren. 2002. *Sortir de la « Grande noirceur ». L'horizon personnaliste de la Révolution Tranquille.* Sillery: Éditions de Septentrion.

Meunier, E.-Martin, and Sarah Wilkins-Laflamme. 2011. "Sécularisation, catholicisme et transformation du régime de religiosité au Québec. Étude comparative avec le catholicisme au Canada (1968-2007)." *Recherches sociographiques* 52 (3): 683–729. doi:10.7202/1007655ar

Noll, Mark A. 1992. *A History of Christianity in the United States and Canada.* New York, NY: MacMillan.

Putnam, Robert, and David Campbell. 2010. *American Grace: How Religion Divides and Unites Us.* New York, NY: Simon and Schuster.

Rawlyk, George A., ed. 1990. *The Canadian Protestant Experience: 1760 to 1990.* Burlington, ON: Welch Publishing Company.

Smidt, Corwin E., Kevin den Dulk, Bryan Froehle, James Penning, Stephen Monsma, and Douglas Koopman. 2010. *The Disappearing God Gap? Religion in the 2008 Presidential Election.* New York, NY: Oxford University Press.

Smith, Christian, Kyle Longest, Jonathan Hill, and Karl Christoffersen. 2014. *Young Catholic America: Emerging Adults In, Out of, and Gone from the Church.* New York, NY: Oxford University Press.

Thiessen, Joel, and Sarah Wilkins-Laflamme. 2020. *None of the Above: Nonreligious Identity in the U.S. and Canada.* New York, NY: New York University Press.

Watts, Galen. 2022. *The Spiritual Turn: The Religion of the Heart and the Making of Romantic Liberal Modernity.* New York, NY: Oxford University Press.

Whitehead, Andrew L., and Samuel Perry. 2020. *Taking America Back for God: Christian Nationalism in the United States.* New York, NY: Oxford University Press.

Young, Pamela Dickey, and Heather Shipley. 2020. *Identities Under Construction: Religion, Gender, and Sexuality among Youth in Canada.* Kingston, ON: McGill-Queen's University Press.

Zubrzycki, Geneviève. 2016. *Beheading the Saint: Nationalism, Religion, and Secularism in Québec.* Chicago, IL: University of Chicago Press.

APPENDIX A

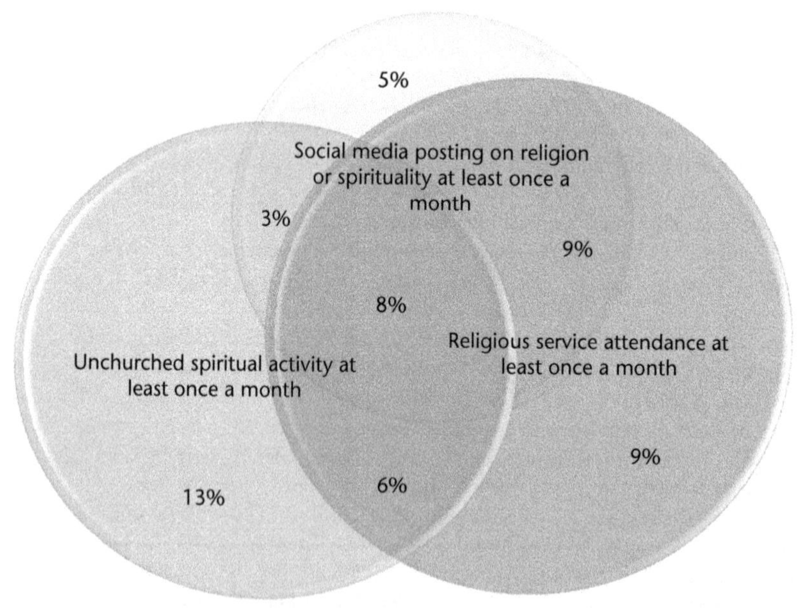

FIGURE A.1 Rates of monthly or more frequent religious or spiritual activities, respondents 18–35 years old, United States and Canada, MTS 2019

INDEX

Note: Page numbers in *italics* indicate figures; page numbers in **bold** indicate tables.